THE LIFE OF NEWMAN

THE LIFE OF NEWMAN

THE BUST BY WESTMACOTT

THE LIFE OF NEWMAN

by

ROBERT SENCOURT

Abuse is as great a mistake in controversy
as panegyric in biography.

NEWMAN TO COLERIDGE

dacre press
westminster

First published in 1948

PRINTED IN GREAT BRITAIN BY ROBERT MACLEHOSE AND CO. LTD.
THE UNIVERSITY PRESS, GLASGOW

PREFACE

It was Fr Henry Tristram of Newman's own Oratory at Edgbaston who first pointed out to me that, although it is more than 50 years since Newman died, no full account of his life has appeared. Wilfrid Ward's volumes are well known, but they say very little of the forty-five years Newman passed in the Church of England doing some of his greatest work. Barry wrote a valuable study, Mr Lewis May has made a delightful portrait; but neither of these is a biography. Yet Newman was the most important Churchman of his century; he is a living power still not only in one Church or in one country, and it is time the development of his power should be traced from the beginning of his life to the end.

The year 1845 was the year he left the Church of England: in 1945, it is still apposite to see why he did so, and what the change meant.

Newman claims attention principally for six reasons:

As a reformer of the Church of England.

As a man who alters England's attitude towards the Roman Catholic Church.

As a central and salutary exponent of Roman Catholicism.

As a classic writer on University education.

As a master of style.

And, finally, as one who foresaw events.

All these aspects of his life are treated here. It is the intermingling of all these with one another which explains both the grandeur and the fascination of his sermons.

But this book aims not only at telling Newman's story succinctly and explaining his mind. It offers some fresh material. I am grateful to the Provost and Fellows of Oriel College and to the President and Fellows of Magdalen College at Oxford for opening their archives to me and allowing me to quote from unpublished letters. I am still more indebted for a similar favour from the Principal and librarians of Pusey House. And I should also here express my debt to the President of Trinity College for accounts of the material in his possession and to the Warden of Keble for an unpublished letter. Canon Ollard of St Georges, Windsor, has placed at my disposal his collection of Newman's letters to Copeland. The Rev Dr Hutchinson of All Souls has aided me greatly. The staff of the Bodleian Library has helped me to find some useful items. Yet another who has helped me is Canon Cross of Christ Church. Not least, I have had the advantage of reading many very apposite works in St. Deiniol's Library, Hawarden—among these many are marked by Gladstone who for sixty years showed a personal interest in all that had to do with Newman. But above all this book owes a special debt to Fr Tristram. For many years he has been studying Newman; and he knows far more on this subject than anyone else.

He suggested the lines it should take; he has most graciously read it in type, and made many corrections, and suggestions which I gratefully incorporate, and he has kindly arranged with his superior that I should publish for the first time new portraits of Newman.

It will be perfectly plain that a book which has the approval of the Birmingham Oratory is that of an orthodox Roman Catholic who accepts the position Newman took up as an Oratorian. Welcoming the collaboration of Anglican scholars, I hope and believe that at the same time it represents him with equal sympathy in his life in the Church of England.

CONTENTS

PART ONE

PART TWO

CONTENTS

ILLUSTRATIONS

★

All the illustrations are due to the courtesy of the Birmingham Oratory. They are reproduced from photographs by F. R. Logan, Ltd. Only the Westmacott and the George Richmond have been published before.

ix

BIBLIOGRAPHY

The main sources for the *Life of Newman* are these:

Letters and Correspondence of John Henry Newman, 2 vols., edited by Anne Mozley, 1892. (A.M.).

Contributions Chiefly to the History of the Late Cardinal Newman, 1891, by F. W. Newman, 1897. (*Contributions.*)

Life of Edward Bouverie Pusey by H. P. Liddon, 4 vols., 1893–7. (Liddon, *Pusey.*)

Reminiscences by Thomas Mozley, 2 vols., 1881. (T.M. *Rem.*)

Apologia pro Vita Sua, by J. H. Newman, 1864. (*Apologia.*)

The Oxford Movement, by R. W. Church, 1890. (Church, *Oxford Movement.*)

Correspondence with Keble and Others, by J. H. Newman, 1917. (*Correspondence.*)

The Life of Cardinal Newman, by Wilfrid Ward, 2 vols., 1912. (Ward, *Newman.*)

William George Ward and the Oxford Movement, 2 vols., 1889. (Ward, *Ward*, I.)

William George Ward and the Catholic Revival, 1893. (Ward, *Ward*, II.)

Cardinal Wiseman, by Wilfrid Ward, 1887. (Ward, *Wiseman.*)

The Life of Cardinal Manning, by Purcell, 2 vols., 1896. (Purcell, *Manning.*)

The Life and Times of Archbishop Ullathorne, by Abbot Butler, 1922. (Butler, *Ullathorne.*)

An Essay in Aid of a Grammar of Assent, 1870. (*Grammar of Assent.*)

*

Other titles without authors refer to Newman's other works. The words in brackets above indicate the citations for the footnotes. The Author has also drawn on unpublished papers in Oxford (Pusey House, *unpublished.* Oriel College, *unpublished*, etc.). He has also sometimes put into italics for the sake of condensation a phrase that summed up others.

PART ONE

CHAPTER I

THE CALL OF OXFORD

I

Those who look towards Oxford from the low hills around see, amidst the glistening pinnacles and towers which rise above its roofs and groves in a singular array of beauty, one spire rise above the rest, eminent in height and queenliness. It is that of St Mary the Virgin. The church is hardly less renowned than one of her Vicars. He indeed rises among English clergy in his century to a height signal, undisputed, arresting. He was in his age the most telling of preachers, the most chaste of writers; but his hold over the Church of England cannot be divorced from the touching story of how he left her, and, while loving Oxford most intensely, was driven away from it by magnetism he could not resist. For who can forget that in 1845 he was received into communion with the Pope of Rome?

Even so, however, he aroused new questioning in every quarter —till finally his countrymen after new scrutinies united to acclaim him.

His published works amount to many volumes: the records of his life are not scanty either: but no one has yet attempted to balance together a life lived half in the national Church and half in the international one, nor has any yet considered what his change means after a hundred years.

Here, with certain new touches from the archives of Oxford, are the outlines of his story.

About his early mind hovered what was never to leave it—the aroma of Israel. This is not to say, as some have said,[1] that he had Semitic blood. There were in his features strong outlines which some have suggested to be Jewish. Rumours were abroad that the original form of his name was Neumann: and so many Jews have

[1] Barry: *Newman*, 9.   Bremond: *The Mystery of Newman*, 1.

come into England from Germany that this name could well suggest—though it certainly would not prove—a Jewish connection; but these rumours are themselves mere fancies; all that we know of the Newmans is that they came to London from Norfolk: and there is no reason to doubt that they were as solidly English as the banking firm into which a Newman entered at the end of the eighteenth century—the firm of Ramsbottom, Newman and Ramsbottom.

It is, nevertheless, true that this Newman was a freemason, and entertained Jewish friends.[1] He had the mentality of the business man. And his eldest son, John, the original of this portrait, might have been seen, perhaps, when he was about nine years old, sedate in Bloomsbury Square, while another boy some five years younger was playing there, a boy whose glossy curls, dark skin and Oriental features attested a Jewish origin no one questions.[2] This younger boy was later to sway England, and captivate the Queen, as Benjamin Disraeli.

As for young Newman, the influence of Israel came to him, not vaguely from distant ancestors, but direct from the Bible. He was trained in it insistently when he went to stay, as he often did, with his aunt, Elizabeth Newman, at Kew, or when he was with his mother. For she too was a lover of the Bible, and Newman never forgot what the Englishman of his generation gained from reading the Bible. 'It has attuned their minds to religious thoughts: it has given them a high moral standard: it has served them in associating religion with compositions which, even humanly considered, are among the most sublime and beautiful ever written, and especially it has impressed upon them the services of Divine Providence in behalf of man from his creation to his end, and, above all, the words, deeds and sacred sufferings of Him in Whom all the Providences of God centre.'[3] God's providence, he wrote, is the special doctrine held with real assent by the mass of religious Englishmen.

Mrs Newman for her part was of French descent. She belonged to a Huguenot family, named Fourdrinier, a family which in the

---

[1] T.M. *Rem.* I, 12.   Barry: *Newman*, 9.   [2] T.M. *Rem.* II, 407.
[3] *Grammar of Assent*, 54.

London of George III kept up a tradition of business integrity, artistic skill, and rigid Protestant religion. Their profession was engraving.

2

Jemima Fourdrinier married her Newman husband in 1799— when Bonaparte was rising to supreme power in France to give a new sense to its revolution, making it into a sort of amalgam with the tradition of army officers, and therefore with the Church, while England—and her bankers—organised against him. Even England tasted the ferment of revolution: there was talk of human rights: in relation to the common man, and the business man, government, tradition, authority, and the Church were often discounted. At the same time, the poets and novelists cultivated a sense of romance, a love of the past, a return to nature, a zest in wonder and mystery, that counteracted the claims of the middle classes with their interest in money or the mills.

3

Jemima Newman's eldest boy was born in 1801. He could remember seeing the body of Nelson brought up the Thames after the battle of Trafalgar.[1] He talked, too, to an old man who had worked for Alexander Pope.[2] As a child he was already quiet and phenomenally sensitive, liking the space and quiet of his aunt's dignified house at Kew, finding it hard to give in to his mother when she refused to allow him his own way;[3] finding it hard to stop eating when he got in among the gooseberry bushes on a summer morning;[4] terrified at the idea that as time went on he would have to go to school; terrified still more at the thought that after that he would have to get married.[5]

The family grew to be six—three boys and three girls. And Mrs Newman brought them all up elegantly and well. Though,

---

[1] T.M. I, 12. Ward: *Newman*, I, 14.
[2] Edward Bellasis: *Coram Cardinali*, 8, 9.   [3] A.M. I, 16.
[4] *Historical Sketches*, 65.   [5] *The Month*, March, 1891, p. 311.

like her sister-in-law, Elizabeth, she based everything on the
Bible, she turned eagerly to a new poetic romance which appeared
in 1809. It was called the 'Lay of the Last Minstrel' and celebrated
the love which a Scotsman of the border country felt for Jarrow
and Vale of the Tweed. It was inscribed to the head of the poet's
clan, the Duke of Buccleuch.

In this romance

> Visions of the past
> Sustain the heart in feeling
> Life as she is.

They meant much to John—a boy already at eight years old given
to books, and delighting in the realms of marvel and of distinction
they opened: he was a boy with already marked features and a
peculiar temper. He was haunted by the unknown, the occult.
He was fascinated by talismans. His only toys were the symbols
of romance. Life seemed to him a dream and he an angel, while
other angels devised the outer world in a game of make-believe.[1]

When he was no more than ten years old, some curious taste
actually induced him to draw the Cross and beads which the
Catholics had fingered as they repeated their prayers and pon-
dered the mysteries of their religion, and—like the Catholics
again—he crossed himself when going into the dark.[2]

How did such fancies come into his brain? He would never
have dreamed of having anything to do with a religion which he
had been taught to abominate. At that time Protestant children,
when they heard of Roman Catholics, looked on them 'with a
sort of awful curiosity and dismay'.[3] John Newman was certainly
Protestant: he loved his Bible: he was trained in his mother's
strict Huguenot tradition: his standards were superior, his habits
serious: he lived in the pride of a conscious purity, trained in the
fear of God.

His parents had heard of a boarding school at Ealing which was
run by an Oxford man, and which they were told was modelled
on Eton. It was so highly successful that, preferring it to Winchester, they sent their son there. John continued as he had begun,

[1] *Apologia*, 56.   [2] *Apologia*, 56.   [3] Church: *Life and Letters*, 8

quiet, bookish and sedate; he loved music and learnt the fiddle; though he formed one close friendship,[1] he mixed little with other boys. If he went to the swimming-pool on a summer day, he would watch the others disport themselves, but he himself did not undress.[2] He played no real games: words were his sport. All his spare time was given to reading and writing—writing farces and quizzes: each term he brought out a paper called *The Spy*.

He remained apart, nursing dreams of some unusual leadership —the leadership of a secret society he would one day form.[3] There were—to tell the truth—some unhealthy things about him, and before he was sixteen there had been some sort of decline from his fastidious standards, and his early piety. This decline haunted him all his life. 'I was living a life of sin with a very dark conscience, and a very profane spirit,'[4] he wrote in after years. In a book where he drew much on his own experience he wrote of one who had been betrayed into some kind of shortcoming, having a lively sense of responsibility and guilt, though his act be no offence against society; of distress and apprehension, of compunction and regret though in itself it was the occasion of pleasure; of confusion of face, though it had no witnesses, of self-reproach, poignant shame, haunting remorse and chill dismay at the prospect of the future.[5] Finally in his *Meditations* he asks: 'Was any boyhood so impious as for some years was mine? Did I not in fact dare Thee to do Thy worst?'[6]

4

At the age of sixteen he was left for a time at his school alone. Suddenly, in the solitude, his mind was overcome with a new conviction of the reality, the nearness of God, and above all of His wisdom and might. Then his conscience awoke again to assume an unrelenting sway. His whole consciousness recognised the authority of his experience. From that moment his convictions were unshakeable.

[1] Hans Hamilton, *see* Ward, II, 414.
[2] *Contributions*, 3.
[3] *Contributions*, 5.
[4] *Correspondence*, 314.
[5] *Grammar of Assent*, 105.
[6] *Meditations*, 100–1. *The Paraclete*, ii.

Now when a clever and sedate boy is religious, he is marked as one apart and in a certain sense superior. Others feel it: he is not unaware of it himself. To this sensitive and already self-conscious boy, so strictly trained in early youth, the experience of conversion gave not a radiant and abounding charity, but a sense of the awfulness of God, of His wrath, of the need to appease it by the effort of a holy life, and of the pressing danger not only for himself but for others, of eternal damnation. Fully and eagerly, to use his own words, he took Calvinism into his religion. With its exacting standards, and its rigid judgments, it stamped its grim impress on his soul. In his malleable years his mind was hammered into shape by a scheme which suited only too well his temptation to feel himself exalted and apart; and it was played upon by the good Protestant chaplain of the school who, though not himself a Calvinist, trained his pupil in uncompromising books: the *Private Thoughts* of Bishop Beveridge, and Law's *Serious Call to a Devout and Holy Life*. A new strictness came into the boy's dreams: he continued to peer into the lives of those around him and was not reassured.[1]

He was felt to be able enough to make a speech before Queen Victoria's father, the Duke of Kent. His voice was breaking but he got through it well, and the Duke praised him for his gestures.

By this time he had learnt all the school could teach him; and his father decided to send him the following year to the University. They thought of Cambridge, but their vicar, being an Oxford man, pressed the claims of Oxford:[2] so it was westward through Maidenhead and Henley that in the December of 1816 the banker drove his eldest boy over the Chilterns at Nettlebed and Nuffield and across the Thame at Dorchester, and, as evening fell, to Iffley and along the country road which gave them their first view of the towers and spires of Oxford before they drove into the famous street Oxford men call the High.

[1] See H. F. Stockley: *Newman, Education and Ireland*. Mr Stockley bases his evidence on a MS. note in one of Newman's books.
[2] A.M. I, 27.

5

About that fair line of buildings above the bare trees there was a dignity that caught the eye of Turner and had become a legend. Wordsworth, coming there a year or two later, was enthralled. Her spires, towers and domes, rising from groves and gardens, were, he said, a presence to overpower the soberness of reason. As he paced the long avenues, or glided along the stream-like winding of that glorious street, he felt that by this sumptuous rival his beloved Cambridge was outdone.

Who can describe the charm of Oxford? For hundreds of years men have come, as they come still, in the freshness of expanding youth to find freedom and cultivate friends in a society still select and privileged, in circumstances of tradition, learning, elegance and ease. The excellence of Oxford was that it combined in the cause and guise of learning the amenities of both city and country, both the manor house and the club. In the spacious grounds of their colleges men lived like country gentlemen: servants and tradesmen offered them a friendly respect: they had leisure and good cheer: but the charm of the place was connected with its delightful groups of buildings. Each college in its hall, its chapel, its quadrangle was at once both a preserve of quiet, and a centre of youth's social joy. But placed together and containing within them the Cathedral, the parks, the Sheldonian theatre, the old Clarendon building, the Bodleian Library, and its round Radcliffe Camera, they combined with many churches in an harmonious contrast of the Middle Ages with the Renaissance, of the Gothic style with the Baroque, in an atmosphere of stateliness, pleasantness and peace.

To these buildings each of many centuries added its peculiar contribution to the general effect of age, taste, continuity and comfort. There each member lived in his rooms on separate staircases ascending from the court or quadrangle, yet came together with others to chapel and to hall. Porters and servants combined to make life easy yet keep it under control. In each of those colleges, dons and undergraduates lived (unless they were

very poor) the life of a gentleman and, within the limits of rule
and convention which called them in at night and demanded
punctuality in hall and chapel, did very much as they felt inclined.
So it was that the minds of privileged hundreds of young men
ripened, for three years, in an atmosphere of leisure. It struck Manning in 1827 as a sort of intellectual Elysium—awful and stately
and beautiful.[1]

Lamb had already observed in Newman's boyhood that even
the butteries and sculleries were redolent of antique hospitality.
the kitchen fireplaces were cordial recesses: in those ovens pies
had been baked for four hundred years. Amid the libraries he
seemed to inhale learning, and the odour of their old moth-
scented covering was as 'fragrant as the first bloom of those sciential
apples which grew amid the happy orchard'.[2] Hazlitt, arriving
there at the same time, took a still more romantic view. 'Rome
has been called the Sacred City,' he wrote, 'might not our Oxford
be called so too? There is about it an air resonant of joy and hope:
it speaks with a thousand tongues to the heart: it waves its mighty
shadow over the imagination: it stands in lowly sublimity on the
"hill of ages" and points with prophetic fingers to the sky: it
greets the eager gaze from afar, with glistening spires and pinnacles adorned that shine with an eternal light as with the lustre
of setting suns; and a dream and a glory hover round its head as
the spirits of former times, a throng of intellectual shapes are seen
retreating or advancing to the eye of memory: its streets are
paved with the names of learning that can never wear out: its
green quadrangles breathe the silence of thought, conscious of the
weight of yearnings innumerable after the past, of loftiest aspirations for the future. Isis babbles of the Muse, its waters are from
the springs of Helicon: its Christ Church meadows, classic,
Elysian fields. We could pass our lives in Oxford without having
or wanting any other idea—that of the place is enough.'[3]

Newman came also to imbibe the air of thought, to stand in the
presence of learning. He held high converse with Oxford's tute-
lary genius. Entering Trinity, he became a citizen of no mean

[1] Purcell: *Manning*, I, 43, 11.   [2] Lamb: *Essays of Elia,* ' *Oxford in the Vacation.*'
[3] Hazlitt: *Complete Works* (1930), X, 970.

city; he found himself surrounded with what Hazlitt called 'the monuments and lordly mansions of the mind of man, outvying in pomp and splendour the courts and palaces of princes, rising like an exhalation in the midst of ignorance and triumphing over barbaric foes'.[1]

In young Newman all these impressions were mastered by something else, something which, though paramount enough, escaped many undergraduates altogether. It was the tradition which went back to the medieval abbeys, and looked on learning as the handmaid of religion.

Newman's chief end in Oxford was not pleasure but piety. As he drove into the city he repeated in awed enthusiasm the words: 'Thou shalt guide me with thy counsel and after that receive me with glory. Whom have I in heaven but thee, and what do I desire upon earth in comparison of thee?' He had come to the University in short as to a shrine.[2]

6

'Those preachers', he wrote afterwards, 'who make comfort the great subject of their preaching seem to mistake the end of their ministry. *Holiness* is the great end. There must be a struggle and a toil here. Comfort is a cordial, but no one drinks cordials from morning till night.'[3] It was in that spirit, still Calvinistic, that he lived his Oxford life. His indulgences were few: his work incessant. A boy who at home loved fun and affection, he broke immediately from society that was uncongenial or seemed tainted. And the legacy of the eighteenth century was not edifying as far as ordinary boys or men were concerned. Schools were bad, and boys in them filled their young minds with brutal and distasteful things. Cruelty was common.

The public schools were 'heathenish at the best, at the worst nurseries of vice'.[4]

[1] *ibidem*.   [2] A.M. I, 48.   [3] A.M. I, 87.
[4] Tuckwell: *Pre-Tractarian Oxford*, 103. Cf. Ward: *Ward*, I, 128.

7

In the June of 1817 he entered Trinity as an undergraduate.

His tutor, Mr Short, sent him an undergraduate called Bowden to explain the customs of the College, and take him into hall at five o'clock to eat his dinner. He found there dons sitting at a table on a dais, a few portraits on the walls, long oak tables and at them, sitting as they chose to sit, a number of boys of eighteen to twenty-one, regaling themselves with salmon, or haunches of mutton and lamb, with beer served up in old pewter cups or earthenware mugs. There were also gooseberry, raspberry and apricot pies.

Being younger than the others there, he was also different; and they looked at him curiously without speaking. One went so far as to ask him in to wine: they drank, and drank, and their talk took a line he did not like. He was glad to escape when he heard the bell for prayers. His eyes gave him trouble, and as always when he could not read easily he was low-spirited.

Yet if only he could find congenial friends, how quickly his soul expanded and threw out a special fragrance—and in Oxford there are few indeed who fail to find in time one or two congenial friends. Bowden found something extraordinarily attractive in this very young undergraduate: Newman returned the feeling: and the two were always together. They read their books together: they ordered meals in one another's rooms: they sat together in hall: if they went out to walk or row on the river, still they were together. They wrote a poem together on the massacre of St Bartholomew: continuing his school project of The Spy, Newman induced his friend to help him bring out a periodical called The Undergraduate.[1]

That Oxford was still the Oxford of past centuries. The time was still long before the days of trains. There was not a single house between Magdalen bridge and Iffley, two miles away. One came from hills direct to the city of colleges: and though the new

[1] A.M. I, 28.

canals were bringing more trade to the city, nothing but one area
of hideous cottages disturbed its dignity. So comfort had joined
hands with learning, and both with dignity to give to youth a
time of quiet and leisure. They either rode or drove tandems or
jumped their horses on Bullingdon Green: for the rest lane and
road provided exercise, on sunny summer days the river. Therefore Oxford was above all a place of talk; talk was its sport—talk
assisted by ample supplies of port and sherry. Scholarly, elegant,
self-indulgent, whimsical—dons and undergraduates might be any
or all of these. But they belonged to a society which was like a
unique collection of clubs, with the great world as their background in London or the counties, and around them that scene
where garden, grove and college combined into a dignified
felicity.

Such a combination of beauty, pleasantness, peace, taste, freedom and prestige struck the fancy of John Newman as ideal. From
those first summer days he desired never to leave it; and as he
looked out of Trinity and saw the snapdragon growing on the
wall, he took it as a symbol of his own natural adaptation to the
place, and prayed that he might stay in it for ever.[1] Such was the
dream that—interspersed with the glow of intimate friendship—
filled his mind.

8

He laboured at his books and indulged ambitions. His father at
first thought of his becoming a lawyer: but then in 1818 came one
of those reverses of fortune by which providence changes a career.
His father's bank got into difficulties: they paid all they owed, but
the bank could not go on. And Mr Newman had to start again as
a brewer at Alton in Hampshire. Later when he found his son
failing to obtain high honours, he no longer pressed the law as a
vocation: and the young man then announced that he would seek
admission to Holy Orders.

This would but give him a securer claim to perpetual residence
in Oxford: for almost all the dons were clerics. His academic

[1] *Apologia*, 369.

career had prospered. In 1818 he won a scholarship at Trinity: his college approved him. 'Oh, Mr Newman,' said his tutor to the father, 'what a treasure you have given us in your son!'[1]

Mr Short would like to see Trinity attain a reputation for its scholars: here was the opportunity—and John Newman was not blind to his own talents. 'Few', he wrote to his father, 'have attained the faculty of comprehension which I have arrived at from the regularity and constancy of my reading, and the laborious and nerve bracing and fancy expressing study of mathematics which has been my principal subject.'[2] One evening he climbed with a friend on to one of the towers that they might make observation of the stars: Newman, however, looked not at the stars but at the colleges. To their dark shadows, lit by gas lamps, he turned the fascinated gaze of ambitious curiosity, for in one of them surely he would live as don, and he longed to know in which.[3]

Not being a brilliant classical scholar, he must read on and on. But in all cases where nerves and brain are involved we find that fevered and intense effort can defeat itself. Newman's efforts were overdone. When in November, 1820, he sat for his final examination, he could not show the calibre of his mind. He was utterly stale, and the examiners could not give him their honours of first, or even second class. All that was left was to put his name as satisfying the examiners in classics: in physics and mathematics he failed altogether.

For what afterwards could he hope? Mr Short was very disappointed. And yet when a year later, Newman, still living in Oxford on his scholarship and coaching, heard that there was a vacancy at Oriel College, then the most brilliant in the University, he decided to risk his chances. Short, naturally, was dubious. The Dean of Trinity wrote to the young man's father that in the final competition 'the struggles of the best have failed'. Yet Newman insisted, with a sort of intuition. 'Hope', he wrote, 'leads me on,' just as it had done when he sat for his scholarship at Trinity.[4] *Pie repone te.* In the days of April, as harassed and almost sinking he wrote in the hall at Oriel, he had noticed the words on a

[1] A.M. I, 34.   [2] A.M. I, 69.   [3] *Loss and Gain* (1848).   [4] A.M. I, 67–9.

stained-glass window, and he had regained his temper of ease and calm.

No sooner had the fellows of Oriel begun to read his papers than they noticed the work of an unusual competence. They saw quickly that though he was not a first-rate classical scholar, his work showed those signs of original and independent judgment for which they searched.[1] They made inquiries at Trinity as to whether the virtues of the candidate had been recognised there. They received an answer which encouraged them: and on 12th April, 1828, as Newman was playing his violin in his lodgings near Trinity, the Provost's butler entered with the message that his presence at Oriel was immediately required. The butler pressed his message on the violinist, and before long Newman was hurrying into Oriel, there to receive the congratulations of the Provost and Fellows.[2] Among those was one fresh, smiling face, so intelligent and so fine that he had noticed it with a sort of awe in the streets of Oxford. It was that of one already honoured above most men at once for the brilliance of his mind and the purity of his life: John Keble. When Keble came forward to shake hands with him, the young Newman could for shyness and shame have sunk into the floor.[3]

The news of the election had spread round Oxford, and at Trinity the bells were set ringing—at Newman's expense—till undergraduates, who had stayed up to work, complained that the clatter had spoilt their day's reading.[4] So did the young man of twenty-one, the youngest don in Oxford, find that he was secure in the position he had coveted above all; the most brilliant intellectual society in the University, the most flattering prospects, were at his command in a position of prestige and ease. He was established in the leisure, and beauty, and the amenities of the city which at first sight he had loved.

[1] A.M. I, 73-4.   [2] A.M. I, 71-2.   [3] Apologia, 76.   [4] A.M. I, 72.

CHAPTER II

THE FRIENDSHIPS OF ORIEL

I

When Newman became a Fellow of Oriel, he entered a society which for twenty years had been remoulding the University by the force of some remarkable minds. The first of these had been Eveleigh, Provost from 1781. He very soon began to urge his college that the Common Room must be less a genial club than the centre of vigorous brains. Having done this he set to work to make examinations serious tests of excellence; and from him comes therefore the system which is now in its turn a bugbear to educational reformers of the present day. From him, in fact, and the Oriel Fellows comes the Oxford system of Honour Schools which has moulded for almost a hundred and fifty years ruling brains in England and the British Empire. The first of these schools was held in 1802.

It was as far back as 1787 that the Provost looking for ability had rejected all the formal candidates and appointed a boy of seventeen who was a scholar of Corpus.[1] This boy, Copleston, had an independent brain and grew soon to have an imposing personality. What delighted him was vigour and independence which recalled his own, and it was for men so endowed that he was ever on the look-out. The enterprise of his choice, the bracing effect of his influence, and the power of his sumptuous and confident personality combined to make this don at Oriel the most remarkable contemporary in either University. 'In that society which owes so much to him, his name lives and will ever live for the distinction which his talents bestowed on it, for the academical importance to which he raised it, for the generosity of spirit, the liberality of sentiment and the kindness of heart with which he

[1] Tuckwell: *Pre-Tractarian Oxford*, Ch. II.

16

adorned it, and which those who had least sympathy with his mind and character could not but admire and love.'[1] His memory ranged wide: his expressions were authoritative and terse: his presence genial and impressive. His voice rang commanding with the resonance of a bell. Such a don soon became a figure in a wider world.[2] He knew the poets and the Whig leaders, and he was recognised as the most substantial and majestic figure in the whole of Oxford.

In his college each don was, as we saw, a personality to vindicate his choice. Of these one was no less than the Arnold who as headmaster of Rugby was to be the strongest among the teachers of his time, a man of obstinate lip and chin, shaggy black hair, thick eyebrows, warm even passionate affections, intense moral zeal and personal piety. Newman was, in fact, elected to the fellowship he left vacant. Another was the tall vigorous figure of Richard Whately. From the time he came to Oriel in 1805 he had fallen under the spell of Copleston, the Provost, who entered into his aspirations and drew out his mind, trained him also to thrust hard and express himself precisely. He loved Shakespeare and Scott. Elected a Fellow in 1811, he delighted to talk and talk. When a youth thanked him for being so painstaking in giving him instruction, he answered that he liked to have an anvil to beat out his thoughts. If we want to catch the point and zest of his talk, we cannot do better than read his *Historic Doubts about Napoleon I.* In a delightful skit he pointed out how incredible the whole story was. This was his way of vindicating the Bible from the sneers of sceptics.

When he taught, he abominated those who learnt by rote, and demanded that a pupil should answer in his own words the thoughts which he had reached himself. He was both a critic of weak argument and a lover of originality. Conquering the shyness of his youth, he jumped into flamboyance. His gestures were tumultuous, his talk quick and overpowering, while in his dress he was unconventional, if not unkempt. When he walked round in the winter in a long white coat, with a white beaver hat, and wielding a strong stick, he was known as the White Bear. None

[1] *Idea of a University,* 157.   [2] Tuckwell: *op. cit.,* 47.

the less so able was his work on logic that it remained the best text-book on the subject for twenty years.[1]

Both Copleston and Whately were independent judges and thinkers, accepting the dignity of the Church in which they were ordained, but, while remaining conservatives, testing everything by the tests of their own vigorous thought. With them was another personality more elegant and gracious though hardly less impressive. This was Hawkins, a man of remarkably fine features, brilliant eyes, strong conservatism and elevated learning. But he too was a man always on the look-out for precise and intelligent expression of originality. So in an age when conversation was one of the chief occupations of dons, the young Newman found himself among men, who needs must train him well—to think, to talk, to write.

2

When first living among them as a Fellow, however, Newman was so shy that they almost questioned their choice. But Whately made friends with him, and poured out his talk till Newman, who was a good listener, felt at his ease. And gradually they began to change the tenour of his mind: he ceased to be the pious and narrow Protestant, moulding his rules of life almost entirely upon his feelings for his Redeemer. These intellectuals began to show him the importance of a Church: they showed him that when the Apostles preached, they preached a doctrine not alone of faith, but of faith joined to baptism in which a human creature was born again to the life of the Spirit. And at the same time as his mind opened to the idea of signs and mysteries, he learnt from the *Analogy* of Joseph Butler to look upon the outward world as an index to things unseen, to believe that as conscience was fixed in the psychology of man as his supreme director, so there must be in eternity a supreme ruler and judge. This, argued Butler, was the reasonable supposition to hold: there was not only every reason to think there was an immortal life, but that in it things were governed by similar principles, and the whole heavenly scheme based on analogies to those of earth.

[1] Tuckwell: *op. cit.*, 27.

Gradually the scope of Newman's mind was changing, ripening and solidifying; Protestantism was being exchanged for a transcendentalism which looked on the outward world as symbols of things unseen, and while at the same time he found and expressed his thoughts in ways that would be approved by the most critical and exact thinkers. Hawkins taught him in fact to weigh his words and be cautious in his statements. He taught him to be extremely precise and outline his meaning sharply, so that there could be no equivocation.[1] Hawkins was a man of the most exact mind, with all a don's ruthlessness in asserting academic standards. So it was that the Newman who had come so early to Oxford, who had been trained by it so assiduously in those malleable years when most boys are still at school, was stamped yet again with its academic exactitude. Already his letters, which were sometimes simple and naïf, had at times a formal, bookish tone which in talk would give that impression of superiority, of intellectual nicety and of conscious rectitude which would easily earn for a boy the name of a prig.

While adored by his mother and sisters, Newman was so far unable to cope with the world. He lacked the ease and bonhomie of the country gentleman or the officer. His nearest approach to it was the culture of the university man, combined with the mixture of shyness and superiority which mark the youth whose religion has made him too squeamish for a corrupt world. He himself speaks of a serious and gloomy temper bordering on mawkishness.[2] To his capacities for intense and intimate friendship, and the vibrancy of an emotional temperament, trained in music and above all the plaintive music of the violin, he had not wholly lost what he owed to his narrow, rigid evangelical piety, which was very moral indeed, yet trusting entirely to Christ's atonement for salvation. Into this Calvinism had brought its astringent flavour; a precision of energy which made his thoughts and conduct as firm and exact as the hands of his ancestors when they were engraving. He wrote his thoughts with the incisive fineness with which they had cut their designs in polished steel. Yet with his precision and his sensitive self-consciousness were in-

[1] *Apologia*, 64–5.   [2] *Loss and Gain* (1848), 2–3.

stincts alien and pioneer. There were eager imagination, fierce
feeling, and the taste for romance, with a temperament unrelent-
ingly individual.

3

His first serious essay completed his literary training. He wrote
for an encyclopædia an article on Cicero, and Cicero he said long
afterwards was the only master of style he ever had. Cicero's
mastery said Newman was in his clearness.[1] So monuments of
classical prose completed the influence of Hawkins and the dons
in training to artistic precision the phenomenal yet disciplined
eagerness of his mind.

And though he suffered from recurring toothache, though his
weak eyes compelled him to use large spectacles, and his face was
thin, his complexion was good, while his hair remained thick and
strong even to old age. And so full were his reserves of nervous
energy that, after finishing with pupils at ten in the evening, he
slept only for four hours, and then walked eighteen miles before
breakfast to have a look at his old tutor's pupils. The fibres of
Newman's constitution were evidently strong.

Already his features were marked. His Roman nose (some, as
we saw, had thought it Jewish) gave boldness to his profile beneath the huge metal-rimmed spectacles. His forehead was broad
and smooth. His eyes shone with a tender light, but what was
most peculiar in his countenance were the lips. Full yet com-
pressed, they marked in their peculiar lines not only a passionate
nature relentlessly controlled, but in that control the consciousness of a high self-confidence[2] in which some detected an unpleasant touch of scorn.[3] Yet the whole face of the man spoke of
a something not only refined, not only noble, but of a gracious
and exalted spirituality. For he carried with him the marks of a
converse with heaven: when he was first at Oriel this was already
noted, and the Provost with another don meeting him on a walk
one day turned to him with a kind courtesy, and bowing said

[1] A.M. II, 477.   [2] Froude: *Short Studies on Great Subjects*, IV.
[3] George Harris: *Autobiography*, 105.

'*Nunquam minus solus quam cum solus*'.[1] He spoke of a dominant characteristic—an habitual sense of the Divine Presence, going before him and guiding him like the pillar of cloud.[2] He had a sense of God being with him, not externally, not merely in nature or in providence, but in his inmost heart and in his conscience.[3] God was a supreme reality, as luminous and self-evident—or almost so—as his consciousness of, and his preoccupation with himself. Such was the nature, shy, timid, awkward and reserved —but with reserves of immense power—which Whately and his friends at Oriel sought with boisterous geniality to mould for the uses of this world.

Newman had already made up his mind that he should live a single life: with his vocation to celibacy went a marked distaste for the intimacy of married life. Besides he was convinced that he must live austerely a life of sacrifice. Again and again he thought of going into the wilds as a missionary. But the call came from no further away than the other bank of the Cherwell.

There was already a growing suburb with a little church, St Clement's, and there he first worked as curate, reading on Sundays a portion of the Anglican Service, and calling on the parishioners to persuade them to come to church. Whately found him another task: it was to be his Vice-Principal in another subsidiary centre of learning in Oxford, St Alban's Hall.

There he came in closer contact with undergraduates than at Oriel, for at Oriel he was not yet a tutor. In this atmosphere, his mind gave up its narrow creed, and was inclined to treat religion in that more arbitrary, free and rational way which he came afterwards to stigmatise as liberalism.[4]

While the Oriel dons took a modern personal and critical view of religion and truth, Newman soon came in contact with a Canon of Christ Church who was Regius Professor of Divinity. Lloyd was suspicious of and hostile to the Oriel Common Room, especially of Whately. He, for his part, laid great stress on history, tradition and Church standards. While Whately called the fathers

---

[1] Never less alone than when alone. *Apologia*, 74.
[2] *Loss and Gain* (1848), Pt. II, Ch. IX, p. 178.
[3] *Parochial Sermons*, XVI, 225, 6.   [4] *Apologia*, 72.

'certain old Divines', and called orthodoxy simply 'one's own doxy', Lloyd wanted a respect for authority; and with young Newman this stout old Canon would profess to be scandalised. He was free and easy in his ways and a bluff talker with a rough, lively, good-natured manner and a pretended pomposity relieving itself by sudden bursts of laughter. He would walk up and down asking questions, gathering answers, and taking snuff as he went along; then sometimes when he came to Newman he would put on a satirical expression, stop and fix his eyes on the young Protestant, as if to look right through him, and then make a feint to kick his shins and box his ears.[1] Newman was aware that all this was a proof of friendship; but he felt nevertheless embarrassed about his Protestantism, he began to see that the prayers he knew best all came out of Roman Catholic books.[2]

4

A change came over him in 1824; in a mood of solemn yet tender joy, he had been ordained first deacon and then priest. His essay on Cicero had been noticed and admired. He had written two others; one on Apollonius of Tyana, another on miracles. All were praised. And then in 1826 when Whately resigned, Newman was made a college tutor. His intercourse with young men gave him confidence. He preached before the University. He was made a public examiner. 'It was like the feeling of spring weather after winter,'[3] wrote Newman, and he came out of his shell.

In this happy change, friendships played a great part. As an undergraduate he had lived almost exclusively with Bowden. To Bowden, now in the Isle of Wight, he then returned. And soon after he came back he found at Oriel a new and delightful friend. In 1826 there had been elected Fellow of Oriel a young Etonian, enthusiastic, engaging, friendly, a youth of most romantic temperament and graceful versatility of mind, who united with his brilliant originality and enterprise of view a gentleness and tenderness of nature, a playfulness, a give and take in talk, a free elastic

[1] A.M. I, 111–2.   [2] I. Williams: *Autobiography*, 37, 47.   [3] *Apologia*, 74.

force and winning generosity which made those to whom he opened his heart love him. Those that knew him could not speak of him but in warmest terms of admiration and affection. He had, said Newman, an intellect as critical and logical as it was speculative and bold. He united with fine taste a quick and piercing precision of thought.[1] Yet it was in talk he was gifted rather than in writing, for his mind was brimful and overflowing with views, both deep and multitudinous, which crowded and jostled against each other in their effort for expression. Ideas and projects came from him like a shower of meteors.[2] To this was added a face, boyish and frank but well bred and expressive. His eyes, grey like Newman's, were not exactly piercing but bright with a light which shone from within, and though habitually soft, they could rapidly assume an expression either of attention, inquiry, amusement or even disgust. He had an interest in everything: when he was out sailing, skating, riding on ponies with his pupils, he showed not more entrain than when he talked philosophy to them.[3] When his grave sentences were played out, he was apt to burst into a light low laugh. Added to this he was both handsome and affectionate.

Newman soon found that he was the most attractive and delightful person he had ever known. They lived on terms of what Newman called intimate and affectionate friendship, Hurrell Froude began to revolutionise Newman.[4] For what were the most arresting subjects of his thoughts but hatred of the reformers and admiration of the Church of Rome? The only good he would admit in Cranmer was that he burnt well. He delighted in the idea of the power and glory of the ancient Church. He loved the tradition and dignity which robed the ancient mysteries and scented the atmosphere of history with the perfumes of worship. He was fascinated by the saints, by the Middle Ages, by the Mass. He recognised with an intense and worshipping enthusiasm both the Catholic Church and her wealth of holiness. He hated the Whigs: he hated the French revolution. He taught Newman to detest all that was called Liberalism.

[1] Blachford: *Letters,* 5.   [2] T.M. *Rem.* I, 303.   [3] Blachford: *loc. cit.*
[4] *Apologia,* 75. 'I was, in particular, intimate and affectionate.'

Nor was this all. There was in the ardour of this young man's temperament a curious mixture of mortification of the flesh, self-preoccupation and romantic emotion. It was one of those natures in which feelings and personal relations become intense, sometimes over intense. It played upon the sensitive ardent nature of Newman as the bow made the strings of his violin vibrant with moving sound. It filled with tenderness a heart that for several years had felt in the place of the incessant companionship of Bowden a desert and a void. Newman was shy and reserved because he had been lonely. Up to that time nothing had shown the dons of Oriel that his mind had any particular bent. But now there came a change. Newman, being loved, felt Calvinism was no longer adequate to his nature.

5

Froude's friendship did not come to him without others. It had been prepared by two other Fellows of Oriel. One had joined the society but a year after himself. Edward Bouverie Pusey had come from Eton and Christ Church. He had a social position and means. He was a sallow young man with a stoop, a sharp pointed nose, slightly sensual lips, in which some afterwards detected a hint of Jesuitry, a growth of dark unshaven hair always on his cheeks, and his hair wet with cold water he applied to cure his recurring headaches. 'I recollect him,' wrote Newman after forty years, 'short and small with a round head and smallish features, flaxen curly hair, huddled up together from the shoulders downward and walking fast.'[1] About him was an air of authority and weight. When he was elected to a fellowship at Oriel, Newman had made some advances, and was assured that Pusey had the root of religion in him. Then Pusey had gone away to Germany to study: when he came back he strengthened in Newman that love of Catholic things which flamed from Hurrell Froude. The two men felt for one another affection and respect.

But what Froude did above all was to bring Newman in touch with Keble. For six or seven years Keble and Newman had met

[1] Ward: *Newman*, II, 95.

without really becoming friends: in the expansion which Froude gave to Newman was included Keble. 'Do you know', he asked, 'the story of the murderer who had done one good deed in his life? Well, if I was ever asked what good deed I had done, I should say that I had brought Keble and Newman to understand each other.'[1]

Before he did so, Keble had made a new claim on the heart and mind of Newman. He had brought out in 1827 a fine collection of religious verse. These verses had the freshness of a flower, the music of a brook. They invested religion with gleams and splendours of magical light. They spoke of symbols and of mysteries. They too breathed the atmosphere of a Church. Newman could not but feel—though he could not analyse—the effect of poetic ideas so deep, so pure, so beautiful, for it is in these words that he describes them. 'I drew near with the reverence which is due to a superior nature: and as my heart was entirely subdued by the captivating strains I fell down at his feet and wept.'[2]

So, quoting Addison, did Newman express in after years the feeling that overcame him after he made friends with the spirit whose happy magic made the Church of England poetical. *The Christian Year* elevated her system into regions of delight, and threw upon them the grace of poetic imagination. Her neglected altars became mysterious in the aroma of perfumed embers, in the light of holy lamps: holiness came to men as not only captivating in its freshness but as associated with her offices.

When Keble saw that Newman had now come to appreciate him, and loved his poems, the hearts of the two men cleaved to one another. And again Newman's confidence increased.

6

These happy experiences of expanding friendship came to him after he had, with Hurrell Froude and Robert Wilberforce, been appointed a college tutor and found yet other fields to display the subdued radiance of his nature. It was found that he could not only teach but could attract young men. The clearness and ease

[1] R. H. Froude: *Remains*. Cf. *Apologia*, 27.   [2] *Apologia*, 77.

with which he spoke, the tact with which he refrained from pressing his own view, the courtesy with which he listened to those of his pupils, the frankness with which he displayed his personal and arbitrary choice, the zest and eagerness of fascination he exerted combined to inspire his undergraduates with devotion, almost awe.[1] He spoke to them about the subjects of the day, of the men and events of the time, of things of general interest, and always with a complete freedom, ease and equality. He walked out with them in the evenings, he joined them in vacations: always he mixed with them as an equal and a friend.[2] Only those who had the highly finished manners of the great world did he rebuff. These baffled him and kept him at a distance.[3] He regarded their polish as the mark of ungodliness, and called them 'the scandal and ruin of the college'.[4] Sarcasm and an ironic tone were his weapons, and the dry words 'Very likely' clapped out to show when he was not amused. It was when he talked alone to the pupils he liked that he opened his heart and won theirs. And this influence he thought a more lasting memorial than any of his books.[5] He regarded this as part of his priestly calling: he needed it also as an outlet for the intensity of his nature.

'Newman went into Oriel Common Room,' wrote Mark Pattison, 'a shy man with heart and mind in a continual ferment of emotion and speculation, yearning for sympathy and truth.

'Thin, pale, and with large lustrous eyes ever piercing through this veil of men and things, he seemed hardly made for this world. But his influence had in it something of magic. It never was possible to be a quarter of an hour in his company without a man feeling himself invited to take an onward step—one of his principles was that every man was good for something, but you must find out what it was and set him to work accordingly.'[6]

To form men exactly to his own views, however, when under the persuasion of Hurrell Froude and Keble and Robert Wilberforce he was becoming a high Tory and very much of a Catholic,

---

[1] J. A. Froude: *Short Studies*, IV, 278–84.   [2] A.M. I, 153.
[3] A.M. I, 152.   [4] A.M. I, 231.   [5] Mark Pattison: *Memoirs*, 4.
[6] Mark Pattison: *The Academy*, July 4, 1882, reviewing the Mozley *Reminiscences*.

was more than Hawkins thought right, and finally Hawkins announced that he would allot no more private pupils to the tutors: to Hurrell Froude and Robert Wilberforce and John Newman. But this did not come till 1830, and even then one cherished and brilliant pupil remained—to be made a Fellow in 1833.[1]

7

Newman had not long met Froude when his nervous energy, either exhausted by so electrical an impact or reacting from other strains, again broke down. He had been doing too much. Friends had to take him away into the country, but before Christmas he had recovered. No sooner had the New Year begun, however, than Mary, his favourite sister, died suddenly at Brighton, and this loss he felt much more acutely than that of his father at London three years before; since then he had been living in much closer relation to his family, for he had found for them first one house, then another, at Brighton. Bereavement had brought him back from literature to a simpler and deeper belief. Such then was his life from 1826 till 1828—busy with new pupils, absorbed with new friends, expansive and conscious of his power to arouse interest and win a following, watching the changes in College, and relaxing from time to time to care about his mother and his sisters. For to them he showed a sympathy and a tenderness which were for them alone.[2]

Then came great changes in College. Copleston was appointed Bishop of Llandaff. Hawkins was elected Provost in his place, Newman was appointed to succeed Hawkins as Vicar of St Mary's.

[1] D.N.B. XV, 120.   [2] I. Williams: *Autobiography*, 176.

CHAPTER III

NEWMAN AT ST MARY'S

I

By his sermons in St Mary's Newman quickly made himself the figure foremost in the eyes of all serious undergraduates. Witness after witness arises to describe the peculiar effect which those sermons procured.

The Church itself is a fine perpendicular church in the centre of Oxford's incomparable High Street. The spire above it, rising in its majesty of grace, expresses with consummate effect the devotion which the Middle Ages gave to the Virgin Mother as the Queen of Heaven. Her figure, with that of her Divine Child, had been set by Laud over the sumptuous baroque portal he had added to the Gothic Church, and to which the leaves then added in autumn the colours of russet and crimson.

Here it was that at four o'clock on Sunday afternoons Newman held his evening service. From the first young men felt the impact of a surprising loftiness of power: in a short time he had become a legend to successive numbers of young men. One after another has described it. From the moment the worshipper heard the service begin, he felt in the familiar cadences of the Prayer Book, in the splendid phrases of the Bible, a new force, solemnity, significance. They felt that holiness had become present among them in its beauty, in its awfulness, in its arresting power. The presence of the man before them seemed to be instinct with the graces of the Spirit. His ascetic thinness, his marked features, his soft shining eyes, his strong yet silky hair, were in themselves significant; but what was his appearance to the cadences of his musical voice, its pauses, and prepared by its pauses, the thrill which passed from it to the congregation in the enthusiasm of wonder in which he worshipped?

'O magnify the Lord our God and worship him upon his

holy hill—for *the Lord our God is holy.*' As the young minister read that invitation, the younger men who listened felt that Paradise was opening and they had caught a secret from on high. Others might make the Prayer Book and its lessons, pompous on one side or unimpressive on the other. He threw over the Bible an indescribable charm of touching beauty. His reading was cogent as a sermon in which you forgot the preacher. It was marred by no effort, degraded by no art. He seemed to pierce his listeners to their very centre. His pathetic changes of tone after his thrilling pauses, made a commentary in themselves. He brought out meanings where none had been expected and threw over all an atmosphere of awe.[1] Sublime in the melody and felicity with which it translated noble Latin into noble English, the English Prayer Book carried from Israel and Rome a voice in which the soul of England found her own ideal.

The impressiveness became more personal when the preacher spoke from the pulpit in the deepening afternoon. From the wide perpendicular window the grey church was suffused with a pale yellow light, the Gothic architecture spoke of an order in which aspiration after something wild and high had grown calm under England's skies. The congregation itself added not a little to the scene. In their variety and their freshness gathered hundreds of young men, glowing with youth and health and strength, young men of a fine strain and graceful in their stature, yet giving their privilege and breeding to the pursuit of culture, and feeling among all these things that the spirit gave them nobler cares than those of their own elegance in England.

2

For it was on their ears that the music of a new evangel fell. The preacher used no oratorical devices; his hands never moved from beginning to the end. His voice sometimes fell and paused. He began as if he were determined to set out his ideas in the plainest and simplest words, words which the poorest and dullest could

[1] Oakeley: *Notes on the Tractarian Movement,* 25.

understand. But gradually the bareness and austerity of phrase took on more brilliant colours; as he went on it seemed as if his body glowed and caught fire within. His zeal consumed him; his imagination poured into poetry. Beneath that quiet calm bearing so strictly controlled, the quickened sympathies of his hearers felt the poignancy of passionate feeling. 'As I hung upon his words,' said one of them 'it seemed to me as if I could trace behind his will, and pressing so to speak against it, a rush of thoughts and feelings which he kept struggling to hold back, and in the end they were generally too strong for him and poured themselves out in a torrent of eloquence all the more impetuous from having been so long repressed. The effect of these outbursts was irresistible and carried his hearers beyond themselves at once. Even when his efforts at self-restraint were more successful, those very efforts gave a life and colour to his style which riveted the attention of all within reach of his voice.'[1] Those who listened were within a charmed ring, under the wand of an enchanter: there was music in his voice, fascination in his eye, and in his spare but lustrous countenance habitual command.[2]

3

What were his themes? The individuality of the soul, the invisible world, particular Providence, the danger of religious excitement, the ventures of faith, warfare as the condition of victory, self-denial, the cross of Christ as the measure of the world, or the emptiness of God's eternity for those who could not appreciate the savour of His holiness. But with these he put within the academic correctness of his style a most telling directness, so that in each sentence delivered as though it were an end in itself, there was a power that touched the quick of a young man's soul.

Taking some scriptural incident or character as a text, he spoke to undergraduates about themselves, their experiences, their temptations. His illustrations were inexhaustible. As the eyes of a por-

[1] Sir Francis Doyle: *Reminiscences,* 146.
[2] Wilberforce: *Quarterly Review* (1864).

THE PULPIT AT ST MARY'S, OXFORD

trait appear to meet the gaze of every person in a room, so he seemed to be addressing each of his hearers in the secret place of conscience. 'He laid his finger—how gently, yet how powerfully! —on some inner place in the hearer's heart and told him things about himself he had never known till then.'[1] So wrote an enthusiastic listener. He is echoed by Dean Lake who wrote that 'He seemed to enter into the minds of his hearers and as it were to reveal them to themselves.'[2]

Yet even as he spoke with this searching intimacy, he seemed apart from his congregation. Indeed the aloofness was part of the charm. The sermon seemed like a soliloquy to which his hearers were listening without the speaker being aware that they were there. He seemed to come from habitual dwelling with the unseen, like a friar from abstinence and prayer, to give almost unconsciously the record of what he had seen and known when single with angels and God.

In 1878, Gladstone made an eulogy of him at the opening of a portion of Keble College. A little before this at the Conference in the City Temple, he had paid another tribute to his preaching: 'without ostentation or effort, by simple excellence, he was constantly drawing undergraduates more and more around him', and this the more surprised a man of oratorical effects like Gladstone, because in Newman there were none at all. Judging by merely technical standards, said Gladstone, he would have come to unsatisfactory conclusions. 'There was not very much change in the inflection of the voice; action there was none. His sermons were read, and his eyes were always on his book, and all that you will say is against efficiency in preaching. Yes, but you take the man as a whole, and there was a stamp and a seal upon him; there was a solemn music and sweetness in the tone; there was a completeness in the figure taken with the tone and with the manner, which made even his delivery such as I have described it and, though exclusively with written sermons, singularly attractive.'[3]

---

[1] Shairp: *Studies*, 277.   [2] Dean Lake: *Memorials*, 41.
[3] Justin McCarthy: *History of Our Own Times*, I, 210.

4

To take some passages from those sermons is to see deep into the themes of this singular preacher. His theme was still that of William Law: a serious call to a devout and holy life. But as has been shown, this call came with a combination of personal insight, practical shrewdness, and the chiselling of a sculptor of words. With an artist's skill he engraved every word upon the fleshy tablets of his hearer's heart:

'If we wished to imagine a punishment for an unholy reprobate soul, we perhaps could not fancy a greater than *to summon it to heaven*. Heaven would be hell to an irreligious man. We know how unhappy we are apt to feel at present, when alone in the midst of strangers, or of men of different tastes and habits from ourselves. How miserable for example would it be to have to live in a foreign land, among people whose faces we never saw before and whose language we could not learn! And this is but a faint illustration of the loneliness of a man of earthly dispositions and tastes, thrust into the society of saints and angels. How forlorn would he wander through the courts of Heaven; he would find no one like himself: he would see in every direction the marks of God's holiness and these would make him shudder. He would feel himself always in His presence. He could no longer turn his thoughts another way as he does now when conscience reproaches him. He would know that the Eternal Eye was ever upon him, and that Eye of holiness which is joy and life to holy creatures would seem to him an Eye of wrath and punishment. God cannot change His nature. Holy He must ever be. But while He is holy, no unholy soul can be happy in heaven.'[1]

Or to show the incisiveness of his exhortation, let us take him on self-denial.

'To take up the cross of Christ is no great action done once for all, it consists in the continual practice of small duties which are distasteful to us.

'If then a person asks how he is to know whether he is dreaming

[1] *Parochial and Plain Sermons*, I, 78.

on in the world's slumber, or is really awake and alive unto God, let him just fix his mind upon some or other of his besetting infirmities. Everyone who is at all in the habit of examining himself must be conscious of such within him. Many men have more than one, all of us have some one or other; and in resisting or overcoming such self-denial has its first employment. One man is indolent and fond of amusement, another man is passionate or ill-tempered, another is vain; another has little control over his tongue; others are weak, and cannot resist the ridicule of thoughtless companions, others are tormented with bad passions of which they are ashamed, yet are overcome. Now let everyone consider what his weak point is.

'In that is his trial. His trial is not in those things which are easy to him, but in that one thing, in those several things whatever they are in which to do his duty is against his nature. Never think yourself safe because you do your duty in ninety-nine points: it is the hundredth which is to be the ground of your self-denial, which must evidence, or rather instance, and realise your faith.'[1]

The preacher, always using the effect of reading rapidly sentence by sentence with great clearness of intonation and pausing often for nearly half a minute till each thrust cut home into the quickened conscience, would still more elaborate his point: he would press home the effect of this full measure of obedience, how it would enhance a man's judgment of persons, events, actions and doctrines and his whole bearing towards God and towards man. And then his theme took another turn: the need of exercise to strengthen the will and the habit of perfection:—

'It is right then almost to *find out* for yourself daily self-denials; and this because Our Lord bids you take up your cross daily, and because it proves your earnestness, and because by doing so you strengthen your general power of self-mastery, and come to have such an habitual command of yourself, as will be a defence ready prepared when the season of temptation comes. Rise up then in the morning with the purpose that please God the day shall not pass without its self-denial, with a self-denial in innocent pleasures and tasks, if none occurs to mortify sin. Let your very rising from

[1] *op. cit.*, I, 67–8.

bed be a self-denial: let your meals be self-denial. Determine to yield matters in things indifferent, to go out of your way in small matters, to inconvenience yourself rather than you should not meet with your daily discipline. . . . Try yourself daily in little deeds to prove that your faith is more than a deceit.

'I am aware all this is a hard doctrine, hard even to those who assent to it and can describe it most accurately. There are such imperfections, such inconsistencies in the heart and life of even the better sort of men, that continual repentance must ever go hand in hand with our endeavours to obey.'[1]

At another time he would talk about revivalist emotions. He would point out that aspirations, and impassioned thoughts and sublime imaginings are the excitements that come with freshly awakened fervour, but they must never be mistaken for duty. They are but the invitation to it. There is even a certain luxury in the discovery of our own guilt: but all these things pass: and their only permanent worth is if they cause us to form habits through deeds and will, so that when the excitement ceases and despondency ensues, those habits will be established in the spiritual life. Emotion and passion, he said, are in our power indeed to repress, not to excite: there is a limit to the tumults and swellings of the heart, foster them as we will, and when that time comes the poor soul is left exhausted and resourceless. Let men, therefore, show and resolutely maintain a change of life. Then when they labour in darkness amid the sordidness of the world, unattended by high transport and warm emotion, they would find that resolute consistent obedience is far more acceptable to God than all those passionate longings to live in the light which look like religion to the uninstructed.

Such then were the practical counsels by which the young master of the spiritual life awoke new stirrings among the undergraduates of Oxford.

5

His voice when he spoke of these things was so distinct that one could hear each consonant and vowel. The words spoken in that

[1] *op. cit.*, I, 70-1.

melodious and moving voice fell, as we have said, on the silence
of the Church like measured drippings of water in a vast cave,
and each made music as it fell, till listeners ceded to the charm,
and the sermons sounded like a strain of unearthly music.[1] Never,
said another, did a voice seem better adapted to persuade without
irritating, singularly sweet, perfectly free from any dictatorial
note and yet rich in all the cadences proper to the expression of
pathos, of wonder and of ridicule, there was still nothing in it that
anyone could properly describe as insinuating; its simplicity and
frankness and freedom from the half-smothered notes which express indirect purpose, were as remarkable as its sweetness, its
freshness and its gentle distinctness.[2]

Yet it was not alone the voice and personality of the preacher.
The words themselves were chosen by a man of sure taste. They
were not only correct by the chastened standards of the scholar:
but they had in them the surprise of that excellence which makes
words literature. It was a combination of intense feeling, purity of
form, clearness of meaning, and an inner calm and poise which,
shared with the order of the spheres, imparted to the words themselves the beat and cadences of music. Through them, said one
hearer, shone the speaker's soul. Their height of conception combined with suppressed yet vibrant feeling into a perfection of
style that, like a great poem, suggested the secrets of the heart in
the very rhythm and melody of the words.[3]

6

For there were times when the theme was raised by a deliberate
and conscious art. So it was when in talking of warfare preceding
victory, he compared the souls of the elect to competitors display-
ing their skill as runners or singers or dancers before a king:—

'It is as though all of us were allowed to stand round His Throne
at once and He called on first this man, and then that, to take up
the chant by himself, each in his turn having to repeat the melody
which his brethren have gone through. Or as if we held a solemn

[1] Shairp: *Aspects of Poetry* (1881), 16.   [2] Hutton: *Newman*, 207-8.
[3] Shairp, *Studies in Poetry and Philosophy*, 278.

dance to his honour in the courts of heaven and each had by himself to perform some one and the same solemn and graceful movement at a signal given. Or as if it were some trial of strength or of agility, and, while the ring of bystanders beheld and applauded, we in succession, one by one, were actors in the pageant. Such is our state. Angels are looking on—Christ has gone before —Christ has given us an example that we may follow His steps. He went through far more, infinitely more, than we can be called to suffer. Our brethren have gone through much more, and they seem to encourage us by their success and to sympathise in our essay. Now it is our turn and all ministering spirits keep silence and look on. O let not your foot slip, or your eye be false, or your ear dull, or your attention flagging. Be not dispirited, be not afraid: keep a good heart and be bold: draw not back; you will be carried through. Whatever troubles come on you, of mind, body or estate; from within or from without; from chance or from intent; from friends or foes:—whatever your trouble be, though you be lonely, O children of a heavenly Father, be not afraid! Quit you like men in your day; and when it is over Christ will receive you to Himself and your heart shall rejoice and your joy no man taketh from you.

'Christ is already in that place of peace, which is all in all. He is on the right hand of God. He is hidden in the brightness of the radiance which issues from the everlasting throne. He is in the very abyss of peace, where there is no voice of tumult or distress, but a deep stillness—stillness, that greatest and most awful of all goods which we can fancy—that most perfect of joys, the utter profound ineffable tranquillity of the Divine Essence. He has entered into His rest. . . .

'O how great and good it will be, when this troublesome life is over and we in our turn also enter into that same rest! If the time shall one day come when we shall enter His tabernacle above, and hide ourselves under the shadow of His wings; if we shall be in the number of those blessed dead who die in the Lord, and rest from their labours. Here we are tossing upon the sea and the wind is contrary. All through the day we are tried and tempted in various ways. We cannot think, speak or act but infirmity and sin are at hand. But in the unseen world where Christ has entered all is peace.'[1]

And then the great cadences of those Hebraic masterpieces, which glorify the Greek of the New Testament—Hebrews and Revelations—pour in their famous imagery. He sees the eternal throne, with a rainbow round about it like an emerald, and the river of the water of life, clear as crystal, proceeding out of the throne. And this court is our home, to which we are invited by the Spirit and the Bride: to this we strive, compassed with a cloud of witnesses, and finding grace to help in time of need.

7

Who can be surprised that undergraduates said that here were thoughts like no other man's thoughts, and emotions like no other man's emotions,[2] or if after many years they asked: Is it too much to say of such addresses that they were unlike anything that we had ever heard before, and that we never heard or read anything similar to them in after life?[3] or that to those who then found religion such a sermon was like a fountain springing from a rock,[4] and that it left them awed both by the immediate reality of the Christ, and the insistence of His call to live among things unseen?[5]

The preacher himself assumed the romance of a legend. As undergraduates saw him passing in the street, with head thrust forward, and his gaze fixed as though on a vision only he could see, while with a swift graceful noiseless step he hurried by, they felt awed as in the presence of a celestial apparition. And while he ministered among them, their lives, their characters changed. The University assumed a seriousness, a purity, it had never known before—nor has known again. And if the reason were sought, all that men could say was that they believed in Newman.

To his friends, nevertheless, he was anything but solemn. Imperious, ironical, wilful, at times disdainful of convention or the world, he showed yet to all young men he could reach or touch a

---

[1] *Parochial and Plain Sermons*, VI, 231–2. [2] J. A. Froude: *Short Studies*, IV, 275.
[3] Dean Lake: *Memorials*, 42. [4] Froude: *op. cit.*, IV, 284.
[5] Church: *The Oxford Movement* (1891), 164, 168.

gentleness, a devotion, and a sparkle that enchanted them with his company, and made them say his talk rivalled, in its power to hold them, the music and eloquence of his sermons. Many found him the liveliest, the most captivating of friends. He was interested in everything which they thought most interesting. He seemed to have found difficulties just where they found difficulties. He combined in the lightness of his elastic strength the insight of a wizard, the lightness of a fairy and the enthusiasm of a young warrior of flesh and blood. They asked him what he thought, when Gurwood brought them out, of Wellington's despatches, 'Think?' he answered, 'It makes one burn to have been a soldier.'[1]

[1] Froude: *Short Studies*, III.

CHAPTER IV
THE WISDOM OF ALEXANDRIA

I

Theology, through its long history, shows the human mind at work on those mysteries of faith which are for ever eluding because transcending it. The mystery is too great for words to define, and passes beyond them into realms of worship and wonder. And yet since there is a connection between mystical illumination and revelation, a common ground between faith and reason, the knowledge of faith must be expressed in terms such as reason can deal with and safeguard in the realm of its formularies.

For were it otherwise, reason, itself misled, would open dangerous doors into the unrevealed, and men would find themselves sundered not only from one another, but also from those realms of light which, flashing truths on the intellect, enabled them to formulate belief.

Central among the truths so revealed about the Divine nature is the Trinity in Unity. But how can three persons be one? And what is the relation between these persons?

We can go no further till we see the meaning of the word Person. To Catholic theology it is a perfect individual of a rational substance. We consider personality, wrote Newman, as equivalent to the unity and independence of the immaterial substance of which it is predicated. We cannot conceive of a person as more than a mere character yet less than an individual intelligent being. But the word person as applied to the Blessed Trinity must mean a reasonable perfection vitally and essentially connected with another reasonable perfection: and to express it the Greek fathers had taken the word *hypostasis*, meaning the fundamental reality. It must be made plain that the Father, the Son and the Holy Spirit are in God not only distinct as 'Persons', but one in Their

39

Being or Essence, and equal in Their Majesty. All Three are co-eternal and co-equal.

But can you have a Son who is not preceded by his Father or a Word which is not spoken and dies upon the ear? It is plain that such expressions, if the best that revelation could find, are nevertheless inadequate to convey the august equality of the Father and the Son: and certain early theologians pressing them too far denied that the Son was of one substance with the Father.

Such was the error into which the Arians fell, such the error which was considered when the Bishops of Christendom met on the shores of a lake in Bithynia in 325. Making more precise in intellectual terms the mystery of their faith, they expressed it in the Nicene creed. They there proclaimed that the Son was God of God, and Light of Light, being of one substance with the Father, and that the Holy Ghost proceeding from Them was worshipped and glorified together with the Father and the Son in the Trinity in Unity.

Such then was the sublime mystery which Newman now set out to study. It was to trace how an error grew, from pressing the words of revelation into human definitions which made them deceptive: it was to see how the Church in her assembled Bishops added to the Bible terms a more luminous precision: a precision which accorded with the revelation, with the faith, with the mystical experience which God had given to them that believe.

2

In finishing these studies Newman found new and significant views opening on his mounting steps. His idea of the Church was that it not only gave fresh play to a brilliant mind, but at the same time contained within itself that which set it above the plans and jurisdictions of men as something divine:—it reigned supreme because of the authority of *faith*.

Newman's intellect was charmed and stimulated by the writings of Clement of Alexandria as by Origen, and by Dionysius: for Platonic mysticism had subtilised the traditions of his illustrious Egyptian Church. In them he found revealed regions of thought of which the Evangelical writers with whom he grew up had never caught a glimpse. He found the Christian faith both interwoven with the speculations of a generous philosophy and illuminated with flashing genius.

His Evangelical teachers had taught him that pagan nations through one dreary century after another had lived and died and perished in a darkness unrelieved by any gleam of light from Heaven. Only Cowper, the Evangelical poet, had protested in noble lines against this indiscriminating and appalling surrender of this overwhelming majority of the human race to eternal perdition.

In Clement, however, Newman learned that the Church of Alexandria, which was engaged in a hand to hand conflict with paganism, recognised in Greek philosophy a gift from heaven, regarding it as a divinely appointed discipline intended to train the Jews for a larger and more wonderful revelation. In the great Athanasius, whose name is popularly associated with the sternest, the most rigid and the most mechanical form of orthodoxy—he discovered the elements of a theology expansive and profound. If it were too much to say that Newman's tendencies towards 'liberalism', which had been arrested by great sorrows a few years before, now received a satisfaction of an unexpected kind, it is at least true that the keen restless active intellect which was ill at ease under the restraints of Evangelicalism and which for the sake of exercise and fresh air had been breaking away towards liberalism, exulted in the discovery of a speculation wide enough for the most adventurous temperament. He was so fascinated by the Alexandrians that it was intolerable to him that Alexandria should remain under the reproach of being the native soil of the Arian heresy. His history, which was published under the title of the *History of the Arians of the Fourth Century,* is really a continuous polemic intended to show that the heresy had its roots in the Church of Antioch.[1]

[1] *Birmingham Post,* Aug. 12, 1890. (An unsigned article by an Oratorian.)

3

Newman therefore was now separated from his Evangelical beginnings, but the formal Church School which was then its only alternative repelled his spiritual ardour because, in keeping free from emotional enthusiasm, it remained cold and formal. As yet it offered no Catholic practices or pieties: celebrations of the Holy Eucharist were rare. There were seldom any churches open except on Sundays, and then only for a matins and an evensong in which there was much formality and few hymns. His mind was in a ferment. He felt that England needed another Reformation, but in what form he could not tell. When in 1832 he left Europe with the Froudes to travel in the Mediterranean, the anchors of his mind were up, and he must steer his course by such stars as glimmered in his sky.

CHAPTER V

IN ROME AND SICILY

1

The news which reached him along the journey increased his excitement: 'liberalism' appeared to be menacing all that was sacred in the Church, but since it placed individual judgment above authority and tradition, it broke with all that was august and venerable in the State. The authorities in each were lacking in both sagacity and courage, and Newman began to feel indignant both with statesmen and bishops.

2

At the same time his sensibilities were charmed by the colours and lights of the Mediterranean as his culture was kindled to enthusiasm by the monuments and churches of Italy. Both completed what his studies of Alexandria had begun. His eyes were always sensitive to tints and lines. Often as he walked round Oxford his eyes caressed the effects of haze and softened light, suffused with colour. When he first went to stay with the Froudes at Dartington in South Devon, he was amazed and overjoyed at the richness of the vegetation and the warmth of colouring. 'The rocks', he wrote, 'flash into every variety of colour, the trees and fields are emeralds, and the cottages are rubies. A beetle I picked up at Torquay was as green and gold as the stone it lay upon.'[1] The squirrel had taken a ruddy shade into its brown, even his fingers were like the fingers of Aurora, tinged with rose. While he found the exuberance of trees and foliage oppressive, he found the delicate yet powerful scents intensely interesting, and the very petals of the flowers as though shot with white.

[1] A.M. I, 242–3.

3

On the coasts of Portugal, and on the Mediterranean, brighter scenes than these awaited him: the sea was an intense blue, the sky seemed all sapphire; a new vegetation—that of the ilex, the olive and the pine—added the atmosphere of Virgil; and among these stood out not only the monuments of the classic age, but also the yet more significant memorials of the apostles and the martyrs of the time nearest to that of the Christ Himself. When he saw the shores of Spain and Portugal, the memories of Devon dimmed at once. The outline of the Cantabrian mountains was magnificent: the sun shone: the rocky coast glittered: the wind sang: the exhilaration of finding the sun warm, the colours bright, was made keener by the effect of sea air after a bout of sea sickness: the sea itself was grand both in colour and in movement. In these lands every occupation of the eye was an adventure. 'The sea brightened to a glowing purple inclined to lilac; the sun set in a car of gold and was succeeded by a sky first pale orange, then gradually heightening to a dusky red, while Venus came out as the evening star with its peculiar intense brightness.'[1]

So much could he write of the Iberian coast seen from the sea. As with the sun renewing its power, they began their long, long summer days, what were to be the effects of Sicily, of Greece, of Italy, spreading their precipitous declivities, their heights of snow, their velvet landscapes, their delightful cities, named one after another with echoing and imperishable names? On then, past Malta, to Corfu and Patras, till he landed on the Peloponnese. Mists hung over brownish cliffs and black rocks; and above them rose the high snowy mountains which culminate in Erymanthos and hide the vale of Eurotas, with Mistra and Lakedaimon; after these he was led on to an expedition in Sicily to visit the temple of Segesta. 'Little as I have seen of Sicily,' he wrote on February 16, 1833, 'it has filled me with inexpressible delight and (in spite of the dirt and other inconveniences) I was drawn to it as to a loadstone. The chief of it has been Segesta; its ruins with its

[1] Faber: *Oxford Apostles,* 285.

temple. A wonderful sight full of the most strange pleasures—strange from the position of the town, its awful desolateness, the beauty of the scenery, rich even in winter, its historical recollections I contrast with the misery of the population . . . my mind goes back to the recollections as one smells again at a sweet flower.'[1]

But on with the spring to Naples, though it naturally disappointed him after Sicily and Palermo. Here were no theatres of graceful mountains, and he was astonished that people spoke of it when so near were Sorrento and Amalfi and the gorgeous drive over the mountains from one to the other: but every step fascinated him alike by the charms of colour and scene as by the classic memories, which were always to move him to far more enthusiasm than any of his Oxford theology. What was the reason? Was it right? he asked, and the question was elaborated into a sonnet.

> Why wedded to the Lord still yearns my heart
> Upon these scenes of ancient heathen fame?
> Yet legend hoar and voice of bard that came
> Fixing my restless youth with its sweet art
> And shades of power, and those who bare their part
> In the mad deeds that set the world aflame
> So fret my memory here. Ah! is it blame
> That from my eyes the tear is fain to start?[2]

It was amid classic scenes that he was enraptured, fascinated and absorbed by associations and beauty, even while he was repelled by squalor, scandal and a dubious religion; he travelled on with the Froudes, arriving in Rome, with the splendour of spring, on March 3rd.

4

Who could drive over the Campagna into the eternal city without emotion or a sense of history and drama? The isolated ruins preceding monuments, arches, aqueducts: the flat and waste of the Campagna, the sight of the walled city: the passage through the gates: the buildings which have arrested the attention of ages: all

[1] A.M. I, 344. [2] A.M. I, 348.

these led Newman and the Froudes to their inn, and to the beginning of absorbing Roman days.

In spite of all their fervent Toryism, Newman and Hurrell Froude, as Protestants, had been taught to look on the religion of Rome as vile. *St Bartholomew's Eve*, young Newman's first published lines, written when he was only eighteen, had spoken the conventional ideas of Roman Catholic corruption, of the dark confessional where blood-stained murder was 'secure of absolution from a faith impure'. Mistaken worship! he burst out

> Where every crime a price appointed brings
> To soothe the churchman's pride, the sinner's stings,
> Where righteous grief and penitence are made
> A holy market and a pious trade.

Now that he was actually in Rome, the same Protestant sense of outrage at Popish errors remained: 'Popery', he said, 'has eaten into the very system of Catholicism and left it an outside shell.'[1]

Only some great catastrophe could, he thought, remedy the evil. 'By no means short of some terrible convulsion and through much suffering, can this Roman Church surely be reformed; nothing short of great suffering or by fire can melt us together in England with one another.'[2] When he looked narrowly at the people, he doubted if they prayed: they stared about soon after they knelt down; he had seen some in Church laughing, jesting, scrambling to get a sight of what was going on. He was horrified to see them kiss the toe of the statue of St Peter, or give an *ex voto* to a shrine of the Virgin. He was shocked to see a Mass without communicants: for 'the Romanist', he said, 'is taught to believe there is a virtue in the priest's will offering it up to God' as an act complete in itself and availing for souls in purgatory. The grand sin of that system, he argued afterwards, 'has been the degradation of the human mind, the offence is that of obliterating the command, the desirableness and the effort of aiming at high moral excellence, at the perfection of truth, holiness, justice and love. She destroys *personal* religion . . . lest natural conscience should

[1] *British Magazine*, V, 127.
[2] Pusey House, *unpublished*. To Pusey, March 17, 1833.

start from a system which makes evil good, she soothes it with drugs till it becomes insensible. She virtually substitutes an external ritual for moral obedience.'[1]

And the monuments of Rome are not easy to admire at the first glance. So it was natural enough that at first Newman should feel in it the great enemy of God or write 'the first thought one has of the place is awful'.[2]

But for a man with his artistic tastes, his culture, his imagination, how soon the ancient city exerted the infinite seductiveness of her dignity. He enjoyed museums, galleries, libraries, and above all the suavity of Raphael. How many emotions came to him among these trophies of genius!

And then Rome showed things more significant than these, the tombs of the martyrs and of the saints: the worship of an august, ancient and fervent religion. Newman's heart was touched, and he wrote before he had been there a week: *Rome grows more wonderful every day.*[3] What was it that made him feel already that, as a place of pilgrimage and worship, it outrivalled his dear Oxford? Oxford after fifteen years was not so sacred as the eternal city became in two days. 'The effect', he said, 'of every part is so vast and overpowering—there is such an air of greatness and repose cast over the whole.'[4] Shocked as he was at certain things he saw, qualify as he might, insist as he might that Oxford is the first of cities, yet still Rome overcame him: he praised her as beautiful because stupendous.

Did he meet Catholics and come in touch with priests? He did indeed. One copied some Gregorian music for him, and with Hurrell Froude he called on Monsignor Wiseman at the Collegio Inglese; and, anticipating Malines, they actually discussed the question of terms of reunion. Having seen that they must accept the Council of Trent,[5] they felt disinclined to go further. They went to few church services except the Tenebræ at the Sistine Chapel, and their general impression was that every prospect was pleasing but the corrupted heart of man: that the Church of Rome hated them, and in an iron temper would resist concession.[6]

[1] *op. cit.,* 129.   [2] A.M. I, 359.   [3] A.M. I, 359.   [4] A.M. I, 302–3.
[5] R. H. Froude: *Remains,* Part I, Vol. I, 304–7.   [6] *British Magazine,* V, 131.

Newman was haunted still, however, by the beauty of Sicily. He must gaze again upon its cities and its mountains, and so even though it meant parting from the Froudes and almost quarrelling with them, he lingered for a day or two after them at Rome, drove back to Naples, and set sail to the nearest approach to Paradise: spring in Sicily.[1]

5

It was not until April 20th that he sailed from Naples for Messina, where he hired a servant, two mules and a muleteer: he started down the eastern coast, seeing Etna near and white: then on to Taormina. 'I never saw anything more enchanting than this spot,' he wrote. 'I realised all that we had read in books about scenery, a deep valley, brawling streams, beautiful trees, the sea (heard) in the distance. But when after breakfast, on a bright day, we mounted to the theatre and saw the famous view what shall I say? I never knew that nature could be so beautiful, and to see that view was the nearest approach to seeing Eden. O happy I! It was worth coming all the way, to endure sadness, loneliness and weariness to see it. I felt, for the first time in my life, that I should be a better and more religious man if I lived there. The superb view, the most wonderful I can ever see is but *one* of at least half a dozen, all beautiful, close at hand. . . . The hills receded —Etna was magnificent. The scene was sombre with clouds when suddenly, as the sun descended upon the cone, its rays shot out behind the clouds and the snow, turning the clouds into royal curtains, while on one side there was a sort of Jacob's ladder. I understood why the poets made the abode of the Gods on Mount Olympus.'[2] And so on to Catania, Syracuse and back, with his servant Gennaro, an old campaigner, experienced, reliable, sharp-witted and ready. From Catania he struck inland to Leonforte on his way to that fabled field of Enna which Cicero had pictured and Milton had recalled as the haunt of Proserpine. At once he felt ill, and at Leonforte was down with a dangerous fever. He felt for a time that he was dying: yet an inner conviction told him

[1] A.M. I, 377-8.   [2] A.M. I, 397.

he would not die, that there was still work for him to do: he lay there for three weeks, much tormented, sometimes in danger, but with a will to live. Then the fever abated, and on May 25, still very weak, he started to drive to Palermo, and there he stayed three weeks. Strange feelings and convictions assured him that God was leading him on to some august end. And this favour was so sublime that he burst into a flood of tears.[1] Once there had come a glimpse of Catholic worship. At six o'clock one morning, as he was making his way across from wild country, he heard voices in a small church. He looked in and found the people were singing in a way that moved him to the depths. He had surprised them at the mystery of the Mass.[2]

Had his journey to Sicily been a failure? Ah no! He had not reached Girgenti as he hoped, nor Selinunti, but what profound raptures in what he had seen in this Catholic country! He never dreamed that nature could be so beautiful. 'It *is* a country,' he wrote: 'it passes belief. It is like the garden of Eden.'[3]

6

Yet he was longing to get on, to get back to his family, to his dear friends in Oriel. In hot Palermo he felt extremely home-sick. When he wrote in exact detail an account of that time in Sicily, he suppressed the record of his deep spiritual experiences, he only says that at Palermo he began to visit the churches and felt as he had felt at Rome a sense of calm. 'The sight of so many great places, venerable shrines and noble churches,' he wrote, 'much impressed my imagination, my heart was touched also.'[4] Before he left he put down in verse a record of a deep mysterious experience which undermined his Protestantism and offered him a mystical solace in the depths of his being. He might try to repudiate and doubt, but in his heart there was the sovereign power of that communion which is faith, and shines beyond the thoughts and formulations of the mind in a sky above mental cloud. Beyond his Anglicanism, beyond his home-sickness, beyond the

[1] *Verses on Various Occasions* (1868), 131.   [2] *Correspondence,* 318.
[3] A.M. I, 408.   [4] *Apologia,* 126.

shadows of a dream, he espied, though fearfully, the ground of
hopes serenely sweet.

                                  O that thy creed were sound!
For thou dost soothe the heart, thou Church of Rome
By thy unwearied watch and varied round
Of service, in thy Saviour's holy home!
I cannot walk the city's sultry streets
But the wide porch invites to still retreats
Where passion's thirst is calmed and care's unthankful gloom.

There on a foreign shore
The home-sick solitary finds a friend.
Thoughts prisoned long for lack of speech outpour
Their tears, and doubts in resignation end.
I almost fainted from the long delay
That tangles me within this languid bay
When comes a foe my wounds with oil and wine to tend.[1]

'Day after day,' he wrote, 'the priest stands before the presence
of the Invisible, interceding for the people, and renews the com-
memoration of that sacrifice by which the world is rescued.'[2]

7

So much did Newman feel before he left Palermo; such were
the consolations which refreshed him, when his weakened physical
fibres fainted in the unaccustomed heat of a Sicilian June.

On June 13 he started in an orange boat to sail through the
Straits of Bonifacio on his way to Provence and Marseilles. Half-
way across the sea, in the Straits between Sardinia and Corsica,
he stayed for nights and days becalmed in the perfect stillness of
the summer weather. In this enforced quiet, recollecting the
deepest experiences he had known, he wrote lines which he called
The Pillar of the Cloud. They were in time to exert his power upon
all kinds of Christian hearts: they were to extend to thousands,
morning upon morning, and evening upon evening, the divine
graces which had poured in upon his soul, to give his unrest and

[1] Verses on Various Occasions (1868), 131.   [2] British Magazine, V, 126 (1834).

his misgivings that consoling trust which he had discovered in the churches of Palermo, and in Rome. They are the record of that blessed mood in which men conquer their misgivings in the quiet of surrender to the unseen power and the inner light. They are an act of faith, of hope, of love, springing like exquisite blossoms from the tended soil of repentance.

Never in a lyric were so many words of a single syllable so originally woven to haunting effect and strong design. The words taken each in themselves are so simple as to find an easy place in common speech: taken together they weave the ideas of uncertainty as encircling gloom, of youth's natural hopes as garish day, or the unfolding of time as the distant scene, with a serene abandonment to the guidance of the Holy Light. On the one side they recall his lonely journey in the Mediterranean. The lighthouses twinkling across the sea in Corsica and Sardinia through the dark hours of the night, the rocky heights and watercourses he had seen in Sicily, preceded by the bareness of Dartmoor, and some stay in monotonous and marshy lands; finally there were hopes of returning to friends and family he loved.

But it is the property of a great poem to allow persons and particular outlines to fade into the sense of limitless significance among those deeps which call to one another in the souls of men. Vague memories of particular scenes are fused into the suggestion of his torment being calmed by a sense of sustaining communion, enforced by the experience of years; and from the confession of a personal effort and a self-confidence that among eternal things no longer avail, the mood of the believer passes to a certainty which sustains him in resolve and hope.

> *So long thy power hath blest me, sure it still*
> *Will lead me on.*

Such words of power come only from him who has received unusual gifts of grace.

Not only had the words the freshness and the fineness of a poem, they had in them both the simplicity which enables the musician to add to them the melody of his own emotions, and the homely sense which enables numbers to sing them together.

Newman's sermons had already suggested to many the appeal of the spiritual life: but after his visit to Rome and Sicily he added to them a still more haunting and touching quality with a range of power which told that he was being moved from glory to glory, as by the Spirit of the Lord.

CHAPTER VI

TRACTS FOR THE TIMES

I

All the time that Newman had been travelling, his mind was apt to rankle at the thought of enemies who were dangerous to what his instincts taught him to cherish: the idea of continuity of authority in Church and State. Political instincts come to us with the roots of being:

> Every boy and every gal
> That's born into the world alive
> Is either a little Lib-eral
> Or else a little Conserv-ative.

And there was no doubt which Newman was. When a boy is sensitive, fastidious, religious, he cleaves ᐧ to everything that strengthens the defence of respect and taste. He detests everything that vulgarises, desecrates or cheapens the shrines and treasures of his choice. He looks for forces of authority that will defend from battlements and with spears the character, the coat of arms, and the collections of a gentleman. For culture is to him as fine as honour, romance he loves as a bride, and in worship he finds the fountain of noble living.

So had Newman ever been. For this reason his virginal nature shrank from the low talk and common sports of ordinary boys to live apart: for this he cherished silence: for this reason he had a natural loyalty to established power. For this reason his mind was fertile ground to the High Tory ideas of Hurrell Froude: and for this reason he was indignant at the Liberals of 1830. To him Charles X, as an anointed king, had a sacred and prescriptive right to the throne of France: as Newman therefore had driven back through France, he had refused to have faith in a Paris he felt to be revolutionary, or even to look at the tricoleur which sym-

bolised the break with ancient kings. He felt everywhere that men
were setting up their own impulses and whims against that order
in society which enabled the lives of men to be ordered according
to immutable laws for the highest purposes, the eternal values.

2

'In politics', he now wrote, 'they talk much about self-govern-
ment. I have nothing to do with politics, but whether a nation
can or cannot govern itself by the men within it, to the supersed-
ing of king and ministers, certainly the individual cannot. The
first step to govern oneself is to be governed: to obey a rule
whether of belief or of conduct on the ground of the authority of
the Giver—I mean of Almighty God—is the only way towards
gaining inherent power of our own, so as to walk as the sons and
in the image of God. The world, however, has extended its
political theories to religion, and having found it can do without
kings imagines it can do without creeds and without bishops
which God has appointed: it calls this ecclesiastical tyranny and
submission to it degradation.'[1]

Such then was the principle of his conservatism. God had ordained a Church with an hierarchical system: and, as analogy to
this, He had established society under constituted authorities of
government so that men framed together in the corporate work
of society should act not singly but together, in free adherence to
the principle of order. 'Toryism, that is, loyalty to persons springs
immortal in the human breast, and religion is a spiritual loyalty.'[2]

Although Newman was hostile to Liberalism, he admired La-
cordaire and Montalembert. The point on which Liberalism came
into special conflict with his Oxford school was its accentuated in-
dividualism. 'Everyone for himself' was its motto: the individual
was his own Church, his own law, his own authority, he was independent, sufficient in and for himself. But Newman saw keenly
what they were blind to—the height and length and breadth of
things, their manifold interconnection and points of contact, the

[1] *British Magazine*, V, 128 (1834).
[2] Quoted by Keith Feiling: *Nineteenth Century Biography*, 114.

various and changing colours of human good and evil, their subtlety of light and shade. To him all were parts of a great whole: it was only in relation to others that the individual realised himself, became who and what he was. Not that he ignored the claims of the individual as such; for in inner life a man as he reminds us in one of his choicest passages, lives *solus cum solo*.

What he detested was that an individual should assert his choice against the traditional government he viewed as providential: but as he always insisted, what he was always fighting against as Liberalism in religion was that man's opinion should be set up against the dogma, which was the revelation, that had come from God. He believed in religion not as a sentiment but as a dogmatic fact; he believed it as one with sacraments and rites; and he believed the principal seat of this rightness was not in an erring Rome but in the Church of England.

All this he saw threatened by an irreligious paganism which was going to paganise—and to vulgarise—society. As years went on, he felt this modern movement to be sinister indeed. Later he put it all in a classic phrase: 'Phæton has got into the chariot of the sun; we alas! can only look on and watch him down the steep of heaven. Meanwhile the lands which he is passing over suffer from his driving.'[1]

3

Against this tendency he ranged himself in the ardour and enthusiasm of his recuperated health. Often people are stronger in their convalescence than they were before their illness, and Newman was tasting a subtler elixir. He had written after passing Corsica:

> Whene'er in journeying on I feel
> The shadow of the Providential Hand
> Deep breathless stirrings shoot across my breast,
> Searching to know what He will now reveal.

When a man has come into an unexpected inheritance, he feels the support which it gives to his will; if he falls in love, and

[1] *Apologia*, 132.

happily in love, his every prospect is gilded. So it was with Newman. The fountains of his soul were brimming with fresh waters,
his memory rejoiced in the joys and beauties with which it had
been enriched. His sensitive nature had been moved to enthusiasm
as it could never be moved by the mere study of theology: he
penetrated the depths of life by other things than the mere exercise
of the mind. His convalescence joined with an enthusiasm which
gave him an exuberant and exultant energy. He came back to an
Oxford which recognised him as ruler both in intellect and spirit.[1]
He basked in laughter and the love of particular friends. He felt
his work to be momentous and inspiring.[2] His personality was so
radiant that some friends at Oxford hesitated before they spoke
to one so startlingly changed by this new investiture with authority and power.[3] His face shone as skies colour with the dawn.

4

He had only been five days in Oxford when on July 14 Keble
preached in St Mary's before the Judges of Assize a sermon which
some felt historic, for it was announced to be on national apostasy.
He said that the nation was 'becoming alienated from God and
Christ'. There was a government overriding the Holy Church
which was established for the salvation of souls: people no longer
minded about the principles of religion: they preferred to explain
them away. What then was the Church to do but to turn first to
intercession, then to remonstrance, and then to give herself more
thoroughly to piety, purity, charity and justice? Disorder and
irreligion might appear to triumph but a Christian is sure that in
the end victory is his—victory complete, universal, eternal.

Such was Keble's sermon. In itself it was not remarkable: nor
was it generally discussed: only to Newman's convictions un
doubtedly did it mark an epoch.[4] It came from a man who was
revered the more because of his selfless modesty. He who had
sacrificed the most brilliant prospects to the care of Gloucestershire
peasants in a humble cure, lived there gay, unceremonious, bright,

[1] Dean Lake: *Memorial,* 47, 50. Froude: *Short Studies,* IV, 189.
[2] *Apologia,* 112-3.   [3] *Contributions.*   [4] Cross: *Newman,* Appendix IV.

simple as a boy avoiding that his kindness should be recognised, and apparently unconscious that he had made any sacrifice at all: yet writing with such an appeal that his volume of poems was to run through one hundred editions in the next thirty years. Keble's nature was retiring, unselfish, tender: and yet it had the naïf ease and gladness of the saint. When such a man as this said the nation was apostate, it was enough to decide Newman on action.

To this action came an impulse from another country rectory. At Hadleigh in Essex dwelt another leader. Like Keble, Hugh Rose had won academic honours. Like Keble he had a writer's gift. Like Pusey he had been to Germany but only to be convinced that Germany had lost its hold on Christian truth and was already corrupt. Rose now set to work to gather men around him in a movement. In that movement were Hurrell Froude and others of Newman's friends. He felt that something must be done and done at once.[1] But what?

5

While they were hesitating, Newman acted. He began to write tracts. And these tracts came out year by year for several years to challenge the temper of the time, to question what it called progress, to insist that human nature can do nothing without heavenly grace, and that this grace comes from God in the mysteries He has Himself ordained in His Church. Such was the tenour of the tracts. They were, as Church precisely says, clear, brief, stern appeals to conscience and reason, sparing of words, utterly without rhetoric, intense in purpose. They were like the short rapid utterances of men in pain and danger and pressing emergency.[2] Indeed as one looks back on them now, it seems incredible that such bald utterances should have played such a part in history.

The first tract succinctly states Newman's stand: it is that of authority against democracy. If the Church has not the support of education, wealth and connections to attract respect and attention, how can it oppose and conquer a world which prefers to master it and stifle it unless it can add to temporal distinctions *the authority*

[1] Church: *The Oxford Movement*, 98.   [2] *ibid.*

of its apostolical descent? Respectability or cultivation or polish or learning or rank: all those things for which Oxford stood, gave her preachers a hearing with the many: and they were advantages not to be despised: but there was a movement to deprive the Church of these—and then on what could it base its claim to raise men to a life above their own, to confront and overcome their standards of convenience and fancy, but on its supernatural authority as the Church built on the Apostles and elders, with Christ the corner stone?

Men admitted often enough that much was wrong, but they did nothing to remedy it. Now they must choose.

Such was the tenour of Tract One.

6

From the moment it was published there echoed from the high towers and pinnacled city of Oxford to the growing towns and quiet villages of England the sound of trumpet and alarm. Timorous spirits there and in London began nervously to fidget; then to express surprise, dismay, ridicule and at last loud indignation; Newman was asked to be still. But on the other hand his friends were angry and their voices gathered volume like the wind which calls up the storm.

The impulse, tumultuous and urgent, passed from Oxford over England. What did it mean? Where would it lead? From the first moment prophetic voices answered 'It leads to Rome'.

To Rome? But, they answered, there is nothing here but what we find in the Prayer Book, and in our Anglican divines. These are but the essential principles of our own Church. This is to support us against the materialistic, loosening, disintegrating tendencies of the age to a purer spirituality, a stronger effort, a firmer discipline, a more loyal faith. These are the principles which will establish the Church of England in her central strength against the tendencies of the dissenting revivalist on one side, and on the other the stately, the moving, the mysterious impressiveness of Rome. Tractarians claimed to represent central, essential truth. 'Considering the high gifts and strong claims of the Church of Rome,' 'and its dependencies, Newman himself wrote on our admiration, reverence, love and gratitude, how could we withstand it as we do, how could we refrain from being melted into tenderness and rushing into communion with it but for the words of truth itself?'[1] Truth he took to be in the authority of certain Anglican divines; and he felt he must speak sternly against Rome to defend himself from the charge of Popery.

Methodism and Popery, he wrote later, are in different ways the refuge of those whom the Church stints of the gift of grace. They are the foster mothers of abandoned children. 'But if the Church of England would cease to decline from her own standards—the neglect of the daily service, the desecration of festivals, the Eucharist scantily administered, insubordination permitted in all ranks of the Church, orders and offices imperfectly developed, the want of societies for purely religious objects, and the like deficiencies lead the feverish mind, desirous of a vent to its feelings and a stricter rule of life, to the smaller religious communities, to prayer and Bible meetings and ill-advised institutions and societies on the one hand—on the other to the solemn and captivating services by which Popery gains its proselytes. The multitude of men cannot teach or quote themselves.'[2]

7

Newman's personality had now grown to its full stature. Graceful, slender, delicate, almost feminine as he might appear, he yet released from his tension a power as dynamic as the personal fascination which gathered undergraduates around him in an unusual mixture of freedom with devotion and awe. Some he invited to breakfast, others to larger evening parties when he gave them tea: others listened as he ravished their souls with the notes of his violin. Shy and silent as he remained, with much distrust of himself, he yet began to display the abilities of a leader of men: he was regarded inevitably and without dispute as the centre and fountain of the Oxford Movement. 'To his lofty character', says

[1] *Records* No. 24 quoted in *Apologia*, 127.
[2] Preface to first 46 tracts, 1824, quoted by Church: *The Oxford Movement*.

Church, 'he added the force of genius and the statesman's eye, taking in and guiding accurately the whole of a complicated scene.'[1]

8

The men who gathered round him not only enthusiastically admired but loved him, with a return of that warm friendship which was an essential mark of his nature and which suffuses with its intense and sometimes hectic colour the annals of the Oxford of that time. His highly strung nerves, his high temper—fierceness he calls it—the way in which he provoked people to argument, mocked them with the absurdities to which he reduced them, and then cut in with irony: all these made enemies, and maddened them. This only the more amused him: but it made men of weight who knew the temper of England shake their heads. How often, they reflected, are brilliant men unsound! And so, though confident in his own cause, he remained distrustful of himself. And later he wrote that he 'never had the staidness or dignity necessary for a leader'.[2]

The person who gave him ballast was the Etonian who had joined the Common Room of Oriel twelve years before, Edward Pusey. Pusey had what Newman lacked of normal temperament, sedate scholarship, settled position. In 1828 he had become Professor of Hebrew and a Canon of Christ Church. He had also a titled mother, and private means. After years of love he had married and had children. His scholarship was as solid as his character. He was not only a sound man but a very good man, with a warm and affectionate faithfulness. In that bent head, with the damped brown hair, the hairy cheeks, the kindly expression above the round shoulders, the scholarly stoop, there was set the ponderous balance of common sense, that comes so easily to and sits well upon generations of country gentlemen, and goes often with a habit of silence. Pusey cared nothing for smartness; he was marked by learning, seriousness, responsibility, piety.

Newman under Hurrell's influence had become a Tory and High Churchman. The friend of Keble, Pusey had been drawing

[1] Church: *The Oxford Movement*, 114.   [2] *Apologia*, 134.

closer to him, and now in the cause of authority in Church and State, he brought his weight to the support of his old friend in Oriel. 'His great learning,' wrote Newman, 'his immense diligence, his scholarlike mind, his simple devotion to the cause of religion overcame me, and great of course was my joy when in the last days of 1833 he showed a disposition to make common cause with us.'[1]

So it was that the Tractarian movement began, and gathered force, till it rumbled and roared through the countryside of England like a powerful train of armoured vehicles, to attack and to subdue.

9

The commander of the movement still was Newman: Newman, gathering friends round his tea-pot and violin in Oriel, Newman walking every Sunday afternoon down Oriel Street to take his service, to read his lessons, to preach his sermon at St Mary's.

For year by year those sermons were going on: year by year the undergraduates of Oxford were being fascinated and then transformed by the preacher's unique appeal. The tracts and the sermons worked together in the movement, and it was impossible to be interested in one without the other. Some indeed were repelled. In that simple manner they saw something constrained and awkward. That melodious voice, as Justin McCarthy said afterwards, could sound thin and weak.[2] Newman's bearing at first was not impressive in any way—a gaunt emaciated figure, a sharp eagle face and a cold meditative eye often rather repelled than attracted those who saw him for the first time. But even those who came with prejudice and began by disparaging felt the impacts of the extraordinary momentum in his sermons. Terse and swift, they had soon carried their hearers away. The bearing which had seemed at first sight awkward and ungraceful now seemed not only quiet but attractive, and the words had a pathetic power that dealt intimately, yet tactfully and kindly, with the awakened soul.

In the sermons, men heard the living meaning of the reasons

[1] *Apologia*, 136.   [2] J. MacCarthy: *History of Our Own Times*, I, 209.

and bearing of the tracts: the dry technicalities of the cleric were changed by art into an adventure of absorbing moment to youth. In this tingling atmosphere, were judged the questions debated by the controversialists. 'It was no dry theological correctness and competence, which were sought for,' wrote Dean Church, 'no love of privilege, no formal hierarchical claims urged by the writers.'[1] What they thought to be in danger, what they aspired to revive was that which binds the life of man to the Divine, that faith which is the substance of men's hope not only in the eternal but in that daily life in which, if they can transfigure and exalt it, they already have a foretaste of the excellence of timeless things. So men looked, in St Mary's, on the prime mover of the Tracts. They came: they saw: he conquered.

He was most comforting, most sympathetic. He set before persons their own feelings with such truth of detail, such natural expressive touches, that they seemed not to be ordinary states of mind which everybody has, but very peculiar ones. For he and his hearer seemed to be the only two persons in the world that had them in common. Strange insight, strange sympathy which won people to the views on which he refrained from speaking.[2]

'Men used to suspect Dr. Newman—I have done so myself—' wrote Kingsley, 'of writing a whole sermon, not for the text or the matter, but for the sake of one passing hint—one phrase, one epithet, one well barbed arrow which, as he swept magnificently on the stream of his calm eloquence, seemingly unconscious of all presences save those unseen, he delivered undecided as with his finger tip to the very heart of an initiated hearer never to be withdrawn again.'[3]

'Who', asked Matthew Arnold, 'could resist the charm of that spiritual apparition gliding in the dim afternoon light through the aisles of St Mary's, rising into the pulpit, and then, in the most entrancing of voices breaking the silence with words and thoughts which were a religious music—subtle, sweet, mournful? I seem to hear him still saying "After the fever of life, after the weariness

[1] Church: *The Oxford Movement.*
[2] J. B. Mozley: *Christian Remembrance,* Jan. 1846, p. 169.
[3] *What then does Dr Newman mean?* 14.

and sicknesses, fighting and despondings, languor and fretfulness, struggling and succeeding; after all the changes of this troubled unhealthy state, at length comes death, at length the white throne of God, at length the beatific vision".'[1]

10

Did his doctrines develop and change? Hardly. He still insisted on the reality of things unseen and the strenuousness needed to attain to them. And though his influence was interrupted by that excessive sensibility and frequent distrust of himself which came from a certain self-consciousness,[2] he never compromised in sacrificing the flesh to the spirit.

In a famous sermon on the Ventures of Faith, he argued that he who simply lived a normally moral and religious life had given nothing of those hostages of sacrifice which prove that a man really believes in eternal life.

For that one must give up ambition, comfort, accept penances or choose poverty. People would listen to preaching until personal sacrifices were demanded, and then felt it was going too far. There is no truth, however overpoweringly clear, but men may escape from it by shutting their eyes; there is no duty, however urgent, but they may find in their own case ten thousand good reasons against it. But how different are those who have their contemplations, hopes and desires in the invisible world: and to whom death brings back the sight of what they had worshipped, what they had loved, what they had held intercourse with in years long passed away!

It was in this high and unearthly spirit Newman would have them live. For who, he asked, who shall dare to describe the blessedness of those who find all their pledges safe returned to them, all their ventures abundantly and beyond measure satisfied?

He was but returning to a theme on which he had written at Palermo in 1833, in a poem which he called 'Liberalism', and

[1] M. Arnold: *Discourses in America* (1885), 139–40. Cf. *Parochial and Plain Sermons*, VI, 369–70.
[2] Dean Lake: *Memorials*, 51.

another might call lukewarmness. It was already on the theme of
those who refused to purchase holiness and heaven by heroic
effort.

> As for zeal and quick-eyed sanctity
> And the dread depths of grace, ye pass'd them by
> And so ye halve the truth, for ye in heart
> At best are doubters whether it be true.
> The theme discarding, as unmeet for you,
> Statesmen or sages. O new compassed art
> Of the ancient Foe! but what if it extends
> O'er our own camp, and rules amid our friends?

This was indeed the haunting and recurring question of his life.[1]

[1] *Verses on Various Occasions* (1868), 132.

CHAPTER VII

THE ANGLO-CATHOLIC LEADER

I

Besides his sermons and his tracts he gave lectures in St Mary's in the chapel of Adam de Brome. Not from the pulpit but from the desk, listeners heard Newman in the same clear and perfectly modulated voice speaking with a breadth of view, and with force, with daring, with originality on the Prophetical Character of the Church, on Justification by Faith, on Popery and Dissent as worship alternative to the Church of England. The charm of Newman's personality and his prestige lent these lectures an interest which was not inherent in the words themselves; and they too were a part of the movement.

The movement then proceeded: on the one side it preached a doctrine: on the other it set up a standard. An earnest and spiritual life was to lead to and to lead from a proper understanding of the character, the marks, the needs, and, yes, the failings of an ideal Church, that Church of England which, marking the mean of extremes, still seemed to offer hopes of solving England's fundamental problem.[1]

The teaching of Newman and his friends invited new interest in the central figure of the Gospels:—the Christ stood forward once more as the Portrait and Inspirer of Perfection. And with this came a fresh striving to imitate Him in directing and purifying the aims of life, in elevating character, in practising self-discipline, in acquiring control of every impulse, thought and wish, in pursuing in a word that holiness without which none shall see the Lord.

[1] Church: *The Oxford Movement*, 166.

2

Such was the influence of Newman, while he himself remained the tense, impatient, energetic enthusiast who felt in the quick of his being such extremes of joy and pain, of enthusiasm and doubt, of affectionate sympathy and ironic scorn. Beneath his pallid skin his heart exhaled the sweetness and showed the yellow ochre of a freesia. It made Aubrey de Vere compare him, as in cap and gown he glided with singular grace into a room, both to a woman of grace and breeding and to a young ascetic of the middle ages. He was pale and thin almost to emaciation, swift of pace, and when not walking, intensely still, with a voice sweet and pathetic, and so distinct that you could count each vowel and consonant in each word. Though not vehement when touching on subjects which interested him much, he used gestures which were rapid and decisive.[1]

One thought obsessed him: that in the temper of rationalism which had spread from France to England, there was a menace not merely to faith but to morals, to the noblest traditions of civilised life. He anticipated an unprecedented outburst of infidelity all over the world, and felt that he was trusted to play no small part in setting right the perilous and disjointed time.[2]

What really could withstand it but that supernaturally august truth which came to him with Divine authority as Catholicism?

Catholicism! But which was the more truly and essentially Catholic: the reformed Church of England in which he worked, or that venerable, moving august communion which had soothed his heart in Palermo, which filled his soul with admiration, reverence and love? His heart and his head gave to this question conflicting answers: and he was already in tumult within.[3]

[1] Aubrey de Vere: *Recollections*, 256–7.
[2] Aubrey de Vere: *Life*, I, 182. Cf. Pusey House, *unpublished letter to Pusey from Rome*, March 19, 1833.
[3] A.M. 127.

3

We come now to a fresh crisis in Newman's life. For we are approaching a time when Providence gathered together in his fate a number of distinct yet converging events to touch his heart and direct the spirit of his genius.

In his lectures on justification he tried to establish one of the subtlest points of theology in a way that should distinguish Anglican teaching from Lutheran. What does St Paul mean when he says that a man is justified by his faith? Luther said that to the man who believes in Christ's atonement the rightness of Christ was *imputed*, and works were of no account.[1] Catholic theology insists that faith, being a grace, is so profoundly one with the mysteries of grace, that uniting the believer with his Redeemer it imparts to him the rightness of Christ and so sets him right in the eyes of God. He is justified because he is just with the justness of Christ.

Newman already saw how false was the current Protestant view of faith as an emotional enthusiasm over Christ's atoning sacrifice, or a blind trust in it, regardless of an active life of love; he saw also that the view that it was a mere assent of the mind to Divine truth was also quite inadequate; and this he then took to be the Roman Catholic view. Yet he firmly stated the true Catholic doctrine in his own way when he defined faith as an original means of knowledge founded on a super- naturally implanted instinct: it is a secret inexplicable spontaneous movement of the mind which persuades people that in joining the Church, and in living blameless and holy in her graces is the sal- vation of the world.[2] And in the way which is typical of his training in the Bible, of his literary genius, and his power as a leader of men, he works this out by an eloquent Ciceronian appeal to the work of the early Church in ministering to the necessities of human nature, the anxieties of conscience, and the instincts of purity and holiness.

[1] For an excellent account of this see Gregory Dix: *The Question of Anglican Orders*, 15–25. [2] *Grammar of Assent*, 270.

Yet though Newman made certain compromises with the Lutheran doctrine, he does assert most clearly that the essential meaning of justification is *to receive the Divine Presence within us and be made the temple of the Holy Ghost.*[1] This Divine indwelling is the inward gift conveying the virtue of Christ's Atoning Blood. 'What is it', he asks, 'to have His presence within us but to be His consecrated temple? And what to be His temple but to be set apart from a state of nature, from sin and Satan, guilt and peril? What to be thus set apart but to be declared and treated as righteous? And what is this but to be justified?'[2]

He insisted furthermore that this inward gift was one of Divine power and glory. The gift of the Spirit came with power: and the might was in God's glory. 'The glory which thou gavest me, I have given them.' The Spirit of glory, said St Peter, rests upon us, and, added St Paul, 'we are changed from glory to glory as by the Spirit of the Lord'.[3]

4

It was just at this time that Newman, whose mind never worked so much by logic as by the sway of impulses deeper and more complete, found that many events were combining to loosen his moorings in the harbour of conviction. In the first place his friend Hurrell Froude died; and he saw, in the intense clearness that shines in the mind from souls we love as they pass into the world of light, the significance of their lives. That of Hurrell was an instinct for Catholic values. But hardly had his closest friend died, when a yet more profound and intimate loss came to Newman, the death of his mother. For some time she had been looking with pained misgiving on the direction his mind was taking, and he grieved at the idea of disquieting one to whom for thirty-five years he had been attached with affectionate veneration, and who cherished him as her pride. As his mother died just after his sister had married, her death broke up his home and brought him once again alone to the alone.

'We are in great affliction,' he wrote to Pusey. 'I think I have as yet been more wearied from this world than set upon another.'

[1] Newman: *Justification* (1874), 144.   [2] *ibid*, 149.   [3] *ibid*, 164–5.

I trust the late trials I have had may make me really desire and look out for Christ's coming to end this troublesome world.'[1]

His friend Pusey wrote the weightiest of the Tracts: that on Baptism; a great Anglican divine was insisting for the first time for centuries on the full Catholic doctrine of baptism as the completion of faith in the new birth of the soul to transforming grace.

At the same time the movement on which he was engaged gathered force. The tracts ceased to be pamphlets, and became treatises with Pusey's initials attached. Pusey also set to work to publish a library of the fathers of the Church, and away from the University and his college, in the quiet of Littlemore, Newman found himself lonely and alone in the cure of souls. Littlemore was part of the Parish of St Mary's, and there Newman in the course of years built a chapel.

5

To these were added two other events. On the one hand, the very man whose mantle he had taken at Oriel, Dr. Arnold, came out in the *Edinburgh Review* with an article of abuse on the Oxford Movement, abuse so scurrilous that he was almost dismissed from Rugby. He described Newman and his friends as 'conspirators', as 'obscure fanatics', as low worldly clergy careless and grossly ignorant 'carried away by the fanaticism of mere foolery', that fanaticism which he called the peculiar disgrace of the Church of England.[2] Their only prototypes in Church History, said Arnold, were the men who tried to murder St Paul—the enemies and revilers of the holiest names which earth reverences, who are condemned in the most emphatic language by that authority which all Christians acknowledge as divine.[3]

At the same time Newman found himself engaged in violent controversy about the appointment of Hampden. This man, also a Fellow of Oriel, had been a friend of another member of the Oriel Common Room, a renegade priest from Spain, Blanco White; he gave the Bampton Lectures in 1832; he had not only

---

[1] Pusey House, *unpublished*, May 18, 1836.
[2] *Edinburgh Review*, LXIII, 235.   [3] See Liddon: *Pusey*, 382–3.

attacked scholastic philosophy as a farrago corrupted of Plato and Aristotle, but he had insisted that the only source of Catholic truth is the Bible. Now all this sounded like militant Protestantism, and it was less acceptable because it came from a stolid and unprepossessing personality, who contrasted violently with the elastic grace of Froude or Wilberforce or Newman. 'He stood before you like a mill-stone,' it was said, 'and brayed at you like a jackass.'[1] And the Anglo-Catholics tried to prevent him being appointed, they organised a vote, and though they persuaded Convocation to forbid him serving on a board to appoint preachers to the University,[2] they could not prevent the Crown making him Regius Professor of Divinity and a Canon of Christ Church.

6

This appointment was a blow to the Anglo-Catholic cause. Not less influential on the mind of Newman was the return to England of that very Monsignor Wiseman with whom he had discussed in Rome the project of union. Wiseman was a man whose culture was stimulating, whose temper was generous, and who, to awaken souls hibernating in English fog, had brought from Rome a clarion like the spring. In him was alive the spirit both of de Maistre and Chateaubriand, of Mohler and Görres. He could put urbanely yet with profound learning and sincerity the claims of the cosmopolitan Church. He did so now.

[1] T.M. *Rem.* I, 380.   [2] D.N.B. XI, 1148.

CHAPTER VIII

WHAT IS SCHISM?

I

Against these, Newman set out to define his position in words which many an Anglican will welcome and echo still. He defined it as Catholic but not Roman:[1] as taking a middle course between a Rome and a Protestantism which, hurling at one another anathemas, disrupted Western Christendom. 'The English theology would come in with its characteristic calmness and caution, clear and decided in its view, giving no encouragement to lukewarmness and liberalism, but withholding all absolute anathemas on errors of opinion except where the primitive Church sanctions the use of them.'[2] So, invoking divine wisdom, did he proceed in his task.

If Roman Catholics appealed to tradition, Anglicans must meet them fearlessly on the ground of antiquity, for truth is consistent to itself. Rome, he argued, was neglectful of antiquity, and therefore tended to err. Its innovation was a minute, technical and imperative theology, which tended to discourage simple personal surrender to God. It claimed infallibility, but could not say where that resides, and did it not fall therefore to a dependence on each man's private judgment? But if the Church of England, modelling herself upon the Fathers, took up her central position, then she could make the Bible her standard, and meet the hazard of the times. 'For such', he said, 'is God's will, gathering in His elect, first one and then another, by little and little, in the intervals of sunshine between storm and storm, or snatching them from the surge of evil even when the waters rage most furiously.'[3]

Such was Newman's method of meeting his controversy with

[1] *Prophetical Office* (1837), 24, 25.   [2] *ibid* 26.
[3] *ibid*, 422.

Rome which, as he had said in an earlier tract (No. 71), had over-taken them like a summer cloud.

The attitude was new and stimulating. It vindicated Catholicism even while it arraigned contemporary Roman practices. It shewed a great respect for the ideas and traditions of a Catholic Church while claiming that Anglicanism could be consistent with them. It implied that in all Churches there were evils from which God's pity needed to cleanse and defend them. And it urged both that the Anglican Church should undergo a second reformation in going back to principles and practices stated in her Prayer Book but fallen into disuse, and that if she did so she would be in a happier position than any other Communion. 'The Church of England', he said, 'claims to be merely *Reformed,* not Protestant, and it repudiates any fellowship with the mixed multitude which crowd together whether at home or abroad under a mere political banner.'[1]

2

Such then was Newman's argument from 1836 to 1839; and it raised him to his peak of prestige in the Church of England. Churchmen felt an indescribable exhilaration in returning to Catholic traditions and mysteries; how moving it was to think that they, while cherishing their Prayer Book and insisting on its authority, could yet regain that supernal majesty and wisdom, with which the Divine Master had endowed His Apostles when He founded a Church to remain continuously from age to age in one communion and fellowship with the saints and doctors on whom the light of the Spirit had shone with intense brilliancy! In their renewal of enthusiasm, in their renewal of the spiritual life, in the stimulation of fresh ideas and learning, in the romance and beauty which they found associated by the gracious talent of Keble with the offices and doctrines of the Church, revealing at once the evangel of redemption and its interior application to their lives, they felt the holy dew descending on them to fertilise their souls; and many a life put forth the shoots and buds of a wondrous spring.

[1] *op. cit.,* p. 130 in edition of 1877.

These things they could keep in closest loyalty to the temper and claims of England.

There is in Englishmen, as in Frenchmen, a profound conviction that their own country is the best; best not only in its climate and scene, but in the temper and character of its people, and therefore in its national institutions. And therefore they were indisposed to question their Church, and if they did only because of some grounds which would not prevent them finding it better than any Church in any other country. The Oxford Movement, while encouraging the imbedded confidence of their patriotism, yet took them back to something ancient, universal, august, divine. Cleaving to the Church of England and her Prayer Book, they found in them, as they saw in the Bible, at once the highest standards of an English gentleman, and a model of ancient mysteries coming down through the ages, first from the patriarchs and the prophets, then from the evangelists and seers of the glorious Israel of God.

They contemplated, says one of them, 'a Church of England triumphant here below, pure as the earliest day dawn of the faith, venerable as the sagest antiquity, cleansed from medieval accretions, enriched by modern science, daily rising up out of the confusion of the sixteenth century, and delivering itself from secular bonds at no loss but that of diminished revenues; a gradually increased colonial extension, making her the inheritor of a second *orbis terrarum*—and ultimately a reunion with the earlier one'.[1]

The idea was fascinating: it worked like a spell. It began what it continues, to transform the Church of England. It brought back to her with belief in the communion of saints the splendid implications of her belief in the Holy Spirit. She came once more face to face with that article of the Apostles' creed: *the Holy Catholic Church*.

3

Various scholarly men elaborated this doctrine: first there had been Alexander Knox; there were still not only Pusey and Keble, but Rose and William Palmer, and there were brilliant young

[1] Aubrey de Vere: *Recollections*, 261.

men like Froude and Ward and Church and Gladstone—there
was also a cohort of Oxford men in London, of young clergy
everywhere, of undergraduates not yet removed from Oxford,
but spreading their enthusiasm every time they went home for
their vacations. All these centred on Newman, whose speeches
and silence were alike dynamic. It was said of him that if his
mouth were shut, it seemed it could never open; and if open, it
could never shut. The magnetism of his personality, the fame of
his sermons, the ease of his approaches, the freshness and distinction of his style, combined with his dislikes and reserves, focussed
on his name the gaze of thousands.[1]

His methods might be unsystematic and incomplete, but in him
men saw not donnish technicalities, but a sympathy kindly and
encouraging as the sun. He kept arresting and fascinating mind
after mind, with that combination of characteristic gifts, which a
friend describes as 'his habit of mind and way of writing, his ease,
his frankness, his candour, his impatience of conventionality, his
piercing insight into the very centre of questions, his ever ready
recognition of nature and reality, his range of thought, his bright
and clear and fearless style of argument, his undisplayed but never
unfelt consciousness of the true awfulness of everything connected
with religion'[2] he filled the men of his generation with admiring
reverence.[3]

4

What added mustard to his mixture was his acumen in controversy.

A superb cat which all admire for the glossiness of its fur, the
agility of its motions, the independence of its poise, cannot but
charm by the delicacy of its caress; yet, having closely watched
the flitting sparrow, or the furtive mouse, can spring upon them
with overpowering agility and kill them; if annoyed, it can hiss
and arch, ready in swift reprisal to scratch with claws so ruthless
that its opponents are in danger for their eyes.

As a controversialist Newman found himself engaged in a war

[1] Ward: *Newman*, I, 151.   [2] Church: *The Oxford Movement*, 188.
[3] Sir F. Doyle: *Lectures on Poetry*, 123.

on two points. On the one side he was accused of being a Papist, and this suspicion attached to his sermons as well as to the tracts. It not only occasioned the scurrilous outburst of Arnold from Rugby, but from one section of Protestants after another he had been stigmatised as 'a bigot, an ascetic, a high church fanatic and, worse than all, as little better than a champion of Popery'.[1]

5

Yet did he not find though more courteous, yet certainly more formidable antagonists in the very camp of Popery? In 1836 his friend Perceval brought out a book called *The Roman Schism illustrated from the Records of the Catholic Church*. He was reviving the contention of Barrow and of the Anglican Canons of 1603. Here he developed the line which was the innovation of the Tractarians. They did not argue that the Roman Catholic Church was wrong in its essential tendency, but in its toleration of deviations from its own standards.[2] This book contained an attack on a Jesuit, Harding, who was accused of saying that 'Christ was twice immolated, has twice shed His blood, once in the Eucharist, and once on the cross'. That, argued Perceval, was a common superstition, condemned by an article of the Church of England. Admitting that the Eucharist was a sacrifice, however, he abstained from condemning the decrees of the Council of Trent.[3]

6

The appearance of this book with its challenging title coincided with the arrival in England of the work of a scholar competent to present Rome's answer. Nicholas Wiseman, though still at the English College in Rome, prepared for delivery in England his lectures on the Catholic Church, which were reviewed courteously and at length in the *British Critic*.[4] Wiseman himself gave the most considerate attention to the Tracts, reviewing them in three successive articles of great length. In these he naturally dealt

[1] *British Critic*, Vol. IV, p. 380, April, 1836.   [2] *British Critic*, IX, 444–6.
[3] A. P. Perceval: *The Roman Schism* (1836), 395–6.   [4] Oct. 1836, 373–403.

with the questions raised by Perceval. Which in England was in schism: the established Church or the adherents of the Pope? He developed his answer learnedly, urbanely and gradually.

Newman must already have studied in the *Dublin Review* the two long articles which Wiseman had already written in July, 1837, and October, 1838, on Anglican claims in the *Tracts for the Times*. They had been concluded with the words: '*We covet their brotherhood in the faith, and their participation in our security of belief and their being bound to us in cords of love, through religious unity.*'

Each of those articles had been courteous and competent. Neither had shown a conclusion at all likely to overwhelm an Anglican. The final answer did not appear till 1839. Wiseman then found his illustration in the Donatists in their controversy with St Augustine. They too had claimed that Rome was in schism and that they were the Catholic Church. But what was the answer of Augustine? It was that when the world as a whole decides on a particular matter against a certain view held by a particular nation or section, the world as a whole is right. It was the view repeated by Abraham Lincoln in his famous Bloomington aphorism: 'You cannot fool all of the people all the time.' How, asks Augustine, can one national Church say that it alone is right, when all others agree together against it? Of course, it will say that they are in schism, that they are so corrupt that it *must* separate. But, St Augustine asks, who are men to leave God's holy Church because it is corrupt? 'Good men', says Augustine, 'cannot separate themselves from the Church which is the source of all goodness established by God. His guarantees are given not to individual zealots but to a universal Church against which the gates of hell shall not prevail. *Securus iudicat orbis terrarum.*'

Now it happened that Newman read this article in 1839 just after he had been suspecting a similar conclusion in relation to those earlier heretics, the Monophysites. They too had claimed that they were right, and the whole Church wrong. At first, this second article from Wiseman, written not sensationally, but in the soberness of a scholar, did not shake him; but Robert Williams, who brought it to him, was influenced, and kept repeating the sounding Latin words: *Securus iudicat orbis terrarum.*

As in cases where great ideas are at stake, one sentence will waylay and haunt the uncertain man, so that sentence haunted Newman and changed the direction of his life.

7

It provided the answer to the dilemma he had already stated that year in the *British Critic*.

When in later years with travail of spirit he sought to unravel in a string of ideas the innumerable knots and tangles of his mind he emphasised that article. But he already took an attitude and stated a view which contrasted, as dark with light, the Protestant against the Catholic principles.

That article is an *Apologia* in itself. He notes at once that his Anglo-Catholic movement (for so he already calls it) had split the Church of England in two, and that it was accused of undermining the very foundations of Protestantism. But what, he asked, was that Protestantism? It lacked an inward principle of union, permanence and consistency: it was centred on individual choice, and open also to all the wilfulness and malice of our frail nature. Unstable as water, it could not excel. It did not know what it meant by faith or by unity or yet by the Church. It was vague about the sacraments and antiquity. Its foundations were sand. It could not maintain its present insecure position. 'It is', he wrote, 'but an inchoate state or doctrine, and its final conclusion is in rationalism.'[1]

Protestantism, he argued, stood on no entrenched ground, but was on the neutral and undefended no-man's-land between the armies of Catholic truth and rationalism, neither of them owning it, or making account of it, or courting it. It was intrinsically confused and imbecile. It was but an encumbrance on the battle-ground between the real enemies who were marshalling their array. 'Then indeed will be the stern encounter when two real and living principles, simple, entire, consistent, one in the Church, the other out of it, at length rush upon each other.'[2]

[1] *British Critic*, XXV, 419 (1839).   [2] *op. cit.*

8

People might not like this sharp antithesis: they might answer that 'mistiness is the mother of wisdom'. But sooner or later they would have to see that vagueness is an insufficient protection. 'Orthodox Protestantism is not enough between men and women,' said Newman. 'It tires them: it is so very awkward . . . they cannot go on for ever standing on one leg, or sitting without a chair, or walking with their legs tied, or grazing like the stags of Tityrus, on the air. Premises imply conclusions: germs lead to developments; principles have issues: doctrines lead to action. Effects will sooner or later be seen to presuppose causes, correlations to nullify each other; contradictions to exclude each other; the elephant will not for ever stand on the tortoise, or the Barmecide fatten upon empty dishes. The most intense horror of Popery cannot undo facts or legitimate fallacies. And the sooner certain zealous friends of Protestantism understand this the better.'[1]

9

He looked out on the currents of contemporary opinion. He saw on the one side pantheism, on another democracy; on yet another a return to dogmatism, to mysticism or to asceticism: but nothing pointed back to the schools of the Reformation. The Oxford movement was typical of a Catholic revival which had been prepared by poets and spread over Italy, France and Germany.

If all this were so, what should be the conclusion? To most people the conclusion of his line of thought would be obvious enough. If Protestantism was degenerating into humanism, materialism or democracy, which are all the opposites of the primacy of the Spirit, then obviously one must give it up. But, so Newman now said, it must not be for *Popery*. His object was to make the Church of England Catholic. He looked on her as the 'reformed Catholicism of the West'.

[1] *op. cit.*

Newman wrote long afterwards that this essay was his last word as an Anglican to Anglicans. In point of fact that was hardly true;[1] but it certainly points to an unresolved crisis in the development of his thought. It was a line of argument which tends to take people beyond the Church of England. It expressed his native distrust of mass movements, of revolution as against tradition, of men's turning from authority to democracy—that distrust which was at every turn the profound instinct of his mind; at the same time he shewed himself the energetic arguer—schooled by Whately and authority to his logic—to carry reasoning from premises to conclusions. That reasoning was gathering force, like a river in stormy weather.

10

But Newman had by now given proof that his mind was being swayed not alone by logic. In two sermons preached at St Mary's on the first two Sundays of 1839, he had argued firstly that faith was swifter and subtler than reason: that it was based on inclination towards divine things and love of them: that it marked the trend of a whole life and character. But he went further: laying the foundations of his later contributions to metaphysics, he showed that the greatest achievements of human genius are subtler far than logic. Our senses, our memory, our reason itself can each be deceived in the first place, while our conclusions are loftier and more cogent in so far as they elude scrutiny and are inwoven into the fabric of life and events. 'Great objects exact a venture, and a sacrifice is the condition of honour.'[2]

11

New light on Newman's mind is now furnished from Magdalen by the Bloxam manuscripts, left by a former member of the College who was a friend of Newman's.

On March 15, 1840, Newman wrote to Bloxam from Little-

---

[1] Church: *The Oxford Movement*, 244. 'It is clear from what he tells us that his words in 1839 were not his last words as an Anglican to Anglicans.'

[2] *Sermons before the University of Oxford* (1843), 213.

more: 'I am so drawn to this place that it will be an effort to go back to St Mary's. How one is pulled in twain! Why cannot one be in two places at once. However, I have various plans to effect this object of multiplying myself, which when I see you I will detail.

'Everything is so cold at St Mary's. I have felt it for years. I know no one. I have no sympathy. I have too many critics and carpers. If it were not for those poor undergraduates who are after all *not* my charge, and the Sunday Communions, I should be sorely tempted to pitch my tent here. By the bye, would your Dorchester friend, I forget the worthy man's name, sell me some bare ground? Perhaps I might contrive to build a house on it.'[1]

At this time Newman took a very important move. Giving more time to his parishioners at Littlemore, it occurred to him that he might form there a religious community, and retire there to direct it.

He explained his plan on March 17, 1840, in a long letter to Pusey.

'Since I have been up here, an idea has revived in my mind, of which we have before talked, viz. of building a monastic house in this place and coming up to live in it myself.

'It rose in my mind from the feeling which has long been grow-ing on me that my duty as well as my pleasure lies more at Little-more than I have made it. It has long been a distress that I know so little of my parishioners in Oxford, but tradespeople it is next to impossible to know, considering how they have hitherto been educated—at least impossible to me. It has pained me much to be preaching and doing little more than preach—knowing and guiding only a few, say about half a dozen; moreover from the circumstances of the case, however little I might wish it, preaching more for persons who are not under my charge, members of the University. All this is independent of my monastic scheme. I have given twelve years to St Mary's in Oxford, may I not in fairness and propriety give something of my continual presence to St Mary's at Littlemore?

'In such a case, I should have no intention of separating myself
_____
[1] Middleton: *Magdalen Studies,* 45.

THE HOUSE AT LITTLEMORE

from St Mary's in Oxford, or the University. I should take the Sunday afternoon service at St Mary's, if that were an object, and should certainly be in Oxford; indeed I must, as being full of ties as a Fellow of Oriel.

'Next as to this plan of a priory:—I could not be here much without my library—that is what immediately turned my thoughts to a building: and then all we had on former occasions said about it came into my mind.

'I am quite of opinion, first that such a scheme cannot begin in Oxford: nor in London or another great town. Next I think we must begin with a complete type or specimen which may *preach* to others. I am sanguine that if we could get one set up at Littlemore, it would set the example both in great towns, and for female societies.

'Again perhaps it might serve as a place to *train up* men for great towns.

'Again it should be an open place, where friends might come for a time if they needed a retreat, or if they wished to see what it was like.

'And further, if it be any object as you sometimes kindly think to keep me in Oxford, and indeed as I should like, a plan like this fixes me.'[1]

But for a time Hope and other friends dissuaded him from living so much away from College.

[1] Liddon: *Pusey*, II, 135-6.

CHAPTER IX

THE CONFLICT OF DOUBTS

I

In January, 1841, he produced his article in the *British Critic* on the Catholicity of the Church of England. It was occasioned by Perceval's vindication of the validity of Anglican orders.[1] After accepting Perceval's contentions, he engages in a fictitious dialogue through which he contends that if Anglicanism looks suspiciously like schism, Rome looks like overlaying revealed truth with the doctrines of men. Yet even so, after stating his difficulties about indulgences, the prerogatives of the Blessed Virgin and the 'worship of angels', he leaves the final word to Rome: it is said expressly 'I have many things to say unto you, but ye cannot bear them now; howbeit, when He, the Spirit of truth is come, He shall guide you into all truth'. If 'I am with you always' applies not only to the Apostles but to the Church after them, so does the other promise. If we deny the continuance of the Holy Spirit's office after the Apostles' age, why not of His presence also?

Yet even so he wavers once more. Rome, he feels, *has* added to the Creed: and yet again even if that is true, Anglicanism was separate from everything else—so for page after page the theological controversy sways about. It is plain that the writer's mind is in a torment of confusion. But the last word was after all a defence of Anglicanism as having the note of possession and of freedom from party titles—'the note of life, a tough life and a vigorous'; to these he added ancient descent, unbroken continuance, and agreement in doctrine with the ancient Church.

[1] A. P. Perceval: *An Apology for the Doctrine of Apostolical Succession* (1839).

2

Nor did he refrain from attacks on Rome. Strange to say, he accused her of association with a low democracy and pandering to the spirit of rebellion. He was disgusted that she did not insist on the Divine Right of Kings and the High Tory doctrines of Hurrell Froude. And besides he still took the Englishman's view that she was tricky and debased: 'Till we see in them as a Church more straightforwardness, truth and openness, more of obedience to God's least commandments, more scrupulousness about means, less of a political scheming grasping spirit, less of intrigue, less that is hollow and vulgar, less subserviency to the vices of the rich, less humouring of man's morbid and wayward imaginations, less indulgence of their low and carnal superstitions, less intimacy with the revolutionary spirit of the day, we will keep aloof from them as we do.'[1]

So touchy in fact was Newman's Anglicanism that in January, 1840, he refused the proposal of Fr Spencer to pray for unity. Yet the story of Fr Spencer might well have touched his heart. The son of a well-known peer, George Augustus Spencer had lived a life of gaiety before a performance of Mozart's opera, *Don Giovanni,* in Paris converted him to the life of grace. After taking orders in the Church of England, he was converted to Catholicism when staying at Grace-Dieu with Ambrose Lisle Phillipps, the most interesting convert made until then: a broad-minded, cultured and devout country gentleman, Spencer became a Passionist, taking the name of Fr Ignatius. When Fr Spencer came to stay with a friend at Magdalen, Newman declined to meet him at dinner. When Palmer of Magdalen brought Spencer to call on him at Oriel, proposing that if people in different communions would pray for unity in a spirit of real charity, difficulties would vanish, Newman consulted Pusey who was unduly cautious,[2] but to Spencer personally Newman was extremely petulant. He asserted in fact that Spencer in leaving Anglicanism for Rome

[1] *British Critic,* XXVII, 87, Jan. 1840.   [2] Liddon: *Pusey,* II, 135–6.

had in a time of crisis united with the evil against the good. This he wrote in a letter distinctly sharp in tone to Fr Spencer himself.

'To everyone who comes to me with a proposal', Newman wrote to Bloxam, on March 2, 1841, 'for negotiations for the reunion of the Church of England to the Holy See, what is my simple answer? Is it not Address your Bishop, not me? Mr Phillipps, in kind and warm feeling, makes much more of two or three people in our Church and University than he has any right to do. He much exaggerates our importance and influence. Some of us are not even in authority, nor likely to be. To ask us to propose terms of negotiation is to invite us to forget our place, and to take on us the duties of our rulers: let us go to them: they have the care and oversight of the Churches, and none but they. Others than they have no right to take the initiative except where the essential truth of the gospel is in jeopardy. If the *Tracts of the Times* took on them to speak first, it was because their authors felt that heresy was starting all around the Church, if it had not already entered it.

'We are all agreed if Mr Phillipps will excuse me in saying it, in distrusting Rome, as hollow, insincere, political, ambitious and unscrupulous. I am not saying whether or not we exaggerate, but this would be our common impression, and I think it is founded on the undeniable truth that Rome has not upon her at this day, at least to our view, the note of sanctity. We see much of her gaining power by political party intrigue and tumult. We hear much of disputations, much of societies, publications and tracts, but very little of inward religion. We find her authors of this day able controversialists, but how very few can be pointed out who have written any work which evidences any heart, any depth of spiritual experience, or fullness of faith and love. Let them put into our hands the meditations, or the prayers, or the essays, or the sermons which argue the man of God. We cannot but judge them by what comes before us. That there are zealous and devoted persons in this communion I rejoice to believe. Let them employ their exertions not in attempting to convert us, but in improving their own people. If a foreign order is to come into this country, let it employ itself on the English and Irish Roman Catholics. Let it break off their active co-operation with the political party with which they are at present identified. Let them promote a real reformation of life and conduct. Let them and us rival each other in preaching and practising righteousness. And let us see *where* such a course leaves us in the end. Then will be the time for negotiations.'[1]

March 3, 1841

'This I feel most strongly,' Newman wrote to Bloxam a day later, 'and cannot conceal it, viz., that while Rome is what she is, union is impossible. That we too must change, I do not deny.

'Rome must change first of all in her spirit. I must see more sanctity in her than I do at present. Alas! I see no works of sanctity, or, if any, they are chiefly confined to converts from us. "By their fruits ye shall know them" is the main canon our Lord gives us to know true pastors from false. I do very much think that, with all our sins, there is more sanctity in the Church of England and Ireland than in the Roman Catholic bodies in these same countries. I say all this not in reproach but in great sorrow. Indeed I am ever making the best of things before others when the Roman Catholics are attacked, but I cannot deny this great lack.

'This is not the place to go into controversial matters, nor is it necessary, since the previous difficulty of the sadly degenerate state of Rome is first to be removed. But when it is removed, they still would have to explain authoritatively many portions of their formularies which they at present interpret in a sense which seems to me very uncatholic.

'And then, after all, I see nothing to make me think it would be other than a sin for any of us to *leave* our Church; we must make our Church move. If indeed so far from moving she rushed (which God forbid and what it is profane even to suppose) into open heresy instead; and the Church of Rome on the other hand cleared herself of her present faults, in such a state of things I can conceive it being a duty to leave our own Church and join the Roman. I do not feel it a duty on any other hypothesis. . . . The

[1] Bloxam MSS in Magdalen College Library.

D

English heresy will be favourably inclined to a plotting intriguing party: but faith and holiness are invincible.'[1]

3

To tell the truth Newman's nerves were on edge: his mind was confused. 'Who can know himself,' Newman asked later, 'and the multitude of subtle influences which act upon him?' He was in perplexity and dismay. The stars of his heaven were going out one by one, and he felt that though the kindly light was leading still, yet it was leading dimly through his soul's dark night of anguished doubt.[2] He himself wrote long after that when he tried to analyse his mind it was the ripping up of old griefs, and an extreme trial to head and heart. If his own words are poignant, yet they are not more touching than the sympathy with which, fifty years later, an old friend who was with him at the time in Oriel explained the torments of his mind. 'The change of religion when it comes to a man gradually,' wrote Dean Church, 'when it is not welcomed from the first, but on the contrary long resisted, must always be a mysterious and perplexing process, hard to realise and follow by the person most deeply interested, veiled and clouded to lookers-on, because naturally belonging to the deepest depths of the human conscience and inevitably and without much fault on either side liable to be misinterpreted and misunderstood. And this process is all the more tangled when it goes on, not in an individual mind travelling in its own way on its own path, little affected by others and little affecting them, but in a representative person with the responsibilities of a great cause upon him, bound by closest ties of every kind to friends, colleagues and disciples, thinking, feeling, leading, pointing out the way for hundreds who love and depend on him. Views and feelings vary from day to day, according to the events and conditions of the day. How shall he speak and how shall he be silent? How shall he let doubts and difficulties appear, yet how shall he suppress them? Doubts which may grow and become hopeless, but which on the other hand may be solved and disappear. How shall he go on as

[1] Bloxam MSS in Magdalen College Library.   [2] *Apologia*, 179-80.

if nothing had happened, when all the foundations of the world seem to have sunk from under him? How shall he disclose the dreadful secret when he is not quite sure whether his mind will not still rally from its terror and despair? He must in honesty, in kindness give some warning, yet how much? And how to prevent it being taken for more than it means?

'For it is not knowledge and intellect alone which come into play, but all the moral tastes and habits of the character, its liking and dislikings, its weakness and its strength, its triumphs and its vexations, its keenness and its insensibilities which are in full action while the intellect alone seems to be busy with its problems.'[1]

4

Such, in the words of one who was both an enthusiastic admirer, an unwavering friend, and a master of English, is the interior semblance at this time of the palpitating complex genius, compact of nervous fibre, scholarly acumen and poetic sensibility with fervent zeal, who was both the leader of an historic revival in his historic Church, and the central personage of Oxford.

He himself described in *Loss and Gain* the latent conviction that all the time he was proceeding to his inevitable end. He could not escape his destiny. But all the time the slow wheels of time were bringing it nearer. 'And even before that blessed hour, as an opening flower scatters sweets, so the strange unknown odour, pleasing to some, odious to others, went abroad from him upon the winds, and made them marvel what could be near them, and made them look curiously and anxiously at him, while he was unconscious of his own condition.'[2]

[1] Church: *The Oxford Movement*, 234–5.
[2] *Loss and Gain* (1848), Part II, Ch. VI.

CHAPTER X

TRACT NINETY

I

The travail of Newman's mind was now to find expression in the most complex, intricate and sophisticated of his writings, the treatise that brought upon his head the hail and lightning of the storm, and brought his movement into full collision with the authorities—Tract XC.

As the hosts of Midian had prowled around the rising walls of the citadel of Anglo-Catholicism, they had concentrated their attack on its apparent disloyalty to the XXXIX articles, attached to the Prayer Book. The first eight of those articles certainly were incontrovertible statements of Catholic truth; but then their tone changed, and they contained phrases so difficult to reconcile with Catholic doctrine that, taking them as a whole, many an Anglican clergyman has referred to them as the forty stripes save one. It was indeed reasonable and natural for the Protestants to use them as artillery to bombard the ramparts and bastions which their Anglican enemies were raising.

But the truth is that as the Prayer Book itself was a compromise which, while discarding many Catholic forms, yet retained many others, so the articles contained subtleties which, when examined very closely, were like chinks in a wall, so that something very like a Catholic meaning could creep in through them. Perceval had already shown it in one case in his book in 1836. Newman had taken up the hint, and now brought out 'a novel and complicated piece of critical research'[1] applying the idea to the eleven articles that most wounded Catholics.

[1] *Correspondence*, 71.

2

He did not for a moment deny that Protestants had drawn them up: his contention was that they had been drawn up with a certain elasticity of phrase so that if a Catholic tried very hard, he could find a loophole in them; though Anglicans might be speaking with the stammering lips of ambiguous formularies, yet it was possible—if not to train the Church of England to speak plain truth yet—to listen to those of her children who did so.

If an article said the visible Church of Christ is a congregation of faithful men, said Newman, the word congregation was used by many a Catholic doctor; if an article said General Councils of the Church may err, he pointed that what guaranteed the Councils was their being gathered in the name of Christ. If an article said that 'the Romish doctrine concerning purgatory, pardons, worshipping and adoration, as well of images as of relics, and also invocation of Saints is a fond thing, vainly invented', it was referring not to the Council of Trent but scandalous abuses among the populace in certain places. If an article said that 'Confirmation, marriage, penance, holy orders and anointing are not sacraments of the gospel', it merely stated what everyone knew—that they were not mentioned in the gospel. If an article denied transubstantiation, it meant not to deny a real and spiritual change in the Blessed Sacrament, but only a change into an earthly and material body. If an article said that 'the sacrifices of Masses' were 'blasphemous fables and dangerous deceits', it meant only to rebuke a superstitious dependence on a rite apart from its essential unity with Christ's death and reconciliation. If an article said the Bishop of Rome has no jurisdiction in this realm of England, it stated an historic fact, not the ideal of Church Government; and to touch on a point on which Newman felt with a personal acuteness, if in an article priests are not commanded by God's law to abstain from marriage, Rome would not contradict it—and neither, of course, she would, having within her unity many married priests.

Newman's contention was then summed up. It was that the

articles were so constructed by those who framed them as best to comprehend those who did not go so far in Protestantism as themselves. If therefore Catholics wrested out of the articles the meaning they wanted, they were only 'using them for an express purpose for which among others their authors framed them'.

Such in brief is the argument of the tract he published on February 27, 1841. The common man was soon to point out that it amounted to saying that the articles were not necessarily Protestant, but could mean anything or nothing. To the normal Anglican of the time such a view was not merely astounding, it seemed not only an outrageous sophistry: but it appeared at once to prove that the Tractarians, uneasy in the gowns of Oxford and the garb of her Protestantism, were but cunning wolves who had trapped themselves out in the guise of innocuousness to pounce upon and devour little Red Riding Hood.[1]

3

Indeed there *was* something almost insidious in the tone of Tract XC. In dealing with separate articles, it pointed out to the Tractarians only that they could squeeze through certain chinks in the wall: but behind was the claim for Catholic authority to decide what the articles ought to mean: or as Liddon afterwards put it with mildness and tact: 'in less troubled times it seems astonishing that any one should seriously endeavour to interpret a carefully worded set of articles as the standard when the language is that of historical theology.'[2]

That was the tenour of Newman's whole contention. 'My view is this,' he wrote to Pusey, 'that as infants are regenerated in baptism, not in the faith of their parents, but of the Catholic Church, so the Articles are received, not in the sense of their writers, but in the Catholic sense as far as the wording will admit.'[3] Unless the Church of England agreed with antiquity, in other words, it had no claim whatever: but even that was not all—in page after page he brought out references and explanations which

[1] J. B. Mozley: *Letters*, 113.   [2] Liddon: *Pusey*, II, Ch. XXV, 163.
[3] Liddon: *Pusey*, II, 182, the MS. in Pusey House, undated.

defended the Catholicity, not merely of antiquity, but of Trent, and therefore of Rome.

No one reading Tract XC could fail to see that, while merely claiming a foothold, he was using his learning and his subtlety to undermine Protestantism in the Church of England, and lead his communion towards unity with Rome. He was told so plainly by his closest friend.[1]

It had therefore always been reasonable enough for any normal Protestant member of the Church of England to say that the Anglo-Catholic movement (as Newman called it) was being injected into a Protestant body like a virus; but it was now natural to say that the movement's leader was distintegrating the very formulas of Protestantism linked up with the Prayer Book, that he was wresting them from the meaning of those who wrote them and those who for three hundred years had subscribed to them, and twisting them to a purpose clean contrary; and this not by the sophistries of the Jesuit working, however subtly, from outside. Newman, by an insidious treachery, was preparing from within breaches for the open enemy without.

The man who first sounded the patriotic alarm was a member of Oriel. He had come back to Oxford to be curate at Littlemore. He had soon come to distrust Newman. He now heavily engaged, as though to clear up imputations suggested by his unusual name of Golightly. This the young Tractarians altered to Goliath, or shortened to Golly—which they might have rhymed with folly, for reading this tract made him beside himself;[2] he became so obsessed with it that he thought Tractarians were waiting at the corners on dark nights to do him serious bodily harm.

He closeted himself with the Provost of Oriel.[3] He puffed the tract all over Oxford as a 'curiosity'; he bought copies of it to send to all the bishops. He interviewed both heads of houses and ordinary dons. He made such shrewd cuts at the tract as caused a panic.[4] His indefatigable exertions won him the commendation of important bishops.[5] Newman's name was in every mouth, and many a brain beside that of Golightly was affected with his new

---

[1] Frederic Rogers, afterwards Lord Blatchford.   [2] A.M. II, 444.
[3] *Correspondence*, 444.   [4] A.M. II, 330.   [5] J. B. Mozley: *Letters*, 113.

mania. Four leading dons at Oxford, including a future Archbishop of Canterbury, signed a protest. The Vice-Chancellor decided to submit the matter to the Hebdomadal Council. Lord
Morpeth attacked the tract in the House of Commons.[1] At Rugby
Dr Arnold wrote of Newman and his party as idolaters. Lord
John Russell, by asserting that many undergraduates were going
over to Rome, caused a sensation of horror.[2]

In Oxford the heads of houses met and by a majority of 19
to 2 decided to censure the tract: in a spirit which Newman described as smouldering stern energetic animosity.[3] They published
their censure on March 16th, stating that Tract XC did not
explain but evaded the articles, and recalling that members of the
University were bound by statute to accept the articles. The censure said that the tract aimed at reconciling readers with the very
errors the articles were designed to counteract.[4] Like those bearing
against dishonest tradesmen, this notice was stuck up at College
butteries and in other places where undergraduates gathered,
as though meant to protect the young men from a trickster.

4

Newman was wholly taken aback. He had never anticipated
such a sensation.[5] By nature he was a militant controversialist
because he was intensely sensitive. And when a spiritual man
highly strung finds himself an open scandal, he feels at the heart
of passionate agitation a central calm. 'I have quite enough,' he
wrote on March 16th, 'thank God, to keep me from inward
trouble: no one ever did a great thing without suffering.'[6] Many
friends hurried to his support, and Perceval in particular wrote a
pamphlet to defend him. But attacks continued and were pressed
hard.

Newman maintained his equilibrium with the reflection that

[1] Liddon: *Pusey*, II, 165, 168.   [2] Stanley: *Arnold* (1844), II, 102.
[3] J. B. Mozley: *Letters*, 113.   [4] *Apologia*, 173 (1864).
[5] Liddon: *Pusey*, II, 183. 'I was altogether unsuspicious that my tract would
make any disturbance.' Cf. Oakeley: *Tractarian Movement*, p. 45.
[6] A.M. II, 335.

the tract had not been suppressed. For him the central question
was the attitude of his bishop. Richard Bagot was not only sympathetic, generous, kindly, but he was a master of tact. Still, when
a bishop sees that a man has raised a commotion, his impulse is
to calm it. The tract, after all, was tending to endanger and dis-
unite the Church of England. 'I cannot refrain', wrote the bishop,
'from expressing my anxious wish that for the peace of the Church
discussions upon the articles should not be continued in the publication of the "Tracts for the Times". You will not, I am sure,
mistake the spirit and feeling with which this wish is expressed,
but will consider it as the wish of one who has a sincere personal
regard for yourself.'[1]

The Bishop of Oxford refused to support either the University
censure, or the letter of the Four Tutors; but urged on by the
Archbishop of Canterbury, he talked over with Pusey the project
of suppressing Tract XC.

This immediately produced the strongest reaction in Newman's
mind. He felt that if his tract were repudiated then he, with his
view of the articles, had no business in the diocese. On March
26th he was in extreme tension. He poured out his mind to his
young friends James Hope and Richard Church. He sent no less
than three letters to Pusey on that one day. 'I shall be hurt and
discouraged beyond measure', he wrote, in his second, 'if the
tract is suppressed at all. The feeling grows stronger every hour.'

On the same day the bishop wrote to Pusey that he had 'read
over and over Mr Newman's distressed and touching notes, with
no small emotion', that he could not 'put him aside without
hastening to relieve his mind by repeating my earnest disposition
to yield the point he has so much at heart'. The Anglican prelates
therefore allowed the tract to stand, the Archbishop only suggesting that Newman should append to it his former pronouncement
against Rome 'by way of explaining the real views of the
writer'.[2]

[1] Liddon: *Pusey*, II, 185.

[2] Liddon: *Pusey*, II, 201. Though many Bishops denounced Tract XC in their
individual charges, they took no action collectively. The Bishop of Oxford
asked Newman to discontinue the Tracts, not to withdraw Tract XC.

Newman now wrote to his bishop and published a letter which was already an apologia. He insisted that he had not disturbed Anglican doctrines in the tracts, nor Anglican traditions in her services. Everywhere he had sought to promote unity by holiness of life. 'I have nothing to be sorry for, but everything to rejoice in and be thankful for. I have never taken pleasure in seeming to be able to move a party, and whatever influence I have had has been found not sought after. I have acted because others did not act and have sacrificed a quiet which I prized. May God be with me in times to come as He has been hitherto.'[1]

5

So wrote Newman at the end of that anguished month. After the summer term he retired to Littlemore without further cares or anxiety, determined to translate St Athanasius for the library of the Fathers. 'But between July and November,' he wrote, 'I received three blows which broke me.' Firstly he was shocked to hear how many Anglican authorities were prepared to unite with Prussian Lutherans in founding a Protestant bishopric in Jerusalem. M de Bunsen, the Prussian Minister at the Court of St James, in working for an entente between Prussia and England, desired the Anglican Church to recognise the new State Church of Prussia. He proposed that English bishops should consecrate alternately an Anglican and a Lutheran as bishop of Jerusalem. This proposal was accepted by the Archbishop of Canterbury! Who can wonder that every Tractarian was shocked?

'If', wrote Newman to Perceval, 'a number of persons have for years been preaching the existence of the Holy Catholic Church, what is the inevitable and immediate effect of the Church of England declaring that she is *not* that Holy Catholic Church, but to send people to Rome by exhaustion, because there is no other Church. If we deny that we are the Church that does not make the Creed less certain.'[2]

Two minor contests in the following year, 1842, showed New-

---

[1] *Via Media* (1877), II, 410.
[2] Pusey House: *unpublished*. Newman to Perceval, Dec. 28, 1841.

man that Oxford was against him. A strong Protestant, Garbett of Brasenose, was elected Professor of Poetry against his Tractarian friend Isaac Williams; and when Wiseman's old adversary Hampden adopted irregular methods to prevent the Tractarian Macmullen from getting a degree in divinity, he received so much support in the University that for a long time Macmullen was prevented from obtaining his degree.[1]

Thus it was that the difficulty first sighted when he wrote on the Monophysites, which stared him in the face when he read Wiseman's article on St Augustine and the Donatists, advanced once more and gripped him by the hair.

6

In the rising of this new unsettlement yet another blow came. The bishops, one with another, reopened the subject of the tracts. Pamphlet after pamphlet had appeared, following the original protest of the tutors. Some drew from the articles the most extreme of Protestant doctrines: others said that Tract XC accused the framers of the articles of a pious fraud.[2] If the framers intended to leave a chink for Catholic views 'was not this (if it were really the meaning of the framers) paying rather an equivocal compliment to the honesty of Catholics, much like that which we pay to the honesty of a mouse when we bait a trap for it with a bit of cheese, "*because we know it is its nature to steal it*"?[3] Such was the contention of the Oxford don who was to be Lord Sherbrooke. It was not surprising if before thrusts like these, the English bishops on the one side, and Newman on the other, began to feel uncomfortable. For, it was asked, was it not degrading for Catholics by taking advantage of obvious ambiguities to countenance and join with men pouring scorn on things they held most sacred?

[1] Church: *The Oxford Movement*, 276.
[2] Lowe: *Observations* (1841), 213.
[3] Lowe: *loc. cit.* For further attacks see G. Fausset: *The Thirty Nine Articles*. A Country Clergyman: *Remarks*.

7

Still more cogent had been the *Edinburgh Review* in an article it immediately brought out. 'We are not going to discuss whose religion is the better, Protestants or Catholics,' said the great liberal quarterly, 'but one thing at least is quite certain: the above opinions may be right; they may be the most consonant with revealed religion, but assuredly they are *not the opinions of the Church of England*.'[1] That was the traditional Protestant view, and from it the *Edinburgh* pressed the case with a logic which a Newman trained by Whately could hardly ignore:—'If Christ founded a distinct visible society, entrusting the functions of government to certain regularly appointed governors, and in due course invested them with the power of authoritatively attesting the truth, then the Church of England is the offspring of an unjustifiable schism and revolution, and rests at bottom on nothing else but the much decried rights of private judgment. It is vain for the Oxford theologians to say that the Church of Rome has departed from primitive tradition, for on whose authority does this assertion rest, but that of Luther, Cranmer and their colleagues, or on that of the conclave of Oxford? They admit that the Catholic Church was the genuine successor of the Apostolical one, and that every title which the Anglican Church has to call herself a Church is derived through the Roman Catholics. Surely, then, they were directly authorised to declare what primitive tradition was and Cranmer and his party were not.'[2]

Finally the *Edinburgh Review* put the case against Newman himself. 'A truthful man would first have determined what the Articles really mean and then have decided afterwards whether he could honestly remain in the Church, or must secede from it. Mr Newman's method is different. His plan is to make the Articles give out the sense which he has previously put upon them: and to this end he operates upon them with every device the keenest subtlety can contrive.'[3]

[1] *Edinburgh Review*, April, 1841, 275.   [2] *op. cit.*, 273
[3] *op. cit.*, 196.

If indeed Protestantism were all in the right, and Catholicism was a corrupt system tainted by simony, idolatry and hypocrisy, then Newman's tampering with the Articles was indeed an outrage to the conscience. Now to the immense majority of Englishmen at that time, Catholicism was a scandal, and those who professed it still regarded with 'awful curiosity and dismay'. Copleston himself now summed up the feeling dominant at Oriel when Newman arrived there—dominant for many a year afterwards all over Britain. 'Among the vulgar, gross and abject idolatry, worship of the creature more than the Creator; among the more educated, hypocrisy and unbelief—a barter and trafficking in matters of conscience—sin weighed against penance—absolution purchased by superstitious homage and blind submission to the priest, and then made a starting point for fresh sins.'[1]

8

Such was the view general at the time not only in Oxford but in England: and when its crude misconceptions were corrected, there was still very general misgiving, not easily allayed. Pusey, for instance, thought that the claim of Roman Catholicism to be the one apostolic Church guaranteed in her unity and continuity induced her to tolerate scandal: 'This is a sore temptation to her to bend, relax, fall in with unholy ways and usages which promote this her first end. She would further holiness as much as she can: but she cannot afford to do what is right if it would cause the unholy to part from her. She is obliged to temporise, to lure, to condescend when she cannot control.'[2]

9

Such then were general convictions among high-minded Englishmen all around Newman; such were the contentions he had accepted himself from early youth; such were the suspicions which haunted his mind still. Its tendency was to insist not only on authority as divine, but on holiness as the prize of effort—

[1] Copleston: *Sermons of 1841.* [2] Liddon: *Pusey,* II, 215.

effort assisted indeed by divine grace, but still the effort of personal determination. He viewed the life of grace as the exertion of a strenuous swimmer in the vasty deep.

But to the Catholic the life of grace was to enter the bark of Peter, her sails filled by the winds of heaven. It was to yield one-self in trust to the mysterious sacraments, to the prayers of the saints, to the stewardship of ministers, to live as a ship's company under the command of officers and a captain who steered by his knowledge alike of charts, of compass and of the stars, and who, even if crew or passengers misbehaved, would never throw them overboard.

CHAPTER XI

NEWMAN'S NERVES ON EDGE

1

Such was the view which was put before him by Wiseman and Russell. They pointed out that the veneration of saints, as indeed the Church itself, was like a stained-glass window, dark as seen from without, but from within like beauteous pictures transfused with heaven's light.[1]

At the same time Wiseman insisted that to claim that the Church is pure, is holy, or is infallible, still allows the tragic concession that in so far as an institution is visible and human, it will be deformed by the errors of men. The Church, since she is made up of the souls of men, is like them in unceasing need of reform. Let thy continual pity, says her inspired liturgy, cleanse and defend thy Church. There were no doubt many local errors and abuses to correct; much need of reform and grace, much need for generosity, kindliness, courtesy, humility. For must not each say: 'We have all failed and come short of the glory of God'?[2]

2

Wiseman's object was to accept into Catholic unity the Church of England as a body. 'That the return of this country (through its established Church) to the Catholic unity, would put an end to religious dissent and interior feud, I feel no doubt. If to Tractarian views were added the richness, the majesty, the unity of Catholic worship, and the intensive work of Catholic communities, they will be heard by thousands with awe and reverence, and we shall see wonders of reformation.'[3]

Such was the fair promise held out to Newman: it was not

---

[1] Ward: *Wiseman*, I, 403.   [2] *op. cit.*, 404.   [3] *op. cit.*, 406.

scorn and contempt for his dear Church; it was on the other hand a courteous and generous appreciation of all he had cherished in it of good.

3

And how did it apply to his tract on the Articles? Even there Wiseman was clear; like many another failing and defect in the Church of England, they were a just cause of complaint, because of their 'Protestant spirit in the aggregate and their insupportable uncatholicism on specific points'.[1] Wiseman did not endorse Newman's excessive subtlety in dealing with them. After all, his work in the Church of England was to restore her to perfect Catholicism, and that could not be done if schism were to be preferred to unity. For behind schism—as Newman felt all along—was that temper which preferred the judgment of reason to the inspiration of God, the will of the flesh to His grace: in a word, the standards of the world to those of heaven; such was the temper of liberalism.

4

Newman was already haunted by the sense of power in Catholic worship. Its claim not alone upon heart and imagination, but upon movements more mysterious, upon something deeper and more ineffable in man himself—that spirit which is acted upon directly by the Spirit of God, and assuming control over his faculties and senses, gives him experiences which, melting the soul into blessedness and love, are mystical, divine. Newman spoke of awe, mystery, tenderness, reverence, devotedness; he associated these with something else, with an atmosphere he could only call Catholic. And with this mystical apprehension came the appeal and invitation of Catholic courtesy. Ambrose Phillipps wrote a pamphlet. Monsignor Wiseman wrote directly to Newman him-

---

[1] *op. cit.* On page 389 is Wiseman's letter to Lord Shrewsbury, Wiseman alluding to Tract XC as the demonstration that such interpretation may be given of the most difficult articles as will strip them of all contradiction to the decrees of the Council of Trent. The words of Wiseman have not received sufficient attention.

self. He pointed out that the Anglo-Catholics had already found much wrong in the old Protestant tradition of Anglicanism: 'Why not suspect', he asked, 'that a further approximation may yet remain, that further discoveries of truth in what to-day seems erroneous may be reserved for to-morrow, and that you may be laying up for yourself the pain and regret of having beforehand branded with opprobrious and afflicting names that which you will discover to be pure and holy?'[1]

5

Wiseman was not alone. A brilliant young priest at Maynooth, Russell, wrote to warn Newman that he was far from understanding either the subtlety and elevation of the Catholics' belief in transubstantiation or the frequency with which—in their popular unliturgical worship—Catholics addressed the saints: for 'these tender and consoling devotions, far from defrauding the worship of God, on the contrary elevate it and give it that stability which our weak and frail hearts require'. But, argued this priest, even if some reforms among Catholic practices were desirable, who could say that the Church of England was as a whole and always had been perfect in the eyes of an Anglo-Catholic? 'Oh,' wrote this young priest, 'may you find your best reward in restoring to your beloved Church the glory which alas she has lost. . . . I believe with all the fervour of my heart that once again the weeks will be shortened upon our people, that transgression may be finished, and sin may have an end. And I am equally persuaded that in the arduous ways of God you and your friends have been especially raised up, imbued with an especial spirit and fitted with peculiar powers for its accomplishment.'[2]

6

Newman was deeply touched: but if so, his tense nerves were still on edge and his words cut with controversial sharpness. 'I feel as much as anyone the lamentable state of Christendom,' he wrote to Wiseman, 'and heartily wish that the Communions of

[1] Ward: *Wiseman*, I, 377. [2] *Correspondence*, 126.

Rome and England could be one; but the best way of tending to this great end seems to me to be in charity and meekness to state our convictions—not to stifle them.'[1]

7

The situation was indeed complex. On the one hand was an ancient and venerable Church, a matron and her daughters mysteriously and mystically one through ages of time and across a vast variety of languages, customs and tastes. Yet while holy in her doctrine and her mysteries, while apostolic in her authority, yet by the mere fact of being a visible and human institution, she bore on every member of this queenly family, the bruises and scars made by the failings of men. On the other hand was a maiden Church which claimed by immunity from many of these marks and scars to be a fairer creature, but, nevertheless, had a type of beauty few could admire except herself; she lacked the majestic presence of the united family. And what she lacked, she reviled. At that time, as often before, she cultivated an attitude of self-righteous indignation, of contempt for the very family from which she claimed to derive her titles of honour.

The mind of man is more complex than his logic. It is the quality of words often repeated to impose themselves as facts. Propaganda long maintained is dearer to our minds than truth; it stifles and paralyses the play of reason, and makes factions within the judgment.

Such then was Newman's mind as a member of the Anglican Communion. He cherished a thousand misconceptions and prejudices against the international Church, even while she appealed to the depths and heights of his being as a man. He felt a grounded and righteous recoil against certain abuses which, if she did not countenance, she had failed to reform. The tastes and habits of his mind inclined to something chaster, and nearer to Christ's own evangel. The habits of his prayer were direct and absorbing communion with the Highest, such as in fact the loftiest mystics practised. Since the popular devotions some permitted were not

[1] Ward: *Wiseman*, I, 377.

necessarily such as a wise director would specially commend to a soul like his, his own distaste for them may have been a true instinct of his soul. Yet with them and among them was the power that soothed his heart and made him feel nearer to Jesus than he had ever been elsewhere.

8

But beside this conflict within the soul of his worship were moral and personal considerations poignant and intricate. His honour was at stake. He had sworn that his movement was not a compromise with that Rome whom his friends regarded as so foully tainted with error. He had sworn that he was not undermining the Church of England. He had created a following who were working within her a wondrous change, and whose work was impugned every time he appeared to be nearing Rome. To vindicate them, therefore, he showed acerbity towards Rome; then—feeling that this too was against his will—his taut nerves were strained still more.

And with this insurrection in his conscience came other considerations which cut into the flesh nearest his heart. His intensely affectionate nature spread the tendrils of his feelings around his intimate friends, and those for whom he most intensely cared were not all drawn, as he was, towards Rome. On the other hand, the more he moved in that direction, the more they tended to leave him lonely. A few years before, his friendship with Hurrell Froude had drawn him towards Catholicism. Another handsome gifted Etonian at Oriel, an Etonian who had been his pupil when the others were taken away, Rogers, who had come with him to Iffley to live in the vacation, occupied in his heart a place which vied with that of Hurrell Froude himself. He had so longed to see this Rogers a Fellow of Oriel that when he heard in Sicily that the wish was fulfilled, he kissed the paper rapturously.[1] He felt for Rogers one of those intense friendships which were among the peculiarities of his nature. With Rogers there was in Oriel a younger and not less enthusiastic admirer, Richard Church. Neither of these felt inclined to leave the Church of

[1] A.M. I, 425.

England—nor ever did leave it: and still firm within the Church of England at that time was the third of his younger friends, yet another Etonian not less gifted than Rogers, and not less attractive—a young Fellow of Merton, James Hope.

So here, cutting into the flesh of his heart, were these poignant affections with young men, all reinforcing his desire to stay in the Church of England. He hardly speaks of them in recording the tribulations of those months, but we cannot look before and after into Newman's heart without seeing clearly how dear any break with them would cost him.

9

Besides these were his relations with the other two leaders of this historic movement—with Keble and with Pusey. Keble, affectionate and loyal as he was, especially after the publication of Tract XC, never for a moment wavered in his feeling towards the Church of England. Pusey for his part was walking away. This was noticed by Church and others. And though Pusey was most helpful with the bishop in the matter of the obnoxious tract, though he was always courteous, sympathetic and loyal, his temperament was much less tense than that of Newman, and his general attitudes were normally English.

Thus it was that Newman felt that he was having his mind made up for him by the behaviour of others. If others treated him unfairly and seemed to thwart him, he always made a countermove. He now became convinced that he was being forced to change the whole direction of his life.

His time meanwhile was crowded. He was busy not alone with theology but with an immense correspondence. He was carefully considering every detail of his monastic house at Littlemore; he was having long talks with his old pupils, Samuel Wood and Robert Williams. He was also busy with a Presbyterian clergyman, with a man from Dublin, with a friend of Lamennais who talked ecclesiastical politics, with a distant relation, and with two princes from Ashanti.[1]

But time is needed to come to deep decisions of the soul.

[1] T.M. *Rem.* II, 48, 9–207.

CHAPTER XII

INCREASING BEWILDERMENT

I

In the Advent of 1841, Newman preached four sermons in St Mary's on the duty of all to remain in the Church where they were born. Take them for all in all, those four sermons were the most moving he had preached yet. In the first he instanced the many graces given in the Church of England, how at her offices the devout had felt an indescribable influence and almost savour of grace: 'If they at her services have been favoured with the peace and the illumination they needed; if there were any consolation in Christ and fellowship of the Spirit, if many had felt that their souls had been transfigured within them when they came to the Most Holy Sacrament, if any had seen how full of hope the children of our Church can die—O! pause ere you doubt that we have a Divine Presence among us still and have not to seek it. Let us enjoy what we still have, though the world deride us—though our brethren tell us that in their and in our Sacraments we have not what we think we have; though they tell us it is all a dream and rudely bid us to seek it elsewhere; no, they do not need to seek who have already found.'[1]

In his second sermon he spoke of that interior conviction which religion gives in the communion between Christ and the soul. And he contrasted it with the city set on a hill, 'of a nature to dazzle and subdue the mind like a miracle, or like the sun's light in the heavens',[2] and could anyone say that the Church of England, apart and with divided counsels, was that? If not let them hold fast to their inward sense of prayer and to that inward power of conscience which forbade them to move.

[1] *Sermons on Subjects of the Day*, 364. [2] *loc. cit.*

2

And now we come to his third sermon: 'What want we then but faith in our Church? With faith we can do everything; without faith we can do nothing. If we have a secret misgiving about her, all is lost; we lose our nerve, our power, our position, our hope. A cold despondency and sickness of mind, a niggardness and peevishness of spirit, a cowardice and a sluggishness envelope us, penetrate us, stifle us. Let it not be so with us; let us be of good heart; let us accept her as God's gift and our portion.'[1]

In his last sermon, he returned to the subject of internal proofs. That religion, he said, is true which has power and so far as it has power; nothing but what is divine can renew the heart. He found seven good reasons for not changing one's communion, but no sooner had he done so than he proceeded to question them and in fact to undermine them. He spoke of two reasons which may lead a man to leave the communion in which he was born: and though he was ostensibly speaking of dissenters coming to the Church of England, yet it inevitably suggested further surmises. For he said it was sometimes God's will 'to lead them forward through their present creed into a purer one, or, if such be His inscrutable pleasure to save them though not through, yet in it by a mercy overflowing the bounds of His revealed covenant'.[2]

As the year 1842 went on, Newman preached less often, but the doubts congregated like vapours in an inky cloud from which fire would burst. It was with a sense of impending catastrophe that at Littlemore he preached his anniversary sermon in the autumn ten months later.

3

For it is the part of a great master of letters to put into words a power subtler and deeper than the meaning he deliberately intends to convey. His words have a wizard power, opening at once to the hearer the hidden places not alone of the writer's heart, but the secrets of other lives than his, and when their influence is extended,

[1] *op. cit.,* 414. The sermons are printed in a different order.   [2] *op. cit.,* 430.

gathering to themselves the feelings they have awoken. So it was with these sermons. While they argued the cause of the Church of England, they opened everlasting gates and disclosed beyond park and pastures a house of many mansions, not built with hands. For in them men could descry, even through the mists of misgiving, the more intense and vivid significance of the Christ's promise that He was with His own always, even to the consummation of the age; He was guiding them with His counsel and after that He would receive them in glory—and what did they desire upon earth in comparison of Him?

Yet which was more insistent in the preacher's voice—the dim hope or the present pathos? For those who listened heard clearly through the words spoken the anguish which tore the heart of flesh.

4

Distinct from Newman's devotion to the most intimate of his young followers, and his loyal reverence for those associated with him in the leadership of the movement, was deep affection for Oriel, and the love for Oxford as a city and a shrine. His was one of those hearts which are attached to places as a tree is rooted to the ground from which it draws its sap. As a boy he had come to Oxford with exaltation like a devotee approaching the object of a long pilgrimage: there he had found the perfection of companionship, the pleasure of stately surroundings, the honour of academic success, the field for his talent and genius, and finally the rare lustre which shines on him who raises hundreds of young men to the flights of the spirit. But if he gave up the Church of England he must give up all that. And did he really want to give it up? His friends and advisers were all convinced that 'Romanism', as they called the cosmopolitan Church, was a sinister compound of idolatry, hypocrisy and venality. 'I feel furious', wrote Samuel Wilberforce, 'at the craving of men for union with idolatrous, material, sensual, domineering Rome, and their squeamish anathematising hatred of Protestant Reformed men. . . . I have no fear of Prussia and the Protestants.'[1]

[1] S. Wilberforce: *Life*, I, 212-3.

They travelled little: they were convinced that England was not only separate from her Latin neighbours, but in her standards infinitely higher and purer. Newman himself shared these prepossessions. When travelling in Italy and Sicily he had been many times repelled. He felt, though the people were civil and good-natured, they were knaves and their 'popular and esoteric religion as pagan as you can fancy'. 'The people', he wrote, 'are heathen certainly.'[1] And these prepossessions remained. Tract XX had declared that the Papists had 'established a lie in the place of God's truth'.[2] This general horror at the great Church was concentrated in Newman's mind on the invocation of saints and the honour paid to them, especially the Virgin Mary—and as for what Russell had said to him, it took him long to understand.

5

While therefore still recoiling from Romanism, still cherishing his Oxford associations, he was also steeped in the authorised version of the Bible. It was engraved in his memory, and gave harmony to his style. It had been his model and study since early boyhood. How could he be expected to give this up, to give up the felicity of the Prayer Book, the charm, the dignity, the associations, the friendships, the prestige? How could he give up the hope for a revival of the Church of England, the promises he had given to it, and the repudiation of his experience of Rome? How give up the loyalties of Oxford; Oxford on which his whole career was centred; his part as a leader, his ties with old friends, the following of young enthusiasts who revered and loved him, to ally himself with English Papists, whom (to tell the truth) he still distrusted? The idea struck those around him as unthinkable: his own education was against it. And all this had to be dealt with because he could follow either the arguments of reason or the call from deep to deep sounding in the sense of personal veneration, mystery and awe which with an aroma, pungent and affecting as incense, encompassed the altars of Rome.

[1] A.M. I, 372.   [2] Tract XX, p. 3.

6

What did reason say? Reason spoke in the tones of the *Edinburgh Review*. Reason told him that the Bible in itself was incomplete, that it melted into the authority of the early Church; reason asked at what point he could say that the Holy Spirit had deserted the Church, at what point the Apostolic authority was undefined. Reason pointed to an august continuity, reason asked him what there was inherently wrong in relying on those prayers of the saints which, as he read in Revelations, were poured out like vials of odours before the throne of God. What answer could reason give either on the one side to the ruthless historic precision of the *Edinburgh Review*, or on the other to the genial and courteous statements of Russell and of Wiseman? At every turn his mind, long trained by Gibbon, was arrested once more at the compelling pictures of power and success painted by Macaulay, in a famous article of 1838, saying that the unchangeable Church was still there.

What remained was the fact that Newman found himself where he was after the publication of Tract XC. But did he really know where he was? Already those three decisions in the University of Oxford showed that its authority was against him.

While he still had the support of his bishop, he felt more secure. In 1842, however, even the kindly Bagot changed his view. On Monday, May 23rd, he said he could not reconcile himself to 'a system of interpretation which was so subtle that by it the articles might mean anything or nothing'.[1]

7

Already Newman had taken a decisive step. He had left Oriel to live at Littlemore. The attacks on him made by the Heads of Houses had produced a reaction of disgust.[2] Had he any right to force on a university views it did not want to hear?

'There is no sadder passage to be found in the history of Ox-

[1] Liddon: *Pusey*, II, 286–7.   [2] A.M. II, 387–8.

ford,' wrote Church, 'than the behaviour and policy of the heads of this great Christian University towards the religious movement which was stirring the interest, the hopes and the fears of Oxford. . . . it was that of contemptuous indifference, passing into helpless and passionate hostility.'[1]

8

Newman's reasons for going to Littlemore were not only to retire from disapproval, but to join with others in living a stricter life. While the moderate Anglicans were uniting to attack him, his own friends had begun to doubt and criticise. 'There are no friends like old friends,' Newman wrote afterwards, 'but of those old friends few could help me, few could understand me, many were annoyed with me; some were angry because I was breaking up a compact party and some as a matter of conscience could not listen to me.'[2] In these circumstances he moved away from his old friends to younger men who took more extreme views, made much of him, and hummed around him busy as bees. When his old friends wavered, they stood by him; they not only did him kindnesses; they really loved him—and how could a heart as susceptible as Newman's not respond with subtle and far-reaching responses? He no longer knew where he stood. While some men thought him unable to lead, others accused him of shuffling and trickery and even called him 'a liar and a pickpocket'. He and all his friends were watched, hunted down and maligned by colleagues who hurried about with gossip, and who displayed not only implacable fury but unwavering pertinacity. 'They acted', says Oakeley, 'the part of jackals to the nobler beasts of prey. They had their emissaries in the suspected colleges, and their eyes were intent upon every action and on every gesture.'[3]

[1] Church: *The Oxford Movement*, 212. [2] *Apologia*, 279.
[3] A.M. II, 405, and Oakeley: *Tractarian Movement*, 84.

9

It was therefore in a mood of reaction, discouragement and disgust that Newman went out to live his stricter life at Littlemore.
He said in the words of Horace that he had enjoyed himself enough
and the time of departure was at hand. And there he did indeed
live severely, fasting always till twelve, sometimes till five in the
afternoon, giving up the hours to prayer and study, and rising at
midnight to recite the office of the Breviary.

Already the object of suspicion and gossip, he could not make
such a move without being accused of going farther into excesses
of Popery and monkery. The Protestants were more suspicious
than ever. They ferreted into his privacy and reported him to his
bishop. The bishop wrote, with his usual courtesy, on April 12;
Newman replied, with his usual asperity, two days later. He had
in writing to his friends called his community at Littlemore by
the Greek name for a monastery: but in writing to the bishop he
insisted it was not a monastery. Why, he asked, when he joined
with a few others in some poor cottages at Littlemore for prayer
and study should they pry into his rooms? Why should his sacred
and conscientious resolves be subjected to unmannerly and unfeeling curiosity? Again the bishop wrote most kindly—he said
that the calumnies against Newman were cruel and unjust, and
later arranged to pay him a visit as a friend. Newman therefore
turned a deaf ear to the new appeal of Wiseman. As for the
Church, where was it? He answered that it had broken up into
decay, like the Roman Empire![1]

10

We cannot attempt to follow Newman's mind through this
year of 1842. He tries to hold back from Roman unity one of his
young men, yet he doubts his own power to give absolution. He
continues his work on miracles, but that too is confused. If he
had argued in Tract XC that, interpreting Anglican formularies
into a sense clean contrary to that most men had consistently

[1] A.M. II, 399.

believed them to hold, one could capture the citadel of Protestantism from within, his subtlety now brought a havoc of confusion
into his own mind. If we could see all, would we not say that he
desired to change the nature of the Church of England, but was
too sensitive to Protestant attacks to pursue his daring course?

If then, in the temper of an inquisitor, we search into the state
of his mind, there are tendencies of equivocation, and the Protestant suspicions are really justified. But on the other hand, to
understand his mind is to pardon it: it is to turn in sympathy to
a soul tormented by rival claims within his conscience, and by a
will which could not act till every barrier had been broken down.

II

For what is the nature of belief? He always kept insisting that
it is something deeper far than logic. 'Religious truth', he wrote
a few months later, 'is reached not by reasoning, but by an inward
perception.'[1] That was the occasion of his torment. He felt deep
in his heart a preference for an undivided Catholicism: prayers and
tactful comments were drawing him towards it: he was being
harassed daily with attacks and calumnies from his own communion: but the question could be decided only when his will
was clear, and that could not be till his mind was in perfect accord
with his spiritual instincts. It was not enough to hear the mysterious appeal of Rome, it was not enough to see her logical case;
but he had to wait for the time when logic and the inner light
would so react on one another to produce on the one side a
strong revulsion from the Church of England, and, on the other,
a strong and consoling trust in a system which in many particulars
was to his deep spiritual instincts distasteful. But the accord of
faith with reason was not in itself enough: it must come in such
deep tides of experience that he could sunder every tie most dear
with the men and with the life he loved, and leave his enemies to
triumph in their gibes; he must fill those who followed him with
sorrow and misgiving. He must turn and stab his own Oxford
followers in the eyes.

[1] A.M. II, 409.

12

And to do this he must attain between the feelings of his heart, the conviction of his reason and the mysterious luminance of his soul a certainty so living, so tender, so complete in love and trust that it would fill him with joy and peace. How complex is the completeness of a man where mind and feelings are both acute! How much must happen before the whole man moves! No wonder poor Newman said sometimes one thing and sometimes another: that he was in certain answers confused and irrelevant. His nerves were both excited and exhausted: he was bewildered and upset. On him fell not alone the stress of personal decision, but, like the assaults of contending hosts, the issues of Church history. And well might he plead in the anguish of his perplexity that great acts take time.[1]

[1] *Apologia*, 285.

CHAPTER XIII
LEAVING ST MARY'S

I

The conflict was tense within him when with the gilding of the leaves he kept once more his consecration festival at Littlemore in 1842. 'Is it right', he asked, 'to keep holy day when the spouse of Christ is in bondage and the iron almost enters into her soul? We know what Prophecy promises us—a holy Church set upon a hill, an imperial Church far spreading among the nations, loving truth and peace, binding together all hearts in charity, and uttering the words of God from inspired lips; a Kingdom of Heaven upon earth that is at unity with itself, peace within its walls and plenteousness within its palaces, a glorious Church, not having spot or wrinkle of any such thing, but holy and without blemish. And alas! What do we see? We see the Kingdom of God to all appearances broken into fragments, authority in abeyance, separate portions in insurrection; brother armed against brother—truth a matter not of faith but of controversy. And looking at our own portion of the heavenly heritage, we see heresies of the most deadly character around us and within us; we see error stalking abroad in the light of day and over the length of the land unrebuked, nay invading high places; while the maintainers of Christian truth are afraid to speak lest it should offend those to whom it is a duty to defer. We see discipline utterly thrown down, the sacraments and ordinances of grace open to those who cannot come without profaning them and getting harm from them. Works of penance almost unthought of, the world and the Church mixed together and those who discern and mourn over all this looked upon with aversion because they will not prophesy smooth things and speak peace where there is no peace.

'The days of age have come upon us, the evil days when thou

shalt say I have no pleasure in them, the days when the Bridegroom has been taken away and when men should fast—how then in the days of our fast can we find pleasure and keep festival?'[1]

Such then was his mood as autumn chilled through the murk of November into darkling winter in 1842 and, cut off from the cheer of Oriel, he lived miserably at Littlemore, encircled in perplexity and gloom.

2

While pursuing this study in the tension of his fasting and prayer, he had gathered several young men around him in the ferment of excitement; he provided Oxford with a fresh sensation when, early in the year 1843, he retracted everything he had written against Rome. This retraction was published anonymously in a periodical, the *Oxford Conservative Journal*, but it was immediately discerned who wrote it and what it implied. He not only retracted the opprobrious words he had used, since he said that they were to be ascribed 'to an impetuous temper, a hope of approving myself to persons I respect, and a wish to repel the charge of Romanism'. Though it is true that all these were strong ingredients in his mind, nevertheless they implied that in denouncing Rome he had been consciously insincere. But what caused most consternation among his Anglican friends was the tone of his final sentences. They sounded as though he were doubting whether the Anglican position was tolerable at all.[2] And the fact is that, say what he might, he could not decide. Every implication of his every word was scrutinised not only by suspicious enemies but by devoted followers. 'I really do not think you know', wrote Pusey, 'how much people love you and respect you and what sympathy they feel with you.'[3]

3

The next thing that happened that year was that Pusey preached in Christ Church on May 14 a sermon on the Eucharist. Three

[1] *Sermons on Subjects of the Day*, 432–3.   [2] Liddon: *Pusey*, II, 299.
[3] Feb. 4, 1843, *op. cit.*, 300.

days later he heard that he was accused of having in this sermon preached heresy, and was to be tried for it before a tribunal of six Doctors of Divinity appointed by the Vice-Chancellor. That tribunal found him guilty: he was suspended from preaching before the University for two years, while the Provost of Oriel questioned his veracity and honesty. On June 11, Pusey wrote a letter to Newman ending with the words: '*Draw me out of the net that they have laid privily for me, for thou art my God.*'[1]

4

If such things could happen to a man so careful as Pusey, what would Newman's position be? For months, he had been considering whether he should not resign his living. For more than a year he had been debating in anguish whether he was not being pushed out of the Church of England; one thing after another led him to the conclusion that he could not honestly continue preaching at St Mary's. In a long correspondence with Keble, his 'kindest and dearest friend', he confided on May 4, 1843, 'at present, I fear, as far as I can realise my own convictions, I consider the Roman Catholic Communion the Church of the Apostles, and that what grace is among us (which, through God's mercy is not little) is extraordinary, and from the overflowings of His dispensation.

'I am far more sure that England is in schism than that the Roman additions to the Primitive Creed may not be developments, arising out of a keen and vivid realising of the Divine deposition of faith.'[2]

So far had he got before Pusey was accused of heresy! And he gathered then that the Oxford authorities were determined to 'put down Catholicism at any risk', and that exasperation on both sides was intense;[3] he was afraid that those who held his doctrine would find no place in the establishment and must look elsewhere.[4] 'I do despair of the Church of England,' he wrote a few months later to his sister, 'and am so evidently cast off by her, and am on the other hand so drawn to the Church of Rome that

[1] Liddon: *Pusey*, II, 336.   [2] *Correspondence*, 219.   [3] A.M. II, 414-5.
[4] *Correspondence*, 233.

I think it safer as a matter of honesty *not* to keep my living.'[1]

One of his main reasons for arriving at this decision was that Lockhart, who had been living with him at Littlemore, went over to Loughborough and joined the Rosminians. This gave him a shock, and he knew that gossip would make it a cause for scandal. He was impressed too with the knowledge that, while the Church of England was repudiating him, countless churches and religious houses on the Continent were beseeching heaven to receive him in the household of the Saints.[2]

He went up therefore to London to prepare the legal instrument of his resignation from St Mary's on September 19, 1843; he returned by train to the station then nearest to Oxford, Steventon.

5

And who can doubt that in *Loss and Gain* he echoes the sorrow of his return in his nervous tension? He decided to walk the twelve miles from Steventon. 'After he had passed through Bagley Wood the spires and towers of the University came on his view, hallowed by how many tender associations, lost to him for two whole years, suddenly recovered—recovered to be lost for ever. There lay old Oxford before him, with its hills as gentle, and its meadows as green as ever. At the first view of that beloved place, he stood still with folded arms, unable to proceed. Each college, each church, he counted them by their pinnacles and turrets. The silver Isis, the grey willows, the far-stretching plains, the dark groves, the distant range of Shotover, the pleasant village where he had lived—it was Iffley with its Norman church, where Froude and Rogers had joined him for intimate hours, where his mother had died—wood, water, stone, all so calm, so bright, they might have been his, but his they were not. Whatever he was to gain by becoming a Catholic, this he had lost; whatever he was to gain higher and better, at least this, and such as this, he could never have again. He could not have another Oxford; he could not have the friends of his boyhood and youth in the choice of his manhood.

[1] A.M. II, 125.   [2] Liddon: *Pusey*, II, 460.

E

'As he mounted the well-known gate, and proceeded down into the plain, he was overwhelmed by his distress. It seemed to him that there was no one to greet him, no one to sympathise with him; there was no one to believe he needed sympathy, no one to believe he had given up anything, no one to take an interest in him, to feel tender towards him, to defend him. He had suffered much, but there was no one to believe that he had suffered. He would be thought to be unfeeling—not to be undergoing suffering.[1] So it seemed to his torn heart: he remembered only the gibes and taunts; he forgot the enthusiastic followers who sympathised most deeply; he thought only of those who told him rudely that he was giving up Oxford for a whim.'

6

But when Newman himself came down into Oxford, though so many faces were changed, yet there were many devoted admirers still, and they gathered round him, first at St Mary's where he preached that 'the just shall live by faith',[2] and on Monday, September 27, at Littlemore for the seventh consecration of his chapel there: Newman had long since learnt to make his sermons most touching and moving. With dahlias and passion flowers decorating the chapel, with the children in the new frocks he had given them, and the benches filled with friends till the place overflowed, with Pusey officiating at the altar, Newman rose to the pulpit to deliver as an Anglican, in words that echoed afar, his last reproaches to the Church of England. 'O my mother,' he read, his tones more thrilling than ever before, 'whence is this unto thee, that thou hast good things poured upon thee and canst not keep them, and bearest children, yet darest not own them? Why hast thou not skill to use their services, nor the heart to rejoice in their love? How is it that whatever is generous in purpose and tender or deep in devotion, thy flower and thy promise, falls from thy bosom and finds no home in thine arms? Thou makest them stand all the day idle as the very condition of thy bearing with them; or thou biddest them be gone where they will be more

[1] *Loss and Gain* (1848), Part III, Ch. III.   [2] Edward Bellasis: *Memorials*, 62.

welcome; or thou sellest them for nought to the stranger that
passes by. And what wilt thou do in the end thereof? ...

'O loving friends,' he said at last, pausing long before he recalled his own offices among them, showing them a brighter
world than this, encouraging them, sobering them, illuminating
them, comforting them. 'My dear friends,' he said again, and the
pause was longer still,[1] 'remember such a one in time to come
though you hear him not and pray for him that in all things he
may know God's will, and at all times he may be ready to fulfil
it.'[2]

The preacher's voice was low, but though at times he faltered,
every word came with his ringing clearness to cut his hearers to
the heart. Few were the eyes that had no tears in them, and as the
service continued the voice of his friend at the altar at times broke,
and stopped; and many a tear had gathered in his eye before at
last he gave Newman the Communion. So much did all these
friends love one another, and love Oxford, and love their
Church.[3]

7

Newman at this time found his most unnerving tormentor in
his boldest liegeman. For he had now in his train Oxford's pet
buffoon. From the time he had been a boy at Winchester, young
William Ward had been awkward and ungainly. No one could
call him coarse, for his soul was marked by a strong purity; no one
could call him vulgar, for he belonged to a family with a distinct
position and connection. But on the other hand he had none of
the elegance which the fastidious Newman found endearing.
From early childhood he had made a habit of the theatre: above
all he delighted in opera bouffe, and ran round Oxford humming
its airs. His room was always in that sort of confusion which,
defying the duster, soon wins the name of pig-sty; he dressed very
badly, and more than all he at once became phenomenally fat.

[1] Edward Bellasis: *Memorials,* 63–4. These give a different text from Newman's.
[2] *Sermons on Subjects of the Day,* 464.
[3] Liddon: *Pusey,* II, 375–6.

Lurching in and out of Balliol, where he was a don, he at every turn displayed wit and provoked it.

Yet underlying his roars of laughter was serious piety; he sought and received ordination.

A ton of flesh, he moved through dons' rooms making outrageously unconventional conversation, humming his opera tunes, and bursting into guffaws of laughter; yet he combined with all his boisterousness not only strong convictions but a 'continual heart-bleeding from being unloved'.[1] Direct and honest to the extreme, he would have seemed brusque were he not so genial: but his strong point was in seeing with sharp distinctness what he did see, in driving principles to their conclusions, and with a roar of laughter in reducing the contentions of his opponents to the absurd. From acute pangs alike and ruthless syllogisms he would pass in a moment into a pirouette, to which his incomparable clumsiness added a charm all its own. It was as though a young elephant was essaying the ballerina, or as others said, as though the soul of an archangel had entered the body of a rhinoceros. Flinging himself at the knees of an astonished don, he would pour out the plaint of a lover in desperation. Nor did the young clergyman disdain an impersonation of Cupid so noisy that a servant would be sent up to investigate. 'It's honly Mr Ward, sir,' was the answer. "'E's a-hacting of a cherubim.'[2]

The Falstaff of Oxford had of course been a Protestant, and when he attended Newman's lectures in Adam de Brome's chapel, his running comment was so rude and the faces he made so grotesque, that Newman had his seat turned sideways. Then suddenly, for his mind was apt to jump though his body was clumsy, he changed his direction, and if anything was abhorrent to him it was to stop short.[3] He took upon himself the mantle of the departed Hurrell Froude. The proprieties of Protestantism, at once punctilious and prosaic, he flung to the winds in gestures as comic as any of his favourite farces. He joined the band which believed in Newman, and suddenly found that the ritual and music of the Church were more satisfying than the gayest of operas.[4] He was

---

[1] Ward: *Ward*, I, 135.   [2] *op. cit.*, I, 40.   [3] Ward: *op. cit.*, I, 84.
[4] *British Critic*, LXVII, art. 1.

still a ruthless logician: and soon his syllogisms were driving him towards the dogmas of Rome. When in *Loss and Gain* Newman describes Mr Campbell who 'has many good points, but he runs theories and rides hobbies and drives consequences to death',[1] we detect his fractiousness with Ward. It was torture for Newman to be dragged on the grinding chains of syllogisms when his heart hung back, drawn by a thousand dear attachments, and instinct still was hesitant. Had he not read in Coleridge that

> Whispering tongues can poison truth
> And life is thorny, and youth is vain,
> For to be wroth with one we love
> Doth work like madness in the brain?

While Newman was withdrawing his tract expressing doubts of Rome, and pleading with Keble that she was a sister Church, Ward said, 'No, unless you insist on her corruption, you will find her attractions irresistible: if I cease to distrust her, I must rush into her arms.'[2]

'As to the fathers,' Newman wrote to Pusey, 'I *do* now think, far more than I did, that their study leads to Rome. It has thus wrought in me. But of course I *ever* have thought it required a safeguard to keep it from Rome, because in the history of the Church their theology *has* led to Rome on a very large scale.'[3]

8

The melodrama introduced by Ward plays its true part in the next two years of Newman's crisis. Ward's articles in the *British Critic* had been so charged with gunpowder, that the periodical exploded. It was left to his irrepressible voice to find expression in a series of papers which soon became a book as unwieldy as his own figure, and which he called *The Ideal of a Christian Church*. '*The Ideal*', says Church, very justly, 'is a ponderous and unattractive volume, ill-arranged and rambling, which its style and

[1] *Loss and Gain* (1848), 274.
[2] *op. cit.*, 248–9.
[3] Pusey House: *unpublished*. Newman to Pusey, Dec. 18, 1843.

other circumstances have caused to be almost forgotten.'[1] But when it appeared in June, 1844, it was the sensation of the year.

Written by an Anglican clergyman, it not merely disparaged the English Church but loaded her with unmannerly scorn; it found the ideal in that very Romanism on which England on the whole looked with horror and contempt. He took the disgusting scenes which had shocked him as a boy at Winchester to be typical of Anglican morality and insisted that the Church of England was as corrupt as she was heretical. At the same time he boasted that he could become the most thorough Romanist while still remaining an Anglican clergyman.

It was too much. Gladstone voiced in the *Quarterly Review* the normal English reaction. If Ward deemed it his duty as priest in the Church of England to pronounce the heaviest of all judgments upon his ancestors and progenitors in the faith, wrote Gladstone, he should not suppress their defence. 'Children should not strike a parent until they have heard her.'[2]

The English might have become materialistic, complacent, compromising; they might have refused to pay the price of holiness; they might have confused material prosperity with spiritual blessedness; but the book was so extreme that it antagonised those whom tact might have persuaded. Newman realised at once that it would not help his cause. 'He was', says Church, 'moving undoubtedly in one direction, but moving slowly, painfully, reluctantly, intermittently, with views sometimes clear, sometimes clouded by that terribly complicated problem, the answer to which was full of such consequences to himself and to others.'[3] And 'in this fevered state, with mind, heart, soul, all torn and distracted by the tremendous responsibilities pressing on him', first to be bullied by an adherent and his logic, then to have to face in Oxford its sensational consequences—such was the double weight which Ward was now pressing on to the lacerated shoulders of his leader.

[1] Church; *The Oxford Movement*, 323.   [2] Ward: *Ward*, I, 300.
[3] Church: *The Oxford Movement*, 315.

CHAPTER XIV

THE STORM BREAKS

1

Newman had been run down all through the spring of 1843. The rigour of Littlemore in Lent had been more than his system could stand. His doctor had insisted on him taking more care of himself: and loss of stamina seriously weakens a man's power of decision. From the logical point of view he already saw things clearly enough, but he lacked confidence in himself.

'These facts will make a very dry work,' he wrote to Pusey early in 1843. 'Comment there cannot help being; for what is comment but the colour which the individual writer gives them? And I fear that a wish to be united to Rome is part of the feeling of mind and comment with which I should write, did I write. . . .

'For years I have been anxious that people should not have confidence in me because I have not confidence in myself.'[1]

2

Before he could act decisively, his powers must be firm, his health sound enough for his mind to bring into accord the complex interaction of his personal responsibilities, his tenderest feelings, his prolonged studies and his inner experience. For out of all these is the web of conviction woven. As for Ward's book, it

---

[1] Pusey House: *unpublished*. Undated. Newman to Pusey, Vol. II, 174–5.
'I suppose it is possible', he wrote on the Vigil of St Matt., 1844, 'for a Church to have some profound wound, which, till treated, infallibly impeded the exercise of its powers, and made attempts to act futile. How should we feel if we saw a man with a broken leg attempting to walk?' (Also unpublished in Pusey House.)

tormented him like a swarm of flies. He was repelled by its unfairness, annoyed by its construction, and at the same time hurried
on by its arguments.

Yet how could he hurry? Had he not been appalled at the in-
stance of a Magdalen don named Sibthorpe, who had gone over
to Rome, then after two years come back? On such a question he
insisted no one should make a final move in less than three years.[1]
He would take every precaution. He would read all the great
Anglican classics: Hooker, Bull, Pearson or that noble work
Jackson on the Creed: he would see what Laud said on tradition.
He would read Bingham's Antiquities, Waterland on the Use of
Antiquity, Wall on Infant Baptism, and his friend William Palmer
on the Liturgy. He would go back to Jeremy Taylor, and with
him read Wilson and Horne.[2] He would consult the controver-
sialists, Barrow on the Unity of the Church, Leslie's Dialogues on
Romanism, and Bramhall.[3]

3

While he was thus weighing out his questions his old friend
Bowden fell ill, and died. 'I sobbed bitterly over his coffin,' Newman wrote, 'to think that he had left me still dark as to what
was the way of truth and what I ought to do in order to please
God and fulfil His will.'[4] 'There lies now my oldest friend, so
dear to me,' he wrote to Keble, 'and I with so little faith or hope,
as dead as a stone, and detesting myself.'[5]

This is the accent of nervous exhaustion, of a man worried,
under-nourished, over-tired and sad. It echoes on through the
autumn in the long letters he kept writing. 'What I have asked
myself,' he wrote on November 21 to Keble, 'is, "Are you not
perhaps *ashamed* to hold a system which is so inconsistent, so un-
tenable?" I cannot deny that I should be ashamed of having to
profess it—yet I think the feeling, whatever be its strength, is not
at all able to do so great a thing as to make me tear myself from
my friends, from their good opinion, from my reputation for

[1] *Correspondence,* 269. [2] *Loss and Gain* (1848), 299.
[3] *op. cit.,* 244; 325 [4] *Apologia,* 359. [5] A.M. II, 438.

consistency, from my habitual associations, from all that is naturally dear to me.

'You must not suppose I am fancying that I know *why* or on
what, or on what *motive*, I am acting. I cannot. I do not feel love
or faith. I feel myself very unreal.'[1]

'I have gone through a great deal of pain,' he wrote three days
later to his sister, 'and have been very much cut up. The one pre-
dominant distress upon me has been this unsettlement of mind I
am causing. This is a thing that has been haunting me day by day.
And for days I had a literal pain in and about my heart. It is the
shock, surprise, terror, forlornness, disgust, scepticism to which I
am giving rise; the differences of opinion, division of families—
all this it is makes my heart ache.

'I cannot make out that I have any motive but a sense of indefinite risk to my soul in remaining where I am. A clear conviction
of the substantial identity of Christianity and the Roman system
has now been in my mind for three full years.'[2]

'You cannot estimate', he wrote at another time, 'what so many
(alas!) feel at present, the strange effect produced on the mind
when the conviction flashes or rather pours in upon it that Rome
is the true Church. Of course it is a most revolutionary and therefore a most exciting tumultuous conviction.'[3]

Then gradually there comes a slackening of his torture; his
health appears to improve. He forms the project of a new work,
which would put in his scholarly and poetic way the conclusions
which Ward was expressing in words too crude to be cogent.
Eight months later, Newman writes to his friend Coleridge at
Eton; his tone, though anguished still, has undergone a change.
'I have no misgivings—every day I am getting more and more
sure what I ought to do. And if so, if I have influence, I cannot
let it stay with me in order to countenance what I feel to be error.
Let it go at once and altogether, if it is useful for nothing but this.

'It is the greatest consolation to me to think that kind and religious hearts are thinking of me in the way which one of your
enclosures describes. O may their prayers be continued—though I
seem to them unkind and not deserving of them.

[1] *Correspondence*, 352.   [2] A.M. II, 445.   [3] A.M. II, 424.

'This I can say, that my great sorrow has been the pain and un-settlement I am causing. It is no use talking about it. It has been like a sword through me; but I am getting better now, and almost think the crisis over—though new trials may be coming.

'Of course it is good as you say to know what other people think of my present state. I wish it, and thank you much for tell-ing me. Yet consider, if any one of our acts—intended acts—were brought before us with that distinctness with which I suppose we shall see all of them in the day of judgment, who could abide it? Who could sustain it? Who could sustain the sight of the conse-quences of any one act he proposed to himself on his own judg-ment to the best of his abilities? Who would put any one of his designs into execution with this terrible sight before his eyes? In mercy are the consequences of our actions concealed from us that there may be room for faith, room for good deeds, room for boldness. We are all walking in the dark and are led on in the dark. Do not doubt all will come right, my dear Coleridge, if we do our part according to the guidance given us.

'Tell me what I could have done which I have not done. I seem to be gaining confidence after the many years of doubt and anxiety—which long state of doubt friends ought in their kind-ness to bear in their minds and sympathise with, even if they do not think it tells in the argument. I have a growing confidence that I am not being left to myself. It seems like want of faith to think that I am not being guided, unless indeed I have committed some dreadful sin which has brought this as a judgment on me, which is a thought which has long weighed on me very heavily. O I trust I am not deceiving myself when I say this is not the case —but, if not, how should it be other than right in acting on so very long a conviction as that which obliges me to acknowledge that Christ's home is elsewhere, and that I must seek Him there?'[1]

4

What had happened in the month between these two last letters? He had long since recovered his power to do successful

[1] Unpublished Letter in Oriel College MSS., June 27, 1845.

work, and Oxford had furnished him with a dramatic scene. On February 13, 1845, the conservatives of the University of Oxford had met in the Sheldonian theatre to deprive the author of the *Ideal* of his degree: or, to speak technically, to vote for his 'degradation'. The University was in no uncertain mood. Making their way through slush and snow, the Masters of Arts, many of them famous in England, crowded the Sheldonian. A moonfaced young clergyman mounted into the rostrum, and spoke boldy and with confidence, repeating at least twenty times the doctrines of the Church of Rome. The advocate of celibacy spoke with the more confidence because, though his hearers did not know it till the day was done, he had just become engaged. He had not long finished speaking when votes of censure and degradation were passed amid loud roars. Further roars of laughter greeted the announcement of his engagement and were renewed until the evening.

Meanwhile the Sheldonian heard the proposal of another resolution: the condemnation of Tract XC.

But at this point the two Proctors rose and, taking advantage of an ancient rule, forbade the resolution.[1] They had saved the absent Newman from a gratuitous insult. Alone at Littlemore he continued to work out his decision.

5

Above all he would trace out fully the question of the Holy Spirit gradually enlightening the Church. He had sketched it already in a sermon preached on the Purification, 1843, and published later that year, with other sermons on religious belief. He would put down precisely what he had suggested in writing to Keble. And so he set to work on the most learned and subtle treatise he had yet written—his essay on the Development of Doctrine. The main idea is one which of course he had perforce often touched,[2] the plain fact that the doctrine of the Church had been gradually defined. 'Christianity', he began by saying, 'has been long enough in the world to justify us in dealing with it as

[1] Ward: *Ward*, I, 342.   [2] *Loss and Gain* (1848), 325.

a fact in the world's history.'[1] It took some time for the Church
to define the doctrine of the Trinity. Following the Jesuit Petavius
rather than the Anglican Bull, he elaborated the view. 'Time is
necessary for the true comprehension and perfection of great
ideas.'[2] Ideas, in other words, develop—as men grow—gradually.
But to ideas as they so develop one can apply certain tests: is the
original idea preserved? Are the original principles continued?
Can they assimilate ideas foreign to themselves? Is there an early
anticipation of a later development? Is there a logical sequence in
the development? Does the new element help to strengthen and
conserve the former one? And finally how long does the new
element last?

These seven tests Newman applied to Church history. They
answered him that if the Holy Spirit guides the Church, then
Rome is right: that if he were to accept the Apostolic succession
or the Canon of Scripture in the New Testament or the Real
Presence, no less must he accept Papal Supremacy and the Invocation of Saints.[3] For all these came together into the Primitive
Church. He became in short convinced that if he were to accept
the ancient fathers, he must accept Rome as he found it through
the ages. It was to them both in fact and history far nearer than
any alternative.[4] As the Medieval Church was one with the
Nicene, so 'the Roman Catholic Communion of this day is the
successor and representative of the Medieval Catholic Church'.[5]
Who could deny that? 'If then there is now a form of Christianity
to which Christian nations are antagonists; which is driven out of
some countries; which is in certain cases surpassed in virtue and
intellect by the heretics it condemns; which has negligent bishops
and is contaminated by heresies—and that amid its disorders and
fears there is but one Voice for Whose decisions its people wait
with trust, one name and one see to which they look with hope,
and that name Peter and that see Rome, such a religion is not
unlike the Christianity of the fifth and sixth centuries.'

---

[1] *Development of Doctrine*, Introduction, 27.
[2] Cf. Dr F. L. Cross: *Newman*, 107.
[3] Letter of July 14, 1844, quoted in *Apologia*.
[4] *Development of Doctrine*, 138.   [5] *loc. cit.*

6

The argument went on: relics, holy water, penance, purgatory, monastic life, veneration of saints, all came into the Church of Fathers. And the Blessed Virgin? What did the early Church say of her? 'There was a wonder in heaven'; 'a throne was seen far above all created powers, mediatorial, intercessory; a title archetypal; a crown bright as the morning star; a glory issuing from the eternal throne; robes pure as the heavens and a sceptre over all.'[1] He looked with a new fervour on the scope of the Church in her glory: 'The sanctification or rather the deification of the nature of man is one main subject of the theology of St Athanasius: Christ, in rising, raises His saints with Him to the right hand of power. They become instinct with His life, are of one body with His flesh—sons, kings, gods. He is in them because He is in human nature; He is in them by the Presence of His Spirit and in them is He seen.'[2] . . . Nay, those who did not recognise the queenly supremacy of St Mary in the world of angels could hardly raise their eyes to the immeasurable heights in which the Creator reigns above all that it has entered into the heart of man to conceive: for the Christ is God of God and Light of Light.

7

The Roman Catholic Church was accused of being corrupt. That from time to time corruptions had crept in, who could deny? Error and heresy had in fact done their *worst*; but such a 'corruption is of brief duration, runs itself out quickly and ends in death';[3] while the Church remained true amid all heresies to the mystery of revealed truth, and moved forward energetic, persuasive, intent on maintaining intact her doctrine of the nature of God the Father, of His co-eternal Christ, and His co-eternal Spirit.

'And is it not utterly incredible', Newman asked, referring to the Church, 'that with this thorough comprehension of so great

[1] *Development of Doctrine*, 406.   [2] *op. cit.*, 402–3.
[3] *op. cit.* 446.

a mystery, as far as the human mind can know it, she should be at that very time in the commission of the grossest errors in religious worship and should be hiding the God and Mediator, whose incarnation she contemplated with so clear an intellect, behind a crowd of idols?'[1] Meeting the complexity of human nature, the great Church had gone through fire and water, but God had brought her out continuous, undivided, incomparable, infallible, into a wealthy place.

The creed of Rome *was* sound.

8

As fasting, solitary, but enthusiastic, Newman pursued for endless hours the study which reflected the cravings of his deep convictions, his whole being grew ethereal, and in this state, he passed gradually from the torments of his years to reach the shining tablelands, where certainty is established in the mirror of the Spirit.

'When', he asked afterwards, 'shall I not feel the soothing recollections of those dear years which I spent in retirement, in preparation for my deliverance from Egypt, asking for light and by degrees gaining it with less of temptation in my heart and sin on my conscience than ever before?'[2]

He solved his problem in finding that flood of light which enabled him to express his enthusiasm in a new combination of defined thought with poetry and pathos. This manifested not only his academic instinct and the poise of his genius but also a celestial grace. To him truth was truth only when he could cherish and adore it as one with beauty and with mystery in words of life.

Before he had come to the end of this book, one after another of his company had left the Church of England, and among these were his closest followers at Littlemore itself, including that one friend whom God had given him to love when He took every other friend away. And still from his heart the hot quintessential drops of bitterness in partings were being squeezed out as the

[1] *Development of Doctrine*, 449.
[2] *Difficulties of Anglicans*, Lecture III, p. 69.

THE ORIEL PORTRAIT BY GEORGE RICHMOND

berries ripened on the hedges and the apples reddened in the orchards.

On August 22nd, Pusey's birthday, Newman had hung a miraculous medal round his own neck.[1]

At Michaelmas his mind was almost made up, and with October he welcomed the festival of the angels whose guidance and society he had long cherished. Then he steeled himself to take the plunge. He wrote to one friend after another, letters which would not be posted till the deep waters had closed over him. 'Dear Mr Provost,' he wrote on October 3, 'I place in your hands the resignation of my fellowship. Yours faithfully, John H. Newman.'[2] With that one sharp sentence the dearest tie of four and twenty years was cut.

9

Never is the silvered beauty of Oxford so touching as when the creeper turns crimson on her walls, blue mists enfold her distances, and auburn leaves fall revolving through the evanescent sunlight of the mellowed year. But all know then that they have ended their summer evenings.

Then suddenly on October 8, 1845, the trees were shaken by a tyrant wind, and the rain poured down to fill the pools and beat against the windows. And on that day a saintly Italian priest, Padre Domenico Barberi, who wore on his cassock the image, as he bore in his heart the love of Jesus Crucified, drove down from Staffordshire along wet roads to alight at the *Angel* in Oxford; he was then driven out through the dark and stormy night to Littlemore.

He had only just taken off his overcoat and seated himself by the fire to dry his clothes when the door was opened by a man of pale face and emaciated figure, who moved swiftly into the room, flung himself at the knees of the Italian and, asking to be received into the one true fold of Christ, began to pour out with sobs the long story of his soul.

[1] Pusey House: *Unpublished Letter*. Newman to Pusey, Aug. 22, 1867.
[2] I have not seen this letter but quote it on the authority of Percy Simpson, D.Litt., formerly Fellow of Oriel, who saw it in the Bodleian in the special exhibition of 1933.

Thoughts prisoned long for lack of speech outpour
Their tears and doubts in resignation end.

Deeply touched by the humility of the soul confiding in him, and by the fine delicacy of such a conscience, the Italian listened long; but he could not pronounce the words of absolution except to one already received into the visible Church after an act of faith. And the time came when the stream of anguished words must perforce be stilled. After the effort he had made Newman was so utterly exhausted that he could not walk to his room unaided.

Only next morning did the story come to its desired end, and one day later, in the little Catholic church near Magdalen bridge in that parish of St Clements where he had first ministered in the Church of England, he made his Catholic communion.

In the might of howling winds, while clouds discharge their burden, is a wild exhilaration. But who shall describe the tempests of the soul, or their end in clear and shining calm? Deep was the peace that came to Oxford's leader when, after twelve historic years, he made his own the promise of Palermo. Through those charged years and their gathering gloom the kindly light had led him on, till he at last had seen that the power to soothe his soul, which vibrated from and around those altars where still his Saviour found a home, was one that he could trust.

PART TWO

CHAPTER XV

TACT AND GENEROSITY

I

After 1845, Oxford's temper swiftly changed. The gossip no longer centred round the steps of Golightly or the novelties of Newman. Speculations in theology, says G. V. Cox, were exchanged for speculations in railway shares;[1] young men, thinking how they could become rich quickly, turned to the Whigs, and in a word Liberalism swayed the University, whilst earnest young men from Rugby still breathed the name of the dead Dr Arnold.[2]

What of Newman's own friends? Thwarted, saddened, calumniated, still they persevered, persevered in Pusey's view of religion, and of the Church of England, persevered in the sense of Tract XC; persevered in following on where Newman, while still an Anglican, had led, and refusing personally to break with him. Yet Newman had shaken England as never before. 'It is impossible to describe', writes Mark Pattison, 'the enormous effect produced on the academic and clerical world, I may say throughout England, by one man changing his religion. But it was not condemnation; it was a lull—a sense that the past agitation of twelve years was extinguished by this simple act; and perhaps a lull of expectation to see how many he would draw with him. Instead of a ferocious howl, Newman's proceeding was received in respectful silence, no one blaming.'[3] No one blaming? Some, of course, were scandalised. The Provost of Oriel in acknowledging in kindest tones the letter of resignation had said that he hoped Newman would be saved from the worst errors of the Church of Rome, 'such', he said, 'as praying to human mediators and falling down before images, because in you, with all the great advantages

[1] G. V. Cox: *Recollections*, 238.   [2] Church: *The Oxford Movement*.
[3] M. Pattison: *Memoirs*, 212–3.

135

with which God has blessed and tried you, I must believe such errors to be most deeply sinful. But may He protect you!'[1]

Hawkins trusted even where he did not understand. It was true of them all. 'My dearest Newman,' wrote Keble, 'you have been a kind and helpful friend to me in a way in which scarce anyone else could have been. You are so mixed up in my mind with old and dear and sacred thoughts that I cannot well bear to part with you; most unworthy though I know myself to be; and yet I cannot go along with you. I must cling to the belief that we are not really parted—you have taught me so, and I scarce think you can un-teach me—and having relieved my mind with this little word, I will only say God bless you and reward you a thousandfold all your help in every way to me, unworthy, and to so many others. May you have peace where you are gone, and help us in some way to get peace, but somehow I scarce think it will be in the way of controversy. And so with somewhat of a feeling as though the spring had been taken out of the year, I am always your affectionate and grateful John Keble.'[2]

2

And Pusey? Pusey, more than any other, was to carry on and establish in the Church of England the transforming work which Newman had begun. His words, most of all, take us to the secret of Newman.

'How devotedly he worked for our Church! How he strove to build her up! It looks as if for some good purpose our Church had failed: that an instrument raised up for her had not been employed as God willed and so is withdrawn. There is a jar somewhere. One cannot trust oneself to think whether his keen sensitiveness to ill was not fitted for these troublous times. What to such duller minds as my own seemed as a matter of course, as something of necessity to be gone through and endured, was to his, as you know, "like the piercing of a sword". . . .

'It is the intensest loss we could have had. They who have won him know his value. It may be a comfort to us that they do. Our

[1] *Correspondence*, 388.   [2] *op. cit.*, 386.

Church has not known how to employ him. . . . He is gone unconscious (as all great instruments of God are) what he himself is.
He has gone as a simple act of duty with no view for himself,
placing himself entirely in God's hands. And such are they whom
God employs. He seems then to me not so much far from us as
transplanted into another part of the vineyard where the full
energies of his powerful mind can be employed which here they
were not. And who knows in the mysterious purposes of God's
good providence what may be the effect of such a person among
them? You too have felt that it is what is unholy on both sides that
keeps us apart. It is not what is true in the Roman system against
which the strong feelings of ordinary religious persons among us
are directed, but against what is unholy in her practice. It is not
anything in our Church which keeps them from acknowledging
us, but heresy more or less within us. As each, by God's grace,
grows in holiness, each Church will recognise, more and more, the
Presence of God's Holy Spirit in the other and what now hinders
the union of the Western Church will fall off.

'It is perhaps the greatest event which has happened since the
communion of our Churches has been interrupted that such a man,
so formed in our Church, and the work of God's Spirit as dwelling
within her, should be transplanted to theirs.'[1]

So by tact and affection did Newman's Anglican friends keep
his influence for the Church of England, and in spite of his resentment recall his sympathies. His own mind was mixed. He kept on
imploring his friend Henry Wilberforce to leave the Church of
England: when on the anniversary of his conversion he addressed
his friend, Miss Parker, about her complaint that converts like
Ward were doing harm, he wrote to her:

'I cannot leave your kind letter unanswered though I have little
to say to the purpose. Certainly I do think that the converts
have been so unkindly treated by those they have left that I cannot
wonder even if they do sometimes (should this be the case which
I am not deciding upon) express themselves severely or unsuitably
in return. If a person finds himself cast off by his relations and left
with his wife almost penniless, with the accompaniment of much

[1] Liddon: *Pusey*, II, 460.

cruelty of words and actions, I cannot defend, but excuse him, if his publications have a tinge of bitterness. And so of other cases which might be described. The difference of position between a convert and a member of the Anglican Church is so great that it is not wonderful that those who are but in that of the former cannot understand it. I can easily fancy the disservice which some words and deeds of converts may do to their own cause, whether by their fault or act, among members of the Anglican Church, and I would do what *I* could to diminish it, but it cannot be helped altogether.

'This day I have been a year in the Catholic Church—and every day I bless Him who led me into it more and more. I have come from clouds and darkness into light and cannot look back on my former state without the dreary feeling which one has on looking back on a wearisome miserable journey. When I was happy in the English Church, it was then when it was *not* English—I mean in those respects in which I could innovate upon the received custom of the English Church, as in the early Communion at St Mary's. On that I shall always look back with pleasure. Is there anything else in which I feel pleasure in remembrance? At the moment I do not think of anything else, nor anything else connected with the English Church. In my dealings with my people, I so keenly felt the want of ecclesiastical authority over them, the need of obligatory confession to know their state that the cure of souls was always a dreadful burden.'[1]

3

But if at one time he thought only of his trials in the Church of England, yet at another he remembered an infinity of consolations in days of confidence and pleasantness, days free from care and anxiety, days when no doubt of God's love or His providence came to give him fever of thought or gloom of mind; he cried out, 'Can I forget?—I never can forget the day when in my youth I first bound myself to the ministry of God in that old church of St Frideswide, the patroness of Oxford; nor how I wept most abundant and sweet tears when I thought what I then had become,

[1] Unpublished letter in Oriel College Library.

though I looked on ordination as no sacramental rite, nor even to baptism ascribed any sacramental virtue. Can I wipe out from my memory, or wish to wipe out, those happy Sunday mornings, light or dark, year after year, when I celebrated your own Communion rite in your church of St Mary's?

'O my dear brethren, my Anglican friends, I easily give you credit for what I have experienced myself.'[1] How many touching associations came back! He knew how many remained looking for encouragement and sympathy in their struggle with godlessness. He realised that the Anglicans had repressed the extravagances of Protestantism.[2] He paid a tribute to the Anglican theologians, Bull, Pearson, Wall, Hooker, Butler—yes, and Paley. But he believed at the same time that the Tractarian movement ought to lead people to Rome, and that, with his so-called novel, *Loss and Gain*, is the argument that he put before his old friends in *Difficulties of Anglicans* when he lectured in 1850.[3]

But the position as he saw it could never be of black against white. He saw it in those precisions and those subleties by which the countenance of truth is outlined and tinted by those who depict her to the life. For it needs a great artist to paint a truth which lives—or to define a truth in relation to an entity so complex as the Church of England, or so infinitely mysterious in its reactions of cogent mystery on human nature as the age-long unity of Rome.

It is a truth which needs adaptation to the case of individual souls; and as Pusey and Keble had foreseen, the great part in history to which Newman was called was to work out the truth in charity: on the one hand proving by his example that the loftiest of Anglicans could not only become a Roman Catholic, but also feel it was the greatest blessing to do so: on the other, still recognising how precisely the Church of England fitted and ministered in case after case to the English character, the English constitution, the English temper. Yet even while he recalled the old associations, he could not help suspecting that Anglicanism was compromising with error.

---

[1] *Difficulties of Anglicans*, 19.   [2] *op. cit.*, 4.
[3] Isaac Williams: *Autobiography*, 32.

So writing to Pusey in August, 1845, for his birthday, he had hoped that his great Anglican friend would go on increasing in usefulness and all good, 'till you have finished God's work upon earth as far as it is committed to you, and have no reason for remaining. He surely is working through you and others in His own way and will bring out all things happily at last.'[1]

[1] Pusey House: *unpublished*. Newman to Pusey, Aug. 22, 1845.

CHAPTER XVI

THE ORATORY OF SAN FILIPPO

I

Meanwhile in the autumn and winter of 1845, Newman lingered on at Littlemore wondering what he should do, and discussing the possibilities with his new friend. For before October was out, he was the guest of Wiseman at Oscott, and later he made a round of Catholic institutions. In the spring it was decided that with his little band he should live near Oscott at a house he called Maryvale. He placed himself and all his projects under the Virgin Mother, whose church in Oxford he had served for fifteen years, and who was also the patroness of Oriel. 'The Church', wrote Wiseman, 'has not received at any time a convert who has joined her in more docility and simplicity of faith than Newman.' 'You cannot think', he wrote later, 'how cheerful Newman is, nor how he makes his home among us.'[1]

Many years before Wiseman had mentioned in the *Dublin Review* his plan for establishing in England an Oratory of San Filippo Neri.[2] This was the freest of the Counter-Reformation orders; to be exact, it was not an order at all but simply a community of men living together under temporary vows and without finally surrendering their private property.

It was to be the most definite and insistent element in Newman's Catholic life, and one to which his works revert again and again.

San Filippo was born in Florence in 1515 and grew up to venerate the memory of Savonarola. He never lost the zeal for a pure and holy life which the great Dominican reformer had preached. After retiring for a time to the neighbourhood of Subiaco, and studying the liturgical monachism of the Benedictines, he had finally come to Rome; living there for sixty years

[1] Ward: *Wiseman*, 433–43.   [2] *Dublin Review*, May, 1839, 429.

the life of a holy priest, he had come in touch with the new idea of a religious society which the Church owed to the genius of St Ignatius Loyola. But San Filippo dreamt of no great organisation.

This was the community which Wiseman now commended. San Filippo 'in his humility had no intention of forming any congregation at all, but had formed it before he knew it, from the beauty and fascination of his own saintliness, and then when he was obliged to recognise it, put it into shape, shrank from the severity of the Regulars, and would have nothing to do with vows, and forbade propagation and dominion.'[1] He realised the value of a community, and would have his priests gather together to learn in charitable intercourse with one another how to attain perfection, and then diffuse their sanctification through their priestly work. His particular object was to consecrate the leisure of Romans. His rule was to go out but little into society: but to draw people back to Church by beautiful services, by simple, moving, and not too long sermons: to recall them also to the sacramental life of Christianity: he set before them the picture of perfection in the example of the Redeemer.

Hope holds to Christ the mind's own mirror out
To take His lovely likeness more and more.

San Filippo was the most modest, the most urbane, the most winning, the most tactful of saints. His rule, said Newman, was love, his only weapon influence. He had made a special study of music—he was a friend of Palestrina—and indeed the Oratorio takes its name from the sacred music performed in his oratories. But he had also his school of mystical piety, that by constant interior prayer the communities should open their spirits to the contemplation of heavenly light till changed from glory to glory as by the Spirit of the Lord.

What a Florentine had begun a Parisian reinforced. Pierre de Bérulle introduced an Oratory into Paris which later, under Charles de Condren and Olier, led to a great revival of religious life in France: it set up in fact a standard of priestly piety which has affected France ever since.

[1] *Office and Work of Universities*, 133–4.

Such then was the influence which, first commended by Wiseman, embraced Newman when he went to Rome, offering in its firm yet elastic pressure a combination of the great Biblical tradition of the Benedictines, the intellectual integrity of the Dominicans with the military and personal enterprise of the Jesuits.

But to an Oratorian, the supreme fact was always that he was a priest. This combined for Newman all that he owed to his colleges in Oxford, to his religious congregation and community in Littlemore with a fresh impulse to disciplined yet mystical piety: and under its influence he walked from year to year the path of peace which leads to perfection, and which attaining holiness diffuses it. Nor was Newman ever tired of referring to San Filippo as his pattern and his head; in verses, in his lectures in Dublin, in the *Apologia*, as well as in many sermons, he refers again and again to the enthusiasm with which he worked out from year to year as an Oratorian his study to be perfect and to follow the luminous example of his founder.

In the autumn of 1846, Newman went to Rome to further his studies, and to renew in his change of spirit that acquaintance with the metropolitan city which had, with Sicily, in 1833, tended his wounds with wine and oil, and sent him to great work like a giant refreshed. He was warmly received by the new Pope, Pius IX, and after careful enquiries, he decided to found an Oratorian Community; all were to be trained by a suitable Italian, and the Pope provided quarters at Santa Croce, the great church beside the Latin Gate, which looks out over the walls of Rome on to the folds of the silent Campagna and so to Frascati and the Alban Hills. He was quickly advanced to the priesthood, and after a few months of novitiate sent back to England to found that Oratory in Birmingham, on which for the rest of his life his heart and soul were centred.

2

Although the Pope and his dignitaries had received Newman with enthusiasm, the courtesies he received in Rome had been interrupted by some roughness. Irishmen from America remembered that he had not long since said hard things about Roman worship and the Holy See. And he himself was still the highly strung genius whose temperamental fierceness had sharpened controversy in Oxford. When they asked him to preach to the English in Rome, he denounced in his sermon those who came to the Holy City without a thought of its sacred character. 'Rome', he said, 'is no place for you. It is the very place where in the whole world Michael and the dragon may almost be seen in battle.'[1]

Italians were more urbane; they did not speak in this way to their tourists; they preferred tact. And even the English Catholics felt uncomfortable. They and the Oxford converts had never understood each other. Even before Newman left England he thought their suspicions cruel:[2] they on their part found it so difficult to see that God gives 'to this last even as unto thee'. And besides they were a little provincial while Newman thought and spoke as one living at the centre of intellectual power.

But in Rome these were passing things. How genially in Italy the sun returns! How happy Newman was in suiting himself to the rule of the gracious Florentine who came to Rome in the sixteenth century, made friends with Palestrina, brought people to listen to the sacred music of his Oratorio, and won them to religion as much by his courtesy as by his goodness. 'Once let a little love find entrance in their hearts and the rest will follow.' That was his method.[3] Wiseman had been right: the Oratorian tradition of popular preaching, of gentle attraction, of affecting music, would well present to the English temperament the appeal of the Catholic Church.

Nor was this his only satisfaction. He made friends with the great Roman theologian Perrone, who was always glad to discuss with him the profound and far-reaching subjects suggested by his *Development of Doctrine*.[4]

---

[1] Ward: *Newman*, I, 155.   [2] Ward: *Wiseman*, 439. *Ward*, II, 16.

[3] Faber: *St Philip*, Third Discourse.

[4] *Rambler*, May, 1859. See note 4 p. 174. This completely belies Strachey's account.

3

After his year in Rome Newman returned to England, establishing his Oratory first at Maryvale, then in Birmingham, and with another community at King William Street in the Strand. It was here that in 1849 he gave those lectures on the 'Difficulties of Anglicans', which Hutton as he listened found so brilliant, even though here and there they were a little perverse.

They argued what indeed Arnold had urged—that the true end of the Tractarian movement was Rome; they were intended to win many more to follow Newman. That they did not do, but they proved how subtle a genius, how able a controversialist the cause of Wiseman had gained. Here was one who could outline with sharp precision, whose precision was cutting, who could evoke enthusiasm, and throw over every consideration those perfumes of style which were the peculiar aroma of his own spirit and genius. He had at first hardly more than one theme—a theme to recur through the years, the character of the Catholic Church and her excellence. He was to depict her lineaments with such arresting power that caricatures of them would lose their currency before the insistent truth of the portrait itself. All her peculiarities, all the reasons why men attacked her, were to receive his attention. He explained, he persuaded, he exhorted; at times he spoke in ridicule and in irony but in a short time he had left a record in England, a most powerful apology for the Catholic Church both as to character and as to claims. This all through was to be his work: when he had been an Anglican he had insisted first on the pursuit of holiness, and then on those Catholic ordinances which, as the means of grace, best led men to attain it. It was so that he had urged the rights of God against those of men and women who were content merely to be themselves, and to do as they felt inclined. Now he was convinced that there was one organic and visible institution which represented with supreme authority the power of the Holy Spirit, and he found in this society an assurance which made his former beliefs seem but the mere ghosts of themselves.

From within the Church of England he had thrilled to the stately music of her liturgy, he had rejoiced in her chants and her choirs, he had hung upon her translation of the Bible, he had even seen in her windows those mysteries depicted which are central in Catholicism. But once he went into the outer air, the storied windows faded, the music of her choirs and organs could no longer reach him, the impression of the graces and mysteries which he had so closely associated with his reading of the Bible became a dim and ghostly memory; he grew accustomed to an intenser atmosphere, to a more fervent and moving worship, to a sense of the close personal reality of saints and angels, to the pressing cogency of rites and blessings and graces, to richer and more classical music, to the broad daylight of Catholic theology, and above all to the closeness of Jesus in the Blessed Sacrament.[1]

4

Newman was still a musician, and he delighted in every opportunity of the best of sacred music. His taste was not Gregorian, but he strongly felt that the music of the Missal had a sublimity which toned and regulated the anthems of other composers. Of these the great classical masters remained, as they had always been, his favourites, and he especially delighted in Beethoven and Mozart. In Gregorian set to harmony, as in the genius of Palestrina—the friend, as we saw, of his patron S Filippo—he saw the perfection of sacred music, the glorious old chants as they met the beginning of the rich classical composers.[2]

Great then was his joy when he found that he could hear in Church that music which had always been one of the well heads of his feeling, and when he could hear instruments concurring in its harmony. None knew better than he what wealth was added to music with the violin and modern instruments; it was, he said, the piano which had made Beethoven the grandest of musicians.

[1] Liddon: *Pusey*, II, 509.
[2] Edward Bellasis: 'Newman as a Musician' in *Coram Cardinali*.

5

Now he discovered what depths and heights were added to his experience in worship, when the most moving classical music could be associated with the supreme office of the Catholic religion, the Sacrifice of the Mass. For here was something which gathered in itself the significance of poetry; grandeur, beauty and awe invested the solemn words, and all the marvels of redemption were applied to the soul in the wholeness of Christ and His sacrifice. Here was summed up the whole story of God in His relation to man.

Very soon Newman began to feel how each day was centred on its Mass. In it, he completed the sacrifice of all his habits, tastes and likings, with his will and his judgment in the ecstasy of faith; by it he was carried on from strength to strength, as by a mighty wind, till he appeared before the God of Gods in Sion. 'To me,' he declared, 'nothing is so consoling, so piercing, so thrilling, so overcoming as the Mass: said as it is among us. I could attend Masses for ever and not be tired. It is not a mere form of words— it is a great action, the greatest action that can be on earth. It is not the invocation merely, but, if I dare use the word, the evocation of the Eternal. He becomes present on the altar in flesh and blood, before whom angels bow and devils tremble. This is that awful event which is the end, and is the interpretation, of every part of the solemnity. Words are necessary, but as means, not as ends, they are not mere addresses to the throne of grace; they are instruments of what is far higher, of consecration, of sacrifice. They hurry on, as if impatient to fulfil their mission. Quickly they go, the whole is quick; for they are all parts of one integral action. Quickly they go, for they are awful words of sacrifice. They are a work too great to delay upon, when it was said in the beginning: "What thou doest do quickly." Quickly they pass; for the Lord Jesus goes with them, as He passed along the lake in the days of His flesh, quickly calling first one and then another. Quickly they pass; because as the lightning which shineth from one part of the heaven into the other, so is the coming of the Son of Man.'[1]

[1] *Loss and Gain* (1848), Part II, Ch. XX, 290–1.

Such then was now, and was always to remain, the great event of Newman's daily life. Holy Communion became to him not what it had been in his youth, a privilege to associate only with the three high festivals of the Christian year; not merely what he had made it at St Mary's—the consecration of his Sundays—but the daily marvel which renewed in him Christ's indwelling, and made his heart one with the magnetic power of the sacramental presence continuously acting from the altar.

If the sense of that great privilege were through lack of the effort of faith, through lack of preparation and thanksgiving, for lack of the recurring effort of holiness to become stale, its power would no doubt diminish, and its mystery be profaned. Newman and his friend Faber issued at the time many warnings of the standard it exacted. But if indeed the consciousness of recurring days is ruled by its majesty, then indeed the Catholic is transformed in the renewing of his mind.

6

In Newman the sensitiveness of a highly strung temperament nevertheless remained: he had not abandoned at a fling the combative and controversial temper which had been so easily roused; the roots of long Calvinism had not all been torn out: nevertheless his passionate nature felt with the old exhilaration a new calm. And with this was still the intimacy of particular friends. For Ambrose St John was always with him. And at this time he wrote a sentence which opens the secret of a new joy. 'It seemed as if the kiss of his friend had conveyed into his own soul the enthusiasm which his words had betokened. He felt himself possessed, he knew not how, of a high superhuman power which seemed able to burst through mountains and walk the sea. With winter around him, he felt like the spring tide when all is new and bright.'[1]

So much did he owe still to his human friends. He now found friendships of a new order; the Catholic Church enabled him to rejoice in the society of canonised Saints. To a devout Catholic these are like familiar friends highly placed in positions in a court.

[1] *Loss and Gain* (1848), Part II, Ch. XX, 295.

NEWMAN AND AMBROSE ST JOHN IN ROME IN 1846

It counted much to Newman to feel that now he could address them personally, and that they would hear him, because all that was of moment to them was seen in their vision of the ultimate perfection.

Though Newman himself always remained an intellectual, he for a time ceded to the novelty of his enthusiasm and accepted legends that faith does certainly not require. He felt he had entered a realm as magical as that which fascinated his follower, Frederick Faber.

Faber was gifted: he had won the Newdigate at Oxford: he had an attractive person: people noticed not only blue eyes, well-formed features and a fair skin, but also pleasing manners; he excited a magnetic power which drew men towards him with its own special attraction; his Protestant brother applied to him a quotation from *Cymbeline*:

> . . . such a holy witch,
> That he enchants societies unto him:
> Half all men's hearts are his.

He was himself not unaware of this power. With it he lured many a soul into the Catholic Church; and in it he regaled them with pictures not only of a Paradise where they would be 'all rapture through and through', but of sweetness and bliss, here and now.[1]

One means to this was to give the English the highly coloured narratives in which a late phase of piety had delighted Southern Italy, where they liked their religion as full of marvels as a fairy tale.

But when these were brought out in Birmingham they jarred on the taste of a very shrewd and wise person who was to play a great part in Newman's career: who already in 1846 had been made a Vicar Apostolic, and who, when Wiseman went to Westminster in 1850, became Bishop of Birmingham.

William Bernard Ullathorne had begun life as a cabin-boy, living a rough life. He had a strong Yorkshire accent. He never could in his speech put the letter h in the right place. But if he lacked the polish of Oxford, he had in its place strong sense, broad

[1] G. C. Faber: *Oxford Apostles*, 229–31.

F

sympathies, excellent taste, and the highest traditions of Benedictine spirituality. He knew perfectly what England wanted from the Catholic religion. He saw perfectly that when the Church of England lost Newman she

> . . . cast a pearl away
> Richer than all his tribe.

Now Ullathorne saw at once that these Italian stories would not do for England: but when he very wisely said so, Newman impetuously rushed to do battle for his friend: 'No one', he wrote to Faber, 'can assail your name without striking at mine.'[1] Things were not made easier, when some of the Oxford converts wrote criticisms—not less cutting for being just—on the shortcomings of Catholic schools. At this point Ullathorne, as Vicar Apostolic, wrote Newman an admirable letter.

'My dear Mr Newman, I can with difficulty refrain from tears whilst I write. I love you so much, and yet I feel so anxious for the spirit recently I think indicated a little—to say the least. I know that yours has been a life of warfare and contest, and that you have had painfully to controvert the authorities under which you were brought up. Habits cling in hidden ways and will come back unknown to us in this poor restless nature of ours.' Ullathorne went on to say that in extreme sensitiveness a certain element of human nature is to be found creeping in: he spoke of the difficulty of seeing the more delicate shades of pride, especially of intellectual pride. From delicacy and respect, he would write as little as he could. He had faith in the humility of Newman and in the power of the Holy Ghost to lead all to follow the meekness of the Saints.[2]

So if Newman began by finding certain things which aroused his temperamental fierceness, he enjoyed certain gratifications. He had established his two Oratories; he had set to work. He had preached more of his admirable sermons; he had given his lectures on Anglican difficulties; he found new powers to soothe and calm him.

[1] Ward: *Newman*, I, 212.   [2] Butler: *Ullathorne*, I, 156.

CHAPTER XVII

A CRIMINAL PROSECUTION

1

Then suddenly out of his polemics flared up a furious attack from the Protestant world; it produced from Italy a renegade priest with the most unsavoury past. Though after flagrant scandals he had been unfrocked, he still found a lucrative appointment in England in denouncing the priests who had found him out. This kind of thing appealed to the taste of the time. A fortune had been made by a book called *Maria Monk* which was brought out in 1836 as the disclosures of an escaped nun about the profligacy of certain priests. But these were nothing to the strictures of Achilli.

Achilli spoke out his denunciations in most lurid terms. Newman exposed his record ruthlessly in his lectures; Achilli in himself was the gross horror and the scandal of the priesthood. When Newman detailed the hideous story, Achilli complained, and a prosecution for criminal libel ensued. This was the notorious case of *Regina v. Newman* in 1852.

2

To substantiate his accusations it was necessary for Newman to collect in Italy a number of women, to bring them to England, and to maintain them there. This presented great difficulties: why, in order to protect an Englishman of whom they had never heard, should Italian women come forward with evidence that stained their own honour?

This Newman could not have compassed but for the help of a devoted friend. When he was at Oriel he found in Maria Giberne an ardent admirer. With a high colour, fine features and a well-formed figure, she made a striking impression. She had come sometimes to Oriel. She made drawings of Froude and Newman.

Becoming a Catholic, she followed Newman to Rome and took a flat in the Palazzo Barberini. Now she set to work in Newman's cause. It was a big business to gather these women together, to persuade them to give their unpleasant evidence, to have them shipped to England, to maintain them there for months while the case was delayed by the prosecution in order to embarrass the accused. But Miss Giberne did not falter: and finally when the case was heard, the defence was ample enough.

Let us review Newman's original indictment: 'I am that Fr Achilli who as early as 1826 was deprived of my faculty to lecture for an offence which my inferiors did their best to conceal and who in 1827 had already earned the reputation of a scandalous friar. I am that Achilli who in the diocese of Viterbo in February, 1831, robbed of her honour a young woman of eighteen; who in September, 1833, was found guilty of a second such crime in the case of a person of twenty-eight, and who perpetrated a third in August, 1834, in the case of another aged twenty-four. I am that son of St Dominic who is known to have repeated the offence at Capua in 1834 and 1835 and at Naples again in 1840 in the case of a child of fifteen. I am he who chose the sacristy of the church for one of these crimes and Good Friday for another. I am that veritable priest who after all this began to speak against not only the Catholic faith but the moral law and perverted others by my teaching. I am the Cavalieri Achilli who then went to Corfu, made the wife of a tailor faithless to her husband, and lived publicly and travelled about with the wife of a chorus singer. I am that Professor in the Protestant College at Malta who with two others was dismissed from my post for offences which the authorities cannot get themselves to describe. And now, attend to me, such as I am, and you shall see what you shall see about the barbarity and profligacy of the Inquisition of Rome.'[1]

3

The trial finally began on June 20, 1851, and lasted five days. The Attorney-General, Sir Frederick Thesiger, and the Solicitor-

[1] Ward: *Newman*, I, 179.

General prosecuted. Newman's counsel was Sir Alexander Cockburn assisted by Mr Sergeant Wilkins and Mr Badeley. Newman could produce evidence for practically every single count of the accusation he had originally made.

The case for the Crown was an audacious one: it was that in every case the witnesses who supported Newman, even though they had come to give evidence most disagreeable to themselves, were committing perjury, and that Achilli was in every case telling the truth. None of Newman's witnesses broke down under examination, but it was obvious that each could give no corroborative evidence in her particular case, and simply because each could not do this their evidence was discounted, even though it was proved that Achilli had been dismissed from Malta for improper conduct and that the ecclesiastical courts had given similar sentences against him. No wonder that in these circumstances *The Times*, on the day it published the judgment against Newman, published also scathing comments on the case.

4

The Times noted not only that the witnesses stood cross-examination well in most unpleasant circumstances, and told a story which had every likelihood of truth. It happened practically always that Achilli had rapidly fled from the towns in which these women had lived. In one case, it was proved by two witnesses that he was living on intimate terms with a woman whom he knew to be a prostitute. The police at Naples, the Inquisition at Rome, the Bishop's court at Viterbo, the Courts of Corfu and the Protestant College at Malta, had all accused him of the same propensity, and after a short residence in England a number of women were already bringing the same charges against him. Wherever he went scandal followed him. 'Now stopped in a procession at Naples by a clamorous mother,' said *The Times* in its irony, 'now dogged at Corfu by a jealous tailor; now solemnly remonstrated with by members of his congregation on account of his maidservant, he is the most unfortunate of men if all these charges have been trumped up without substantial foundation.

The charges can be ascribed neither to Roman Catholic, nor to Protestant malignity, for they began when he was of one religion and continued when he was of the other, and always of the same thing.' Besides that he had made confession to the court in Rome, and refused to proclaim his own chastity on oath. 'Against these positive statements,' continued The Times, 'these accumulative and corroborative probabilities, and these dangerous admissions, there is nothing to be set except the denials of Dr Achilli. . . . Many of the witnesses were poor; but it is among the poor that profligates seek their victims. They could not be corroborated as to the fact, for that is a matter of secrecy; they were not discredited; they were not broken down; they were simply put aside and disbelieved. The principle upon which the case was decided would put an end to all proof by human testimony. Who can hope to be believed when such a mass of evidence has been flung aside as worthless?'[1]

The case was even worse than The Times admitted, for Achilli himself was proved a perjurer. He swore that he had never been unfrocked, while clerical officials proved that he had.[2] He swore that the Inquisition had no jurisdiction over cases of immorality, when it certainly has, and an English Catholic Bishop attested the fact in court. The only comment of the judge (Lord Campbell) on this tribunal unfrocking a priest for gross immorality was that Englishmen could be thankful they had no Inquisition in their country!

5

As for Newman, when he reprinted his lectures, he left a blank where the name of Achilli had occurred; and made an appeal to the judgment of posterity. He had not long to wait. 'No one doubts now', it was said, when twelve years later he published his Apologia, 'as to that celebrated cause: no one but knows what to think of the plaintiff and the defendant, of the jury and the judge.'[3]

[1] The Times, June 26, 1852, quoted in W. F. Finlason: Report of the Trial Regina v. Newman, 205.
[2] Chronicle, June 28, 1852.   [3] Dublin Review, July, 1854, p. 154.

At one point Newman's counsel had actually asked for a new trial. If the law had allowed it, the judges concerned would have given this; but apparently the law did not, and Newman at the end, after being threatened with jail, had been fined £100 with costs. But it opened the eyes of Protestants to what they were doing; for, as we saw, some women who were English Protestants had proved that Achilli was doing in London what he had done in Italy.

Newman's costs, amounting to £12,000, were contributed by admirers so generously that the surplus sum enabled him to buy a property at Rednal outside Birmingham. Nor was this Newman's only consolation. Achilli died repentant, confessing all his sins.[1]

6

One of the chief reasons why opinion had overborne justice at the trial was that Protestants were inflamed by the fact that Catholic bishops were again appointed in England to take the place of the old Vicars Apostolic. It was designated as a Papal aggression; the Catholic cause was making advances, and Newman in celebration of these events preached at Oscott on August 13, 1852, one of the most famous of his sermons, the Second Spring.

A year before he had been invited to Ireland to inaugurate a Catholic university; and for years he was to be the victim of the first of those involved and dubious moves, which so complicated the drama of his Catholic life that he was afraid its true story could never be written.

[1] Capecelatro: *Newman*, Vol. II, Book V.

CHAPTER XVIII

THE IDEAL UNIVERSITY

I

Newman's next move is one that like the others brings in the element of personal combat, and high principles. It is the intermingling of a tussle, a dream and an ideal. The intrigue makes him look like a failure: the ideal flames up like a beacon to give to aspiring youth the signal of a college life which combines the pursuit of learning with eternal things. It gives them at the outset of intellectual careers, the length and breadth and depth and height which are added to the mind when it believes that in Christ all orders of being chime into harmony; and so while a young man feels the impulse of his heart of flesh intermingling with a vocation, he is offered the fuller abundance and firmer poise which come to both soul and body when they are fused together by the love which is the Divine Spirit. This is the reason why all over the English-speaking world Newman is the name which Catholics give to their university societies.

In his own Oxford, he had been to undergraduates the personification and the focus of the Christian religion. When he came to Dublin, he defined the Church and the University in their relation to one another. He taught each what to expect from each.

In Oxford he had insisted that for an undergraduate the supreme preoccupation should be the pursuit of holiness, the supreme truth, eternal truth. He had brought the University of Oxford face to face with the Universality of the Church. He had insisted on the continuity of the sublime system which linked the Greco-Roman world with the formation of European civilisation, and through what it owed to Jerusalem brought both to the personal worship of God.

When he became a Catholic, he found there was another work

156

to do. It was to insist that for Catholics their own system of knowledge should not be narrow or exclusive: that its tradition was that of the humaner letters: that man in his whole record and his whole history, that the world—and with it the stars in the complexity which they disclosed to the scrutiny of the scientist— were the subjects which in Universities, youth, and not least Catholic youth, should prepare to study; he argued for the rights and freedom of the mind. Theology, since it studied divine things, is the queen of the sciences; in the court of studies, hers is the sceptre. But she should not make tyrannic claims, or interfere in business not her own.

What then does it mean for a Catholic to be a student? and what in turn for a student to be a Catholic? Those are the questions Newman now sets out to answer with an eloquence and a precision that set him in a place which in Church history is unique.

2

These answers are the more interesting because, like flowers from soil manured, they arise from projects contaminated by quarrels. The Irish question is involved.

Ireland was an anomaly in the country of the Whigs. Liberal principles insist on the freedom of every Catholic which he on his principles must in turn refuse. This takes us to the heart of the Irish labyrinth. Protestants had by direct force established their ascendancy over a people whose Catholicism they could not undermine. They not only seized the Catholic heritage; they made the Catholics pay to support a worship these considered heretical. After making them pay double taxes, they deprived them of higher education; and they ostracised them from good society. Whatever else was filched from the masses of the Irish people, however, Catholicism could not be taken. Their faith remained— a solid shining diamond.

At last the urgency of justice made itself heard. The Government had endowed the Catholic seminary of Maynooth; it had opened the Irish bar to Catholics; and Peel established the Queen's Colleges to give, as against the Protestant tradition of Trinity

College at Dublin, an education which could be called neutral because it was non-religious. But the Irish bishops demanded something more: they argued that if there was for the few a Protestant University, so for the many there should be a Catholic University, 'Why', they asked, 'should religion be banished from those higher studies with which it is so vitally connected?'[1]

That sounded reasonable enough. And yet there was a complication. All Catholic theologians insist there must be a hell: for logic insists that there must be a possibility of final choice of perdition if there is an absolute freedom of the will: but none could be so presumptuous as to insist who have chosen hell. A Catholic University was required by Catholic principles, for logic insisted on this also as fulfilment of justice; but where were the students to take advantage of its courses?

What is a University? was a question asked in *Cranford*. The answer was given: 'It is a place where young clergymen go to be educated.' At that time the tradition of Oxford and Cambridge was strongly clerical. But the Catholic clergy of Ireland were not to go to Universities; they were kept apart under ecclesiastical discipline: they had Maynooth. Secondary schools, as now understood, were few. The Professions contained few Catholics: the peasantry could hardly afford a University. The demand for it was but an anticipation of a need not yet existing. It was urged by two prelates—a hoary old Irish nationalist, racy of the soil, the Archbishop of Tuam, Mac Hale; the other an able Irish scholar, who having been trained for decades in Rome, thoroughly distrusted popular movements—Archbishop Cullen. 'He had an awkward unimpressive figure and his speech was colloquial and commonplace: but under an unpromising exterior lay a decisive will and an overwhelming sense of authority, which with the mysterious attributes of a delegate of the Holy Father gave his bearing not dignity indeed but an air of individuality and power. His idea of government was said to be simple to crudity: Ireland should be ruled as Rome was ruled,—by ecclesiastics.'[2]

Cullen made his proposal for two purposes of his own: to

[1] Aubrey de Vere: *Recollections*, 265.
[2] *A Tribute to Newman*, 164. Robert McHugh quoting Gavin Duffy.

further a plan of the Pope, and to put pressure on Peel. The story of Newman's disillusionment is put down in a volume printed in 1896, but still difficult to find: *My Campaign in Ireland*. The secret of it is a conflict over the spirit and methods of a University born prematurely.

Newman's arrival in Dublin had been delayed for two years; when he arrived he found the laity indifferent, the clergy hostile and Cullen inscrutable.[1] For five years, says Strachey, in a sentence excessively characteristic and to Ireland insulting—'Newman, un-aided and ignored, struggled desperately, like a man in a fog . . . he had to force himself to scrape together money, to write articles for the *Students' Gazette*, to make plans for medical laboratories, to be ingratiating with the City Council; he was obliged to spend months travelling in remote regions of Ireland in the company of extraordinary ecclesiastics and barbarous squireens.'[2] He had to carve every day for thirty hungry youths, or sit listening for hours while enthusiasts recommended an impossible organist. 'The patience with which he bore such trials was marvellous,' wrote Aubrey de Vere, 'but he had to encounter others severer still. He was always short of money, and he had poor material. It would have been idle, he said himself, to have plunged into the abyss of historical erudition or indulged in the flights of speculation in the presence of gentlemen who have yet to learn such elementary truth as that Jerusalem is not in Africa.'[3] And if he brought over a scholar from Oxford, he aroused Irish jealousy; the object of universities is to a university man education; it is not always for this purpose they are fostered by men of affairs.

In fact one reason why Archbishop Cullen had called Newman over was because he wanted to discredit the Queen's Colleges, and embarrass Sir Robert Peel. That he intended to found a real University, to put its control into the hands of a distinguished Englishman, and to make it, like Louvain, a centre of international culture was not clear; would the project not have served its purpose when, having embarrassed the English Government, it provided a few Irishmen with jobs? Or did Cullen merely think of a

[1] W. F. Stockley: *op. cit.*, 235–6.   [2] Strachey: 'Manning' in *Eminent Victorians*.   [3] Aubrey de Vere: *Recollections*, 275–6.

college disciplined like a seminary? Whatever the answer to these questions, he hoped that in Newman he had found a useful hack, well ridden in, to carry him quietly upon his route. He found himself, however, with a winged thoroughbred, fire coming from his nostrils, and while it nervously pawed the ground, Cullen watched anxiously lest it should fly where he could not but follow it into regions of the sky.[1]

But this took Cullen several years to learn. And Newman himself was not quickly disillusioned. He had been encouraged to go by Wiseman: he received a sign from the Holy See: the Pope himself told Wiseman that to enhance Newman's prestige he would give Newman the dignity of a bishop; but that was the last thing wanted by Cullen, whose object was to manage the affairs, alone and arbitrary. It was not in order to lose authority that, having been Archbishop of Armagh, he was now Archbishop of Dublin.

'You must give up the notion of my continuing at Dublin,' Newman wrote at last on December 17, 1858. 'Dr Cullen has no notion at all of treating me with any confidence. He has treated me from first to last like a scrub.'[2]

And yet there was another side. 'No one could work with Dr Newman here,' said his own secretary, in an outburst of impatience. 'If you accepted his ideas, your service would be very acceptable to him; if not, he took no notice of you.'[3]

Such is the background of the famous passages which Newman

[1] W. F. Stockley: *op. cit.*, 325.   [2] W. F. Stockley: *op. cit.*, 121.
[3] W. F. Stockley: *op. cit.*, 203.

The failure of his project was due to a whole concatenation of causes.

1. There was no charter from the Government. Degrees were unrecognised. In the medical board where degrees were valid, the numbers rose in the first four years as follows: 42, 76, 87, 110.

2. There was no endowment. This meant poor salaries for professors, poor equipment, and a burden of £6,800 a year on the people.

3. The University lacked support from Catholic laity. Some preferred Trinity or Queen's. Some did not want a University. The peasantry could not afford to send their clever boys.

4. The Holy See, Cullen and Newman were all mistaken in expecting support from England.

5. The ideals of Cullen and Newman were in conflict,

wrote on Universities, and which makes students choose him as their hero. 'We sometimes forget', wrote Newman, 'that we shall please Him best and get most from Him, when we use what we have in Nature to the utmost at the same time as we look out for what is beyond Nature in the confidence of faith and hope.' As theology helps in other studies, because God is the author of all good, so other studies bear upon theology, and may tend to bear it down. From this Newman went on to another proposition in defence of his Catholic University: that, like a philosophy, the Catholic creed is a whole. And where the wholes are not in agreement there will be clashes.

3

He then went on to an idea which had often haunted him at Oxford; that while culture has an excellence all its own and of great value, yet it is often distinct from Christianity and can be hostile to it. 'It is well to be a gentleman, it is well to have a cultivated intellect, a delicate taste, a candid, equitable, dispassionate mind, a noble and a courteous bearing in the conduct of life'—to have such was a principal object, at least in England, of going to a University—but one must not confuse it with sanctity or even conscientiousness. It was a question which he had scrutinised at Oxford, on which he had preached at Birmingham, warning thrusters lest they should be 'bad imitations of polished ungodliness'! Culture was related to the acquisition of facts, to professional requirements and to religion. With regard to the first of these, he insisted that facts must be regulated by a principle and a standard into order. 'The mind must be illuminated: it must see deep into history and human nature; it must be unprejudiced and serene; it has almost the beauty and harmony of heavenly con-

6. Mac Hale was always in opposition.

7. Some also found a difficulty in Newman's own character.

Cullen's desire to found a University, and obtain endowment and a charter for it, was open, reasonable and just.

I owe to the Revd. Fergal McGrath, S. J., who has made a special study of this question, the preceding note.

templation, so intimate is it with the eternal order of things.'[1]
To improve the intellect then, we must first of all ascend.

He then pointed out that if you bring young creatures together
in a school or college, they will learn from one another—that
society, like solitude, will teach more than a smattering from
many books. 'Let young minds move freely, and good will
come of it. For Truth', he said, 'is the proper object of the intellect.'[2]

Then what is the exact scope of University education? To be
useful in after life? To provide a professional preparation? Let
us frankly admit that is why young creatures go to Universities,
and why their parents consider it an investment to send them.
The claims of utility had been argued by Lord Jeffreys, Playfair,
and again by Sidney Smith in the *Edinburgh Review*. But the presence of Whately as Archbishop in Dublin reminded Newman
that Oriel had through two of its members—Copleston and
Davison—given a better answer. Literature, Copleston insisted,
enriches and ennobles all the qualities of the mind: it enables a
man to act in any profession with nobler views and better grace;
and Davison had insisted that education must train the judgment
so that no matter what subject a man chooses to grapple with, he
will go right to the point and see things as they are.[3]

4

Newman is coming now to his own main thesis. A University
is to train the mind, so that by his governing mind the educated
man can take his part in a governing class. It gives a man command of his subject. Its art is the art of social life and its end is
fitness for the world. It neither confines its views to particular
professions on the one hand, nor creates heroes nor inspires genius
on the other . . . nor is it content, on the other hand, with forcing
literature on the experimentalist, the economist or the engineer,
though such, too, it includes within its scope. A university training
is the great but ordinary means to a great but ordinary end: it

[1] *Idea of a University* (1873), 139.   [2] *op. cit.*, 151.   [3] *op. cit., Discourse VIII.*

aims at raising the intellectual tone of society, at cultivating the public mind, at purifying the national taste, at supplying true principles to popular enthusiasm, and fixed aims to popular aspirations, at giving enlargement and sobriety to the ideas of the age, at facilitating the exercise of political power and refining the intercourse of private life.[1] In a word, it provides a training in tact and judgment. Young men learn at the Universities to cultivate courtesy and maintain balance. It is the function of a college to make the best of the natural man.

And what is the best of the natural man but that type England then regarded as that of her governing class, another secret of her greatness, the gentleman? Newman never wrote any word that so captivated his countrymen in general as this definition of a gentleman: it won to him the vast crowd of educated men which saw in him their portraits idealised: it was like the portraits which George Richmond was then drawing and painting—a noble similitude of a real man; it showed the Englishman at his highest and finest. It was flattering only in so much as it depicted him in the light of his own ideals. It argued for the rightness of taste, to stand with modesty, as the sentinel of the soul watching continually over its momentous intercourse with the world about it.[2]

'Known as self-respect,' continued Newman, with an exquisite irony, well calculated to suit his Irish audience, 'it is the very household god of the Protestant, inspiring neatness and decency in the servant-girl, propriety of carriage and refined manners in her mistress, uprightness, manliness and generosity in the head of the family.

'It breathes upon the face of society and the hollow sepulchre is beautiful to look upon.[3]

'Refined by the civilisation which it has brought into maturity,' he continues, 'this self-respect infuses into the mind an intense horror of exposure, and a keen sensitiveness to notoriety and ridicule. It becomes the enemy of extravagance of any kind: it shrinks from what are called scenes, it has no mercy on the mock heroic, on pretence or egotism, on verbosity in language or what is called prosiness in matter.'[4]

[1] op. cit., 147–9.   [2] op. cit., 206.   [3] op. cit., 207.   [4] loc. cit.

So it is that Newman introduces his famous picture of the gentleman and compares tact to an easy chair or a cheerful fire, for the gentleman's zeal is to put everyone at his ease. He notices how with modest grace a gentleman seems to be receiving favours when he is conferring them: he is the very figure of prudence and the model of precision. He knows how few are worth his strife. He honours generally the ministers of religion while ignoring its mysteries: but he may even hold a religion in his own way. That is, when not a Christian, he cherishes those ideas of the sublime, majestic and beautiful without which there can be no large philosophy; he may even acknowledge the being of a God—or he may be, like Julian the Apostate, the Church's scoffing and relentless foe.

In every sentence we feel the presence of Oriel and Oxford, and are reminded that Whately would not receive Newman in Dublin; and also that Newman, when preaching on the aims and spirit of the Oratory, insisted on the value of a culture of class.

5

Newman is not yet at the end of his acute contentions. He has yet to give his reasons for allowing the intellect free scope in a Catholic University. If the mind must be free to study God in theology, it must be free to study Nature in science, and to study man in the humaner letters. Science sees how things are done, and does not hurry to postulate the action of the Divine: so then the Church must argue for what she asserts, say, in a miracle or about a moral issue. And a Catholic will respect his Church.

Then what about literature? It is the record of the life and heart of man as man, and not as the recipient of grace. But what a piece of work is man! Anger, daring, revenge and ambition, the splendours of taste and wealth, the senses' delight, the lover's joy, and the exterior world all have their part in him! His genius takes a thousand shapes and undergoes a thousand fortunes. The world is exhaustible, while the elect are few. Literature is not the biography of saints; while surveying in wit and taste the range and complexity of human nature, among things beautiful, moving and sublime, it trains the mind to agility and strength. If then a university is a direct preparation for this world, let it be what it proposes. 'It is not a convent; it is not a seminary; it is a place to fit men of the world for the world.'[1]

Such then was Newman's argument for the ideal of a university. It was a place for the free training of the mind: and the Church should come in and pass her judgments. But she comes in no Puritan mood. She forbids to youth no pleasures that are lawful, no curiosities that are healthy; she desires that they should have life, and have it more abundantly. She is present among men as in nature not to deny the excellence of nature, but to exalt it when possible to grace. She never blinds her eye either to the nobility of man's lot, or yet to what disfigures him. 'Her principle is one and the same throughout: not to prohibit truth of any kind, but to see that no doctrines pass under the name of Truth but those that claim it rightfully.'[2]

Such is the judgment of a great Catholic thinker on the scope of education in its advanced forms. And he attempted to make it a reality for young Irishmen. It is an apologia for Oxford and Cambridge and not only for them, but for the system they complete, the English system of schools and colleges to receive and train a cultured class. The apparent superiority of an aristocratic few who put elegance, finish and the grand air in the place of Christian virtue, Newman had detected, outlined and distrusted.

6

When Newman went as Rector to the Catholic University of Ireland, he went as an Oxford man who had always insisted on the part that personal influence should play in the life of a University or College. And his whole thesis was that a University should develop the growth of soul and mind; not constraining them by narrow or pietistic discipline, but on the other hand cultivating them by free and noble exercise in the pursuit of truth. This, as we saw, brought him into conflict with Cullen, who both mis-

[1] *op. cit.*, 359. [2] *op. cit.*, 234.

trusted Young Ireland and believed that the rigid rule and censor-
ship of the seminary was a safeguard necessary for all. Newman
insists therefore that though a University must exercise discipline,
and watch how students use the liberties she accords, she, as a
tactful mother, will speak not in a peremptory tone, but as one
who by her mild wisdom enlists on the side of duty the ambition,
the tastes and the imagination which make youth impetuous.[1]

The object of a liberal education was, he insisted, intellectual
excellence: and it was his aim to cultivate the faculties till they
attained to beauty and perfection. 'The artist puts before him
beauty of feature and form; the poet, beauty of mind; the preacher,
the beauty of grace', so intellect too has its beauty. If one can
cultivate virtue, so too one can cultivate the mind: and this was
the object he advocated: to open the mind, to correct it, to refine
it, to enable it to know and to digest, master, rule and use its
knowledge, to give it power over its own faculties, application,
flexibility, method, critical exactness, sagacity, resource, address
and eloquent expression.[2]

The secret of Newman's principle in education is in the words
companionship and exchange. The tutor must exercise an influence over his pupil, but he exercises it as a delightful friend:
the pupils, on the other hand, freshen, enlarge and amuse their
tutor and give him the rapture of looking forward into new
modes of living. The tutor offers the wealth of a tradition: the
pupil the ever-recurring novelties of a changing world.

Let the Church then be generous to the instincts of youth; let
her welcome the exercise of the body in sport, and mind in culture, science and learning; but on the other hand, the natural
man's preoccupation with the insistent and challenging claim of
the world's things and the world's facts should not allow him to
forget the dictates of conscience or of faith, which are so easily obscured. 'They are like shadows and tracings, certain indeed, but
delicate, fragile and almost evanescent which the mind recognises
at one time, not at another; discerns when it is calm, loses when it
is in agitation. The reflection of sky and mountains in the lake is

[1] Newman: *My Campaign in Ireland*, 35–6.
[2] *Idea of a University, Discourse V*, Section 9.

a proof that sky and mountains are around it, but the twilight, or
the mist, or the sudden storm hurries away the beautiful image.'[1]
For neither science nor learning, nor efficiency nor taste can speak
the whole truth, nor even the most important truth. Men must
be directed and governed by other intimations: they depend on
a seat of government in another world: sight and sense must
accept as suzerain the Church they have too often fought as an
antagonist.

In all these passages we see not only that Newman was inspired
by a zeal for truth as an end in itself, but that he had also a phenomenal understanding of youth, due to a special sympathy with
it. He gave always his best to young men, and drew from them
their best.[2] And if in Ireland he clashed with Archbishops, he had
his consolation in the company and enthusiasm of his undergraduates, on whom he showered more generously than on the
élite of Oxford his rarest gifts of genius.[3]

7

Among these were still his sermons, and the sermons were still
those of the man who had emanated attraction. The strange force
of his character made itself felt the more quickly because he was
entirely unconventional. His tenderness was displayed in a smile
of magical sweetness, but a sweetness that, far from being soft,
was combined with severity: a severity exacting from others the
high standard of service and sacrifice he himself rendered. He
combined dauntless courage with deep thoughtfulness: he was
both logical and imaginative. What men felt most in him was the
magical power and flavour of his presence. It was a very human
personality, one that imposed upon him a large share of human
sensibilities and perhaps, by necessary consequence, of sorrows,
cares and anxieties. He had also, it is true, a strong sense of humour, but in all serious matters, seriousness was exigent and nothing
came to him lightly, although he had notwithstanding a strength

---

[1] *Idea of a University* (1873), 515.
[2] H. Tristram. *Oratory Parish Magazine*, April, 1932.
[3] R. McHugh: *Newman on University Education*, xxiii.

that raised him under its weight. Silence and stillness but kindled
yet more the interior fires and a narrow limit increased their
force. His nature, one—

> Built on a surging subterranean fire
> That stirred and lifted him to high attempts

was far more likely to be stimulated than kept down by pressure
of any sort. He had vehement impulses and moods, which in the
Apologia he calls 'fierce'; and these were stung into activity by the
sights of oppression or injustice. But his temper was also one that
abounded in sympathy. He was full of veneration. He was worn
now and bent but yet in his swift step there was the same grace
and distinction; in his voice the same peculiar mingling of insistence, emotion and refinement: none could mistake in the
silhouette of his face the same sharp eagle outlines, nor had his
gaze lost its intensity. But though the dark of his hair survived,
his features, as in a tower which had been raised aloft to weather
lightning and fierce wind, displayed in lines and in expression the
signs of wearying conflict; yet when he spoke there was in his
smooth eloquence no roar nor tumult. His voice neither rose nor
fell. Simple, grave and musical it flowed on, a silver stream disturbed by no floods, broken by no cascades.[1]

And what, he asked, is the secret of a preacher's excellence? The
first is the earnest desire to minister some definite spiritual good
to those who hear. The earnestness of tone will come from the
zeal: the master is within. To sit down to compose for the pulpit
with a resolution to be eloquent is an impediment to persuasion;
to determine to be earnest is fatal.

Definiteness is the life of preaching. A good sermon is a talk from
a particular man to a particular set of people on a particular
theme.

First then let a man know his audience; secondly let him not
speak commonplaces but rather reveal some novel aspect of his
subject, and win his engagement by surprise; when speaking to
University men his preaching must be informed and exact. Let
him remember furthermore that as youth rushes easily to excess,

[1] C. V. Duff: *My Life in Two Hemispheres.*

so does the cultivation of the mind lead to doubt and rash speculation.

Newman now advised against the reading of sermons. Since
definiteness was the soul of preaching, so let it be direct; in other
words, it should approach a talk. 'I came', he quoted cogently,
after the example of St Francois de Sales, 'that they might have
life and have it more abundantly.' He was convinced that the
preacher could not do better than take to himself that searchlight
sentence on the aim of the Christ.[1]

8

In his sermon, 'God's will the end of life', he had finely delineated the type with whom, as a scholar from the middle classes, he
had come into collision at Trinity and Oriel. 'They were fashion-
able men; a collection of refined, high-bred, haughty men, eating
not gluttonously but what was rare and costly: delicate, exact,
fastidious in their taste from their very habits of indulgence; not
eating for the mere sake of eating, nor drinking for the mere sake
of drinking, but making a sort of exercise of their sensuality.
Sensual, carnal as flesh and eyes can be, with eyes, ears, tongue
steeped in impurity, every thought, look and sense, witnessing or
ministering to the evil one who ruled them, heartless and selfish,
high, punctilious and disdainful in their outward deportment.'[2]

He was even more ruthless on those who aped them: 'You, my
brethren, have not been brought up splendidly or nobly. You
have not been to the seats of higher education. You have not
learned the manners nor caught the tone of good society; you
have not even the largeness of mind, the candour, the romantic
sense of honour, the correctness of taste, the consideration of
others, and the gentleness which the world puts forth as its highest
type of excellency. You have not come near the courts or the
mansions of the great; yet you ape the sin of Dives while you are
strangers to his refinement.'[3] While on the one hand no one who

[1] These passages are a digest of Newman's essay on University Preaching,
reprinted 1873 with *Idea of a University*.

[2] *Discourses to Mixed Congregations*, 183.   [3] *op. cit.*, 114.

has good sense and humility but may, in any station of life, be truly well bred and refined, a bad imitation of polished ungodliness is despised everywhere for its pointless vulgarity.

But besides aristocracy and this fatal aping of it, Newman knew well that there were gentry. He now defined the position of the gentleman, that type which in English society merged imperceptibly into the aristocracy. He pointed to its intrinsic excellence: he admitted its necessity in its system, and he exposed its deficiencies in relation to Ireland where Catholic gentlemen then were few and Catholic noblemen unknown, where in fact at that time the religion he passionately vindicated was represented either by the masses or by priests rising from among them to exercise among them, perhaps often, the rule of priests—not always, that is to say, as sharers in their joy but sometimes as having dominion over their faith.

Yet in Ireland Newman was widely popular with the priests, and indeed with the Irish as a whole. Preachers of note from all over the country came to preach at his University, and in Dublin his young Irishmen found him that delightful companion who for so many years had drawn Englishmen to him at Oriel. He could criticise without being didactic; he was always stimulating, never dull. And there was in his voice still that rippling music which made it like

> Running water to whose falls
> Melodious birds sing madrigals.[1]

9

When he returned to England, the problem put itself in another form. There the Protestant preponderance had been less ruthless: there a Catholic gentry did exist: there could be seen—in their prestige and in the power of their wealth—Catholic peers. There Catholics already succeeded in the professions. But what did not exist was a due free training for the sons of Catholic gentlemen such as was found in the public schools and completed at Oxford. The Benedictines and the Jesuits certainly had their schools; there

[1] J. H. Pollen in *The Month*, Sept. 1906, p. 320.

were Ware, Oscott and Ushaw, but in all these the classes were
mixed, the polish lacking, and over all there hung the professional
piety of the seminary, with a rather constricted view of human
life. The converts from Oxford noticed these differences at once.
And they published comments on what they noticed.

Meanwhile the English Catholics of the upper classes saw the
drift of Newman's discourses. Here was a Catholic who urged
with unrivalled eloquence the supremacy of their religion, and yet
defined with the art of a master of men the qualities of an upper
class. Evidently he perfectly understood what they wanted for
their boys. The conclusion was obvious. Let there be a Newman
school.

Such was the task to which Newman addressed himself on his
return from Ireland. He founded his Oratory School at Birmingham. It soon won the confidence of parents. It is true that hardly
had it begun when all the masters came into collision with the
matron and, since Newman supported her, all resigned. In a
twinkling he had replaced all who had not withdrawn their resig-
nations. Himself Prefect of Studies, he left the mere administration
to Ambrose St John, who had practical charge till his death.

But the school succeeded well: it not only produced through
decades a delightful type of boy, a manlier, a more English, a more
scholarly and a more gentlemanly boy, but it led to a reform of
Catholic Schools all over England. It was one of Newman's
essential contributions.

Nevertheless, it had to face at the beginning, as indeed long after
Newman's death, the slings and arrows of outrageous malice. The
memory of all that gossip has died away; but in the *Dictionnaire
de Théologie Catholique*—that laborious and magisterial compila-
tion—still one reads that the rumours spread about it were mischievous to such a degree that history would refuse to admit such
vile ideas had ever come into men's minds did not there exist
documents which are irrefutable.[1]

Newman continued to watch the school and to watch the boys
—whose name for him was Jack—but nowhere did he come so
closely in touch with them as when he helped to coach them for

[1] *Dictionnaire de T. C.,* XI, 343.

the Latin play they performed at the end of the summer term. To make these plays perfect in every detail, he spared neither effort nor expense, but it was to his own example the young players owed the final success of their dramas. For here the theological controversialist displayed the range of his interests and the versatility of his temperament. He coached all his principal actors privately; and the boys were not a little astonished to find with what verve the venerated Dr Newman could, up to the time when he became a Cardinal at nearly eighty years of age, throw himself, for their imitation, into the part of a love-sick exquisite of Rome, or a drunken slave.

CHAPTER XIX

THE FRICTION OF DISAPPOINTMENTS

I

He might well have been content with his years in Ireland had they produced only the nucleus of a university; yet once again he produced a series of classic sermons: he wrote also a second novel, *Callista*, a well-written story of the Africa of St Augustine, and starred by some memorable passages. This was certainly an improvement on *Loss and Gain*, which he had written in Rome, and which gives us with some self-revelation an Oxford of repellent, theological undergraduates occupied incessantly with controversy over Catholicism. But *Callista* was not all. Newman's eye was intent also on current affairs, and in *Who's to blame?* he wrote a pamphlet on the Crimean War leading to the conclusion that if it was tragic waste it was due to the popular clamour demanding an unnecessary, and therefore unjust war.

It is not in war that the Englishman is seen at his best, for war is a huge undertaking of the State, while the greatness of Englishmen, Newman insisted, is in their individual gifts, gifts which enable them to balance private enterprise with respect for law and regard for one another, and to co-ordinate the efforts of the people with the traditions of the gentleman whom they respect and whose judgments they accept.

2

So he might have been content to let his brain lie fallow, or to concentrate on his Oratory School. He had plenty to occupy him as Superior of a Community. But no! He had hardly come back to Birmingham, when he first engaged in a fresh polemic, then embarked on a huge and weighty project.

The first was that of a Converts' periodical, the *Rambler*.

Launched in 1848, it had been edited by laymen of original views from the Universities, among them Lord Acton. But when Richard Simpson was editor, he showed insufficient discretion— he had made too many quips and there was annoyance which made Newman miserable.[1] Then he himself was urged to take the editorship, encouraged by his bishop: he did so, vigorously, with large plans, but most unfortunate results,[2] for shortly afterwards one of his articles in it was delated to Rome, and Ullathorne intimated to him gently that he had better give the Review up.[3] Newman did defend himself, but by some mischance the letter entrusted to Wiseman was not delivered, and Newman did not know till years afterwards that the case had gone against him by default.[4]

3

That was one contretemps: the other was still more unfortunate. It had long been felt that the Catholics should have a better version of the Bible than the old Douai translation. The best plan seemed to use the classic English of the Authorised Version, the English which Newman loved so well and which could where necessary be corrected. This was to be a means of bringing the Catholics back to the fundamental classic of their faith, not only a means of furnishing them well with weapons of persuasion, but it should be also a monument of Catholic learning, a glory to the Church. Newman saw the great scope of the project; none better

[1] Gasquet: *Lord Acton and his Circle,* 47.   [2] *op. cit.,* 63, 70–1.

[3] *Rambler,* May, 1859.

[4] Note: Newman wrote 'On consulting the faithful in matters of doctrine'. He argued that when bishops are undecided the people may be enthusiastic. In Rome in 1847 he often saw Passaglia and Perrone (206). 'I am glad to have this opportunity of expressing my gratitude and attachment to the venerable man who never grudged me his valuable time' (i.e. Perrone) (207). Perrone argued that when bishops failed, the people were sustained to uphold the doctrine of the Church. So Newman said there was during the third century 'a temporary suspension of the functions of the *Ecclesia Docens*' (214). This sentence, taken from its context, was delated to Rome as a heresy: the context proved that the *Ecclesia Docens* meant only the bishops, while the doctrinal integrity remained with the whole body of the Church: Newman adopted the view of Perrone himself and of Petavius, as against Hull.

knew the need; none by gifts of scholarship, style and taste was better fitted to give the new translation the stamp and the prestige required. But hardly had he begun when he found that support was ebbing away; and finally the explanation was offered that it would mean a loss of vested interest to the publishers and book-sellers who had stocks of the old version.[1]

4

This second failure left Newman disillusioned, and sometimes, not from wantonness, he was sad as night. Now, fifteen years after his conversion, he was much inclined to think that his Catholic life had been a failure. When he first came to touch with Oscott, it had been hoped that he would lead a great movement of conciliation. Instead of that, a cloud of obscurity had descended on him, an ominous cloud, for by its very blackness it suggested that it was yet to prove the centre of a storm.

So little attention did Catholics pay at the time to the Newman of Universities, that Faber said, and Newman himself felt, that he was put on the shelf. 'O Lord,' he wrote, 'bless what I write and prosper it, let it do much good, let it have much success, but let no praise come to me on that account in my lifetime.'[2] That prayer was being answered almost too well.

In Newman's career, the most lustrous achievements in litera-ture, the most precious contributions to history were being pro-duced while he himself was being neglected, harassed and thwarted. But none can say this is very different from what Church history would lead us to expect. For not until they are wearied and enfeebled, not until they have undergone envy and calumny, hate and contempt and pain, do great Christians leave those records which best serve a generation to come.

When his nerves were overwrought, he turned at times to talk,[3] at times to letters; and occasionally to an old exercise-book he

---

[1] Aubrey de Vere: *Recollections*, 273. Sir Shane Leslie adds that the interests of an American bishop were also involved. See Essay on Newman in *Great Catholics*.

[2] Ward: *Newman*, I, 578. [3] Gasquet: *Lord Acton and his Circle*, 47.

committed the bitterness of his soul in sad self-questioning. But this secret and fragmentary record of his misery is no index to the strong soul which, mastering it, made his demeanour serene and his company delightful.

Saints are apt to pour out confessions. Their high standards and their extreme sensibility of conscience are apt to lead them to accuse themselves of severe failings; and Victorians committed more of such confessions to paper than most. But these apparent failings are really no more than temptations or tendencies which no one else could detect. So it was here. But since Newman's most secret thoughts, and his evanescent moods are documented, we can learn that the aureole of Oxford had faded, and also that, disappointed and depressed by shabby clothes, he felt at times like a tramp wandering on through the dust and the rain till he was unkempt and miserable. Everywhere, it seemed, he had been misrepresented, backbitten and scorned. 'I have had many failures,' he wrote, 'and what I did well was not understood.'[1]

5

Vilified he had certainly first been by Protestants: he now found that he was suspected by Catholics: this in turn awoke his resentment; he was thus tempted to ask for sympathy from those old friends, still in the Church of England, who had honoured and loved him at the beginning and continued their courtesies through the years. Besides, he could not but observe that the temper of Anglicanism was changed, for if he had remained where he began, he would no longer be under suspicion, his principles were after all being accepted: it was becoming recognised that he had been a marvellous leader at Oxford. 'Those very books and papers of mine which Catholics did not understand Protestants did,' he wrote. 'Moreover by a coincidence, things I had written years ago as a Protestant, and the worth and force of which were not understood by Protestants then, are bearing fruit among Protestants

[1] Ward: *Newman*, I, 577. The gloom is expressed in several letters but the few pages on which Ward drew so much for his chapter 'Sad Years' are not a diary, and taken alone would give a false impression.

now. O my God. I seem to have wasted these years that I have been a Catholic. What I wrote as a Protestant has had far greater power, force, meaning, success than my Catholic work and this troubles me a great deal.'[1]

The truth of course was that Newman's delicate constitution allowed many scratches to develop and spread poison through his system till his heart beat high, the aches spread, and he was sick and tired, as people are when their blood is poisoned. He could every morning receive in the Holy Communion the source of life and sanctity, in that blessed Sacrament which he had described as so thrilling, so consoling. But, later in the day, in his hours of mere human consciousness, he felt himself a fractious, touchy, temperamental person; and his depression expressed itself in terms of nervous exhaustion. 'I shrink from every small inconvenience,' Newman once wrote, 'I sicken under every slight affliction, I fire up at every trifling contradiction. I fret and am cross at every little suffering of body.' 'I'm ashamed of myself,' he burst out in dubious verse:

> 'So easily fretted, so often unstrung
> Mad at trifles to which a chance moment gives birth,
> Complaining of heaven and complaining of earth.'[2]

But if that was his mood no one else observed it: in fact if it means anything more than a temptation, it only means that more tears witnessed that cutting sense of the hurt and smart of life which is the unmistakable symptom of neurasthenia, like the sharpness which Ullathorne had suspected might be the pugnacity defending intellectual pride. His melancholy became so well known, however, that not only did his Catholic rivals discredit him, but the Protestants began to bruit it about that his trials as a Catholic were such that he must perforce seek relief in coming back to the Church of England.

[1] Ward: *Newman*, I, 577–8.   [2] *Verses on Various Occasions*, 287.

6

To feel worn out is one thing; to be unstable is another. He was still the dogged combatant who had fought his way up by toil of knees and hands. He was still the believer who read: 'Blessed are you when men shall revile you and persecute you and say all manner of evil things against you falsely for my sake—rejoice and be exceeding glad, for great is your reward in heaven.'

Though to those who thwarted or even disappointed him he could be severe, those who loved him still found him a companion, courteous, considerate, subtle, urbane and winning—the Newman of Oriel, in short, who had captivated Oxford with the lightness of his elastic strength. He was still the close intimate friend of those he loved, yet always dignified and commanding veneration. The Oratory tradition asserts most firmly that he was neither touchy nor petulant. And he was still the eloquent preacher who through the years, in tribute after tribute, had extolled the uniqueness of the Roman Catholic Church, and who was moved to tears of thankfulness and joy at the clearness of her dogma and the impressiveness of her worship.[1] 'In the awful music of her doctrines, in the deep wisdom of her precepts, in the majesty of her Hierarchy, in the beauty of her ritual, in the dazzling lustre of her saints, in the consistent march of her policy, and the manifold archives of her long history, in all of these we recognise the hand of the God of order luminously, illustriously displayed.'[2]

'You who day by day offer up the Immaculate Lamb of God,' he had also asked. 'You who hold in your hands the Incarnate Lord under the visible tokens which He has ordained, you who again and again drink the chalice of the Great Victim—who is to make you fear? What is to startle you? What is to seduce you? What is to stop you, whether you are to suffer or to do, whether to lay the foundation of the work in tears or to put the crown on the work in jubilation?'[3]

[1] Ward: *Newman*, I, 580.   [2] *Occasional Sermons*, 221–2.   [3] *op. cit.*, 213.

7

None knew better than Newman that those who reap in joy must first sow in tears. And because he was passing through tribulation, because he was widely misunderstood, because clerical intrigue, narrowness, prejudice, and conventionality failed to understand the priceless worth of his far-sighted genius as from the peak he surveyed the varied project of a Church which combined with revelation an acceptance of men's reason, culture, science and genius, were men then to say he was falling away from the very faith for which he was valiantly contending? He would silence these dangerous rumours. Once for all, Protestants too should feel the lash of his asperity. 'I profess', he wrote in a letter to the *Globe,* 'that Protestantism is the dreariest of all possible religions. 'Return to the Church of England! No.

'The net is broken and we are delivered. I should be a consummate fool if in old age I left "the land flowing with milk and honey" for the city of confusion and the house of bondage.'[1]

In later years, he was to mention his love for the Anglican chants: in earlier years, he outlined in exquisite pencillings the charms of certain memories—but his appreciation of the Church of England did not mean he regretted the choice he had made deliberately in the face of acute sufferings.

Particular Catholics he might combat, but never for a moment did he doubt that he was building for the future, and that another age would vindicate his efforts.[2] Meanwhile the Church as the visible organ of the Holy Spirit, inspired a devotion that conquered all his being and for her no labours and no words were vain. Let there be in the good fight no failing of valour. His temper still was that which, as he read Wellington's despatches, had made him yearn to be a soldier.

[1] Ward: *Newman,* I, 581.   [2] *op. cit.,* 578.

8

Can one reconcile his sensitiveness with his fortitude? Where is his consistency? When he has given one impression, he often contradicts it by another. He was no lover of generalisations; he saw how many subtleties are interwoven into the mind of man; he recognised that one set of impulses governed him at one time, another set at another time. Always to be qualifying, however, always to insert a counterpoise weakens the sense of power and blurs the distinctness of an outline. Newman as a writer was clear, while as a man he was complex. With the instinct of a writer, he sets out whatever mood or idea he is exposing with all the force and effect he can command. Nor was his disillusionment without value. He had passed through a period of golden dreams when he first became a Catholic: he had indulged views more romantic than facts warrant: then as saddening experiences brought home the human things always associated in the world—and in the Church—with the terrible, sublime and beauteous shapes of truth and mystery, the glamour faded: and he fixed upon Catholic institutions, as on life itself, the unfaltering gaze of a believer's just yet searching judgment; but it cut him to the heart both to forego his dreams and to be accused of doubt and disloyalty.

9

He cherished also old associations; how could he not? He felt most tenderly towards old friends, and in the later sad years it was his solace to remember the ties of affection. His severance from them, he had written in 1860 to William Froude, was a wound that would never heal.[1] 'No one knows but myself,' he wrote to another, 'how great an affliction upon me it has been that you all have so simply treated me as dead.'[2] With his friends at Oxford, even when friendship was renewed, there was pain also in meeting after so many tribulations those whom he had loved.

[1] Harper: *Newman and William Froude*, 125.
[2] Pusey House: *unpublished*. To Copeland, Jan. 23, 1863.

The first of these was one of the last to see him when he left Littlemore, Copeland of Trinity, whom he met in London in the street, and whom in 1862 he longed to welcome, and did welcome, to Birmingham. Frederick Rogers came a year later. As they looked on one another the wearing of the years spoke so suddenly, so unmistakably its affecting tale that Rogers burst into tears, and clung to his friend's hand. When he spoke, it was to say 'How altered you are!'[1] Afterwards the flood-gates of confidence were opened, and the two friends spoke as they had spoken at Oriel thirty years before. He saw Isaac Williams again only at the point of death. 'It was', he wrote, 'as though he had stopped dying till he saw me, for as far as I can make out he never rallied. I believe he lived and died in perfect good faith and without a doubt that he was in the Catholic Church. And that is a great consolation.'[2]

Saddest of all was his return to Pusey and Keble. That did not come till 1865 when one gilded September morning Newman, after a visit to Southampton, walked across from Bishopstoke to Hursley, through the Hampshire woods.

Though Keble himself opened the Vicarage door, neither he nor Newman recognised the other; Keble was nearly seventy-five: as the result of a stroke he had a thickening in his speech, and could not hear when Newman spoke. Newman had to bring out his card. Did Keble then hold out his arms to the friend he loved? He put instead a question. 'Then you did not get my letter?' Keble had written to say it would be better not to come just then, because Pusey would be there. It was awkward. Keble could not shut the door in his old friend's face. So Keble must go and warn Pusey.

When Newman did come into the room, Pusey, in what Newman felt was shyness and suspicion, shrank back into a dark corner; as he looked narrowly and long at his old friend's thin worn face, he saw what twenty years of crosses had done. Newman returned the gaze; he was startled, pained and grieved; at a glance he would have known that face anywhere, but how oddly it too was changed! Twenty years of Christ Church dinners had

[1] Ward: *Newman*, I, 611.　　[2] Pusey House: *unpublished*.

G

also done their work; Pusey's head and features were all as large again as when Newman saw him last; his figure was swelled also, as though seen through a distorting glass, while in his voice there was a new tone, formal and a little pompous, 'a strange condescending tone'. Even Keble felt that Pusey was somehow taking himself too seriously. The talk of the work that followed was kind; and Keble had not altogether lost in his look that sweet, earnest expressiveness which captivated Newman forty years before. But though Pusey felt happy enough, Newman wrote that there was a weight on all their hearts.

Thus the three Oriel leaders of the Oxford movement dined together for the first and last time. And when they had parted, Keble's mind rung with the words of the three witches who met on a blasted heath.[1]

Where was it all leading? Who could tell? For those that live by the heart from youth to age, time cuts into the quick of feeling. Hopes fade and memories hurt. Youth it seems was folly; age is so vain. But is it always vain? Ah! not for those who have found within the King of Heaven, and seen Him in His beauty.

10

To them the Redeemer reveals an intimacy as exquisite as the world is evanescent. Newman could tell it well:—

Till Thou art seen it seems to be
A sort of fairy ground
Where suns unsetting light the sky
And flowers and fruit abound.

But when Thy keener purer beam
Is poured upon our sight
It loses all its power to charm
And what was day is night.

[1] This account is taken from Ward: *Newman*, II, 95–7. Liddon: *Pusey*, IV, 110–2.

And thus when we renounce for Thee
    Its restless aims and fears
The tender memories of the past
    The hopes of coming years.

Poor is our sacrifice whose eyes
    Are lighted from above;
We offer what we cannot keep
    What we have ceased to love.[1]

<hr>

[1] *Verses on Various Occasions*, 291–2.

CHAPTER XX

THE COMBAT WITH KINGSLEY

I

Yet through those many disillusionments and certain mystic consolations, Newman was still the zealot who earnestly waited the opportunity to vindicate his career. At last and suddenly the chance came. His had not been the only movement which was giving life and interest to the Church of England. On the contrary it was odious to some of the most romantic and delightful idealists.

Among clergymen of this type few were more attractive than Charles Kingsley. Born in 1819, he had grown up at Clovelly to open air, the sea, sport and poetry. As a boy, he lived finely in the delights of Devon. He had fallen deeply in love, had married, and he delighted in his children. Sensitive, ardent, passionate in love, he began to compose ballads and romances—both excellent; in him as writer and scholar the spirit of the active knightly Englishman lived anew. He rejoiced both in the impulse of the natural man, and in doing good to the wretched. He joined with Frederick Denison Maurice; earnest and energetic, they planned together:

> How best to help the slender store,
> How mend the dwellings of the poor,
> How gain in life, as life advances
> Valour and charity more and more.[1]

Such men had no sympathy with dogmas, with ritual, with sacerdotalism, with finesse. They combated the Tractarians. Newman they could not understand: and like many Englishmen, Kingsley felt that what he could not understand had something

[1] Tennyson: 'To Frederick Denison Maurice.'

sinister about it. Imaginative, daring, unselfish, he created from history a Protestant ideal, an ideal of Elizabethan chivalry modelled on Sir Philip Sidney, and throwing glamour over the buccaneers; while he painted Elizabethan nationalism in azure and gules, he identified Rome with what he disliked: not only celibacy, not only sacerdotalism, but malignance, furtiveness and bigotry. Among writers Kingsley expressed with rare success the temper of the traditional English gentleman whom Newman had delineated, while he added to it dash, philanthropy, poetry and a lover's joy. These were expressed in a clear vigorous style of high colours, light fancy and warm appeal.

Charles Kingsley had just finished *The Water Babies* for *Macmillan's Magazine* when he sent it a review of a *History of England* by a Froude who was Hurrell's younger brother, who had been in Newman's train, but was now a protagonist of Protestantism. In this review Kingsley added many hard things about the Catholic religion. 'Truth for its own sake', he wrote, 'has never been a virtue with the Roman clergy. Father Newman informs us that it need not, and on the whole, ought not to be.'[1]

2

Later Newman's case was taken up by the *Dublin Review*.[2] 'Why is it', asked a contributor, 'that a man whose genius is so universally admired—whose name will be handed down, at all events, as that of one of the great intellectual and literary glories of the generation—in whose lofty integrity no flaw has been detected—who has always been courteous and forbearing, almost to excess in his controversial dealings, and who has to all appearance withdrawn himself into the quiet duties of his own immediate vocation—Why is it that Dr Newman is so continually assailed by misrepresentation, calumny and every kind of literary unfairness?' His every movement had been misinterpreted. He could hardly take up a book that did not go out of its path to attack him, but all the while that detractors were impugning his reputation, he was earning the respect of better men. 'In his

[1] *Macmillan's Magazine,* Jan. 1864, p. 217.   [2] 1864, Oct., pp. 521–2.

silence and retirement,' said the *Dublin Review*, 'Dr Newman is drawing after him many hearts, and rebuking many intellects that would fain shrink from the light which it has been his providential mission to kindle. This kind of abiding, silent, unsought influence upon the minds of his fellow countrymen is something far greater and nobler than ephemeral popularity or universal applause. It is the glory of genius, softened by the shadow of the Cross.'[1]

3

This time, however, Newman decided that silence was not sufficient answer to malignance. He at once wrote to the editor of *Macmillan's* to complain of grave and gratuitous slander.

Kingsley replied saying that he founded his accusation on a passage in the *Sermons on Subjects of the Day*, published in 1844, when Newman, in speaking of the need of wisdom in safeguarding innocence, had said 'in certain cases, a lie is the nearest approach to truth'.[2] The answer was plain. First then, there was no sermon which approved lying, and secondly, Newman had written, not as a Popish priest, but to preach at St Mary's as an Anglican clergyman to the University of Oxford.

Kingsley's answer to this was: 'Dr Newman has by letter expressed in the strongest terms his denial of the meaning I have put on his words. No man knows the use of words better than Dr Newman: no man, therefore, has a better right to define what he does or does not mean by them. It only remains, therefore, for me to express my hearty regret at having so seriously mistaken him, and my hearty pleasure at finding him on the side of truth in this or any other matter.'

This sounded generous enough, as well as courteous and clever, but it was far from effecting Kingsley's purpose. Newman, with a mind subtle and acute to the highest degree, saw in the answer a chance to get beneath his opponent's fur. He would point out that not only did the sentence quoted above imply that Newman

[1] *loc. cit.*
[2] *Sermons on Subjects of the Day*, 335–43. Newman never used any such expression in the actual sermon.

was extremely skilful at playing with words: he would also insist that Kingsley failed to do the one thing that was required—to admit that Newman never said the words put into his mouth. This provoked Kingsley to write a pamphlet, *What then does Dr Newman mean?*

Controversy is always a diversion. Men watch it as eagerly as they watch the display of skill when champions are matched. Hutton invited attention to this one in the *Spectator*, and soon the intellectuals of England were drawn to admire one of the deftest pieces of controversy ever written. It was soon shown that it was not the convert Newman but the Protestant Kingsley who was prevaricating: that it was Kingsley who had got his facts wrong: that it was Kingsley who had rushed on to unjustifiable conclusions: Kingsley's little attempt to cover little inaccuracies with little subterfuges was, in a word, now ruthlessly exposed. He had begun by suggesting that Newman encouraged deceit. He had a second time instilled the suspicion in using such words as sly, shifty, sententious, cunning, not to say that Newman was these, but that he must take the consequences of his eccentricities if his sleight of hand led on in their direction. What did Newman mean?

'I ask', wrote Newman, in reply, 'why could not Mr Kingsley be open: if he still intended to arraign me on a charge of lying, why could he not say so as a man? Why must he insinuate questions, imply and use query and irony as if longing to touch a forbidden fruit which still he was afraid would burn his fingers if he did so?'[1] The counter-attack was itself barbed, and that was not the end of it. Newman in adding that he scorned lying and quibbling and slyness and cunning quite as much as any Protestant, was only preparing the ground for his final accusation against Kingsley, that Kingsley in saying he was in doubt about all that Newman would write was saying a most unfair thing: he was trying to poison the public mind against his antagonist for all time.[2]

[1] *Apologia*, 16–7.   [2] *op. cit.*, 22–3.

4

That was not all. Kingsley in attacking what Newman had said as an Anglican had suggested that even in the Church of England he had been a papist at heart: a Jesuit in disguise. 'The whole strength of what he says,' Newman wrote to Copeland, 'as *directed rhetorically* to the popular mind lies in his antecedent prejudice that *I was a Papist* while I was an Anglican. Mr K. implies this. The only way I can destroy this is to give my history and the history of my mind from 1822, or earlier, down to 1840.'[1] For did not the earlier doubts about him justify the doubts about him now? That was the most dramatic problem in the career of a man who was as baffling as he was remarkable. 'How could I dare,' asked Newman, 'how could I have the conscience, with warnings, with prophecies, with accusations against me, to persevere in a path which steadily advanced towards, which ended in the religion of Rome? And how am I now to be trusted when long ago I was trusted and found wanting?'[2] The time had come, had it not, for him to write an apologia for his whole life—to state from the beginning to the end the history of his religious opinions.

So it was that Newman produced the most monumental of all his writings. He had no personal bitterness towards Kingsley: he saw that Kingsley had simply made some awkward slips. But by making so popular a writer for the Protestant cause look as though his game was neither skilful nor straight, he could focus the attention of thoughtful England. Then he unravelled as best he could the complex and affecting story of his change. He put in touches so deft that they have taken their place in the echoing phrases of literature. He pictured again the first appeal of Trinity; the intellectual integrity of the Oriel of Copleston. He outlined his first conversion to Calvinism, and the change which affected the deeps of his soul when he first saw Rome and Sicily before writing 'Lead kindly light'. He went on to the Tractarian movement, to

[1] Pusey House: *unpublished.* Newman to Copeland, March 31, 1864.
[2] *Apologia,* 44.

the shock he had received when Robert Williams brought him face to face with Augustine's principles in Wiseman's article. He then told of the harrowing time of perplexity before he threw himself at the knees of the Italian Passionist.

He must collect old letters, consult old friends. Copeland, Church and others came to his support. He wrote with a concentration of effort, passion, and genius kindred to that with which he had written at Littlemore nineteen and twenty years before; and when his personal narrative was told, he set out in his grandest style the permanent sincerity of his belief in the Catholic Church as the supreme contrast to that world, the godlessness of which tore him with distress:—

'To consider the world in its length and breadth, its various history, the many races of men, their little starts, their fortunes, their mutual alienations, their conflicts, and then their ways, habits, governments, their forms of worship, their enterprises, their aimless courses, their random achievements and acquirements, the impotent conclusion of long-standing facts, the tokens so faint and broken of a superintending design, the blind evolution of what turn out to be great powers or truths, the progress of things, as if from unreasoning elements, not towards final causes, the greatness and littleness of man, his far-reaching aims, his short duration, the curtain hung over his futurity, the disappointments of life, the defeat of good, the success of evil, physical pain, mental anguish, the prevalence and intensity of sin, the prevailing idolatries, the corruptions, the dreary hopeless irreligion, that condition of the whole race so fearfully yet exactly described in the Apostle's words "having no hope and without God in the world"—all this is a vision to dizzy and appal; and inflicts upon the mind the sense of a profound mystery which is absolutely beyond human solution.'[1]

It pierced the heart: it bewildered reason. And history made it already more affrighting. Europe, and all minds affected by Europe, were hurrying on to vaster wars, and immenser disasters. Man's genius in its immense enterprise was really about to break down: it was constructing engines it could not control: it seemed

[1] *Apologia*, 367–8.

that in many fine constitutions was a congenital disease that must destroy civilisation as certainly as the body must moulder in the grave or turn to ashes in the furnace. What cure could work for man but something in final contrast to his rank corruptibility, something which was absolute? And as it must deal with the corruptibility of man, must it not be able also to support his mind with a truth that is certain and guaranteed, by some gift to a faculty stronger than the mind itself? Must not faith be given to the spirit? This Newman saw as one of the appendages to the high sovereignty of the Church, which was, he said, 'a supereminent, prodigious power sent upon earth to encounter and master a giant evil'.[1]

5

Arguing always for his own sincerity, he here insisted that he believed wholly the unique prerogative of the Catholic Church, but now, having stated his faith, he vindicated the rights of his reason. It was at this point that he countered the extremists in his own Church. They wanted authority at every moment, and the intellect's daily renewed submission. But no, said Newman, that is not what the thing requires. *Reason* must always *counter* and *complete* what the Church defines. Catholic Christendom is no simple exhibition of religious absolutism, but it presents a continuous picture of authority and private judgment alternately advancing and retreating as the ebb and flow of the tide. He could believe in the infallibility of the Church: but, he insisted, 'it is a supply for a need, and does not go beyond that need'.[2] He did not stop to say that infallibility is indeed a negative word, but he might have added, had he chosen, that it is a word which, far from meaning final or exhaustive, only means preserved from deceit. What he did insist, nevertheless, was that the Church is not infallible in cases of discipline, and that authority, that of Rome above all, is slow to intervene. The mind of Newman, wrote Dean Church, was as deep and subtle as that of Pascal.[3]

Newman had yet another appeal to make. It was that people

[1] *Apologia*, 389.　　　[2] *op. cit.*, 392.　　　[3] Church: *Pascal and other Essays.*

should not judge Catholicism in England by the practices of
Naples. He confessed to a solid preference for the justice of an
Englishman: he preferred even more the directness of an Englishman to the equivocations permitted in certain cases by such an
adviser as Sant Alfonso Liguori. Yet he could quote Jeremy
Taylor, Milton, Paley and finally Samuel Johnson as saying that
in certain circumstances it is allowable to tell a lie. But for his own
part Newman could quote other authorities whom he preferred
to prove that the simple and sincere people were his own choice.
His own Italian father, San Filippo, avoided liars like a pestilence.

Such was the conclusion of Newman's *Apologia*.

6

Its effect was hardly less sensational than his conversion. Once
again it fastened upon him the eyes of thinking England. While
some read from curiosity, others were deeply touched. As no
student could ignore the record, so no person of taste could fail to
see the vigour, the loftiness, or the clearness of the style. In it the
march, swift, yet grave, attested an easy magnanimity, while its
distinction set the writer on a height above that of any churchman
in the country. In spite of his intense concentration upon himself,
the writer's sensitiveness won him sympathy: his combination of
subtlety with openness opened wide and intriguing stretches: his
science touched the heights and depths not only of theology, but
of human nature and of the issues of fate. And who could deny
the dramatic significance of his own story? He had given up so
much to adhere to a Church which herself had an incomparable
power to startle and to hold the eyes of men: and while portraying
in admirable touches the unique background of Oxford, he opened
up with the story of his own heart questions of such moment both
to history and to the soul that his assailant's name was heard no
more.

Some have called this book the greatest biography in the language: but it touches on points too personal to absorb many now.
It is marred to a certain degree by Newman's preoccupation with

himself.[1] But how could he help that? He saw the difficulty from the beginning. 'Mind,' he wrote to Copeland, 'you will be disappointed. It is *not* a history of the movement but of *me*. It is an egotistic matter from beginning to end. It is to prove that I did not act *dishonestly*.'[2] What it must ever remain is a document of history, a casket of jewelled expressions, and a turning point in the career and tragedy of the leading spiritual writer—Kingsley called him the most perfect orator[3]—of his generation.

In an assemblage of churchmen and men of affairs, they began once again in 1864 to explore the problem of his faith and the genius of a man who a year before had been dismissed as a pathetic failure.

[1] Snead Cox: *Cardinal Vaughan*, 215. 'I have read it with a mixture of pain and pleasure.'
[2] Pusey House: *unpublished*. To Copeland, April 19, 1864.
[3] *What then does Dr Newman mean?*

CHAPTER XXI

A SEARCHING OF DEATH

I

In the following winter, his imagination was haunted by the death of friends: he had a presentiment that he might die suddenly himself. In the new excitement of so vast a prospect he found that as an aftermath of his exertions in writing the *Apologia* he was at the height of his powers. In this access of high excitement, he reviewed the experiences which dangerous illness brings: the weakness, the pain, the sense of passing away into the distance, the drama in which his sense had mingled with his returning consciousness, and with all came a vivid realisation of that mighty rite of his Church—the order for the commendation of a departing soul.

For to the Church death is not merely the extinction of the body's vital force: it is a moment of solemn travail to a man's being: all through life, body and soul have been reacting on one another to knit a whole so complex that few can say where flesh begins and spirit ends: and if the soul is to leave the body, it surrenders a vital complexity which has been the means of its conceptions. What does the soul know apart from the body? How, except in terms it has learnt through the senses, can it explain itself?

Its only terms for spiritual things, even the most elusive and mysterious, are those which it has learnt from the body as a teacher. 'In thy light shall we see light.' That suggests a highly mystical experience, but it expresses it in terms of sight. But the soul has such power over sense that it can impregnate sense with a higher significance; the things of the outer world become symbolic. So too with human faculties and feelings; they too are affected by a life higher than their own, and in the life of man things seen and unseen are interwoven: while outward and visible signs are transfused with light divine, shining, as Wordsworth wrote, with a glory not their own.

So it was that Newman brought back from the proximity of death a sense of vanishings which he could suggest in poetry by linking them up with the Order of Commendation, with biological speculations on prehistoric man, and with the dawning of the life to come.

2

To the Church, as to the Hindus, the processes and energies of nature are each linked with the conscious activity of spirit. The avalanche, the flash of sheet lightning across the sky, the earthquake, the virtues of medicinal waters, each suggest the intervention of a distinct intelligence: the very winds are spirits, and flames of fire are God's ministers. And so it is with the processes that disrupt the body from the soul. Disease is linked with devils, comfort and consolation with angels; and the Church, in a wisdom as sure as her tone is appealing, calls personally on saints, angels, principalities and powers to guide the soul through death.

Death is a hazardous combat, not exempt from grisly and ghastly episodes. In it the poor human being, so wrung with physical weariness and pain, so exhausted with the struggle for heart-beats and breath, has to face not only these but the inclinations of exhaustion and of despair: and all these are not mere human weaknesses, but exhibit also the perversity of malignant spirits who seize this opportunity to torment those whom they are not strong enough to menace.

In the agony of death great issues advance. In it a soul can rise to the holiness of a saint; it can fall into the despair of a lost soul or it can remain drugged and impotent on a mere human level, unprepared for the great adventures that confront it, as it passes through the gloom and the marvels of death to awaken to the searching light of timelessness, when coming before the finality of Christ, it sees, concentrated in its meeting with Him, its record in Time.

3

This is the theme on which Newman now composed *The Dream of Gerontius*. He composed it on odd scraps of paper—still to be seen at his Oratory in Birmingham—and pieced together with speed in the dark winter days of 1865. 'It came into my head to write it,' he said, 'I really can't tell how. And I wrote on till it was finished.'[1]

As a poem, it is unique. Gladstone said it gave the most striking glimpse of the other world conceived since the time of Dante.[2] Swinburne saw in it force, fervour, and tense energy.[3] It contains passages of descriptive power: others of tragic strength; and in it too is a most telling interpretation of that doctrine of an inter- mediate state after death where imperfect souls are prepared for final blessedness. All these are put together with a skill which immediately won the admiration of competent critics, and have secured for the poem as a whole a long reign. It enjoyed a new edition practically every year till its writer died: its reputation has certainly not diminished since.

4

It tells first the sense of horror and abandonment which comes with the emptying out of a man's natural forces, when he feels himself sinking back into the blank abyss from which he came.

> 'A visitant
> Is knocking his dire summons at my door,
> The like of whom to scare me and to daunt
> Has never, never come to me before.'

Here, it must be confessed, Newman is drawing out the extreme of effect, for though this sort of fear is of course a common part of the general healthy man's apprehension, it is seldom that of a person actually at the point of death. Now the dying man's voice is interrupted by the office of the Church, as it calls for help on

[1] Stockley: *Dream of Gerontius*, 17.   [2] Sir C. Oman: *Things I have seen*, 93
[3] *op. cit.*, 46.

saints and angels, on martyrs and virgins, and thus suspends for a
moment the storm of the sufferer's bewilderment. After those
present have gone on to plead the efficacy of Christ's redemption
by His own Death, Resurrection and Ascension, Gerontius makes
his own firm profession of faith:

> 'Simply to His grace and wholly
> Light and life and strength belong,
> And I love, supremely, solely,
> Him the holy, Him the strong.
>
> And I hold in veneration,
> For the love of Him alone,
> Holy Church as His creation,
> And her teachings as His own.'

But hardly has he finished, than he is assailed with a fresh access
of terror, which Newman expresses with profoundly moving
power:

> 'I can no more; for now it comes again,
> That sense of ruin, which is worse than pain,
> That masterful negation and collapse
> Of all that makes me man, as though I bent
> Over the dizzy brink
> Of some sheer infinite descent;
> Or worse, as though
> Down, down for ever I was falling through
> The solid framework of created things,
> And needs must sink and sink
> Into the vast abyss. And, crueller still
> A fierce and restless fright begins to fill
> The mansion of my soul. And, worse and worse,
> Some bodily form of ill
> Floats on the wind, with many a loathsome curse
> Tainting the hallowed air, and laughs, and flaps
> Its hideous wings,
> And makes me wild with horror and dismay
> O Jesu, help! pray for me, Mary, pray!'

Once again the office of commendation is heard, and as it dies away, the dying man, worn out by pain, finally commits his soul to God.

As he says the words *Into thy hands, O Lord, into thy hands,* he breaks in with the special invocation of the departing soul that it may go forth in the name of the Holy Trinity, of Angels and Archangels, Thrones, Dominations, Virtues, Principalities and Powers, of Patriarchs, Prophets, Martyrs, Virgins—for all these, as we saw, the wisdom of the Church calls upon by name to help the weakened soul in its extremity, as it engages with the fierce powers that gather upon the threshold of its awful course.

5

It is here that the writer begins to show his finest imaginative gifts. He is picturing the first consciousness of the life beyond death.

> 'I went to sleep; and now I am refreshed.
> A strange refreshment: for I feel in me
> An inexpressive lightness, and a sense
> Of freedom, as I were at length myself,
> And ne'er had been before. How still it is!
> I hear no more the busy beat of time,
> No, nor my fluttering breath, nor struggling pulse;
> Nor does one moment differ from the next.
>
> I cannot make my fingers or my lips
> By mutual pressure witness each to each,
> Nor by the eyelid's instantaneous stroke
> Assure myself I have a body still.
> Nor do I know my very attitude,
> Nor if I stand, or lie, or sit, or kneel
> So much I know, not knowing how I know,
> That the vast universe, where I have dwelt,
> Is quitting me, or I am quitting it.'

He could not tell as he thus passed from the exterior world if he were moving far or on the other hand annihilating distance.

6

And with this sense of leaving distance came another marvel, a sense of strength upholding, but with a uniform and gentle pressure, that bore him onward, while his feelings are enraptured with a sense of song. It is the aid, and the voice of his guardian angel, who tells him the story of a man's life as the angel sees it.

> 'O what a shifting parti-coloured scene
> Of hope and fear, of triumph and dismay,
> Of recklessness and penitence, has been
> The history of that dreary, lifelong fray! . . .
>
> O man, strange composite of heaven and earth!
> Majesty dwarfed to baseness! fragrant flower
> Running to poisonous seed! and seeming worth
> Cloaking corruption.'

Listening to his voice, the soul becomes calm and assured, and seeks from the angel to know more of the fate it enters. Has it not at once to pass to judgment? The angel answers that he is passing forward with extremest speed, a speed not measured by sun and moon or stars, rising and setting in their order, nor by the seasons, nor by the movement of the pendulum. But now all movements are measured by thought alone, and grow or lessen according to its intensity; for 'Everyone is standard of his own chronology'.

And as the soul listens, it is wrapt in serenity. All fear has gone: for it already begins to sense its timeless blessedness. 'I do not believe it would be possible', wrote St Catarina of Genoa, 'to find a joy comparable to that of a soul in Purgatory, except the joy of the blessed in Paradise, a joy which goes on increasing day by day as God flows in upon the soul.'[1]

Even as the departing soul enjoys this foretaste of its Paradise, however, the demons appear, making a fierce hubbub, and yelling uncouth blasphemies and contempt for holy men and holy things.

[1] *Treatise on Purgatory*, Ch. IX.

Yet they could not hurt a blessed soul, either on earth or in this
middle region. For

> 'when some child of grace, Angel or Saint,
> Pure and upright in his integrity
> Of nature, meets the demons on their raid,
> They scud away as cowards from the fight.
> Nay, oft hath holy hermit in his cell,
> Not yet disburdened of mortality,
> Mocked at their threats and warlike overtures;
> Or, dying, when they swarmed, like flies, around,
> Defied them, and departed to his Judge.'

How then, asks the soul, does it perceive anything when sense
has gone? How does it hold communication? It is wrapped in
dreams which, though true, are enigmatical, or at best symbolic.
There still remains some relic or counterpart of touch, taste, sound
and smell. A man whose foot has been cut off still seems to feel it:
and thus will a soul be till at the resurrection it regains its completeness of being.

But still it is consumed with longing for the vision of God, and
this, too, the Angel promises—adding the warning that the vision
will not only rejoice, but pierce, the soul which sees it, as love
pierced the hands and feet of St Francis of Assisi with actual
wounds.

Now they enter the house of judgment, a house so immaterial
and therefore so compact of spirit that

> 'The smallest portions of this edifice,
> Cornice, or frieze, or balustrade, or stair,
> The very pavement is made up of life'.

Even as the guardian speaks, they hear the story of God in His
relation to man and to angels, sung in the angels' ascription of
praise.

7

What is that story? It is the story of the angels who as spirits
decide timelessly their choice of God, while man sways backwards
and forwards among the things of sense and time. Man as a

viceroy and representative of the Divine Majesty meets the
material world but, compromising with it, loses his power to
control it and finds himself amid conditions of being as corrupt
and tormenting as his own heart. He becomes a savage: he lives
like an animal in cave or wood: but gradually in time glimmers
the dawn of his advancement.

> 'He dreed his penance age by age;
> And step by step began
> Slowly to doff his savage garb,
> And be again a man.'

The Divine breath of Spirit was within him; the Providence of
God chastened him; the angels guided him till he regained the
arts, the sciences and social life in a household, a city, a nation. The
angels were tried at once because they were pure intellect:

> 'For them no twilight or eclipse:
> No growth and no decay:
> 'Twas hopeless, all-ingulfing night,
> Or beatific day.
>
> But to the younger race there rose
> A hope upon its fall;
> And slowly, surely, gracefully,
> The morning dawned on all.
> And ages, opening out, divide
> The precious and the base,
> And from the hard and sullen mass,
> Mature the heirs of grace.'

But before man can regain his final blessedness, he must suffer
both in body and in soul: the body must endure the pangs of death,
and the soul, turning chill from the body's companionship, must
naked face a radiance as intense as fire which would consume it
till it became itself a flame. St John of the Cross liked to compare
this double process to that of a damp log brought to a fire: as long
as it was damp, it smoked and smouldered: only when dry could
it be brightly consumed. Such, he said, is the mystic cleansing of
contemplation and of purgatory, till the soul burns with the flame

of selfless and essential love for the Divine, till its whole choice is
perfect holiness. So with the passing soul. It

> 'with the intemperate energy of love
> Flies to the dear feet of Emmanuel;
> But, ere it reach them, the keen sanctity,
> Which with its effluence, like a glory, clothes
> And circles round the Crucified, has seized,
> And scorched and shrivelled it; and now it lies
> Passive and still before the awful Throne.
> O happy, suffering soul! for it is safe,
> Consumed, yet quickened, by the glance of God.'

The glance of God! The guardian angel had already explained
the significance of that meeting of eye to eye, when we shall know
even as we are known. What shall it be for a man to see in perfect
clearness the tenderness and graciousness of God, when knowing
all, he must know also how often he has disappointed Him?

8

The spiritual life, like that of all ardent love, is a life of ever-
quickening sensitiveness: an intuitive sympathy, which enables
two lives to be a constant interchange, and sets on every movement of them the raptures of joy and pain. But here the magic of
meeting glances tells all at once the poignancy and joy of a lifetime of ardour, and sees it in terms on one side of flawless valour,
of self-sacrifice, and on the other of disloyalty, of negligence, of a
dreary dullness of perception, due to self-preoccupation and base
choices. When One fairer than the children of men has offered the
honour of His intimacy, too often His generosity has been put to
shame, and He has been forced to suffer from the vileness of the
soul He seeks to redeem. He has been flouted or neglected in the
person of the human beings who represented Him: for He sums
up in His immediacy the countless benefits which love and charity
confer. Therefore to see Him is to see the reward and significance
of our lives as against the standard of perfection, and this who can

endure but with an agony keen as the consuming fire, which is He?

> 'thou wilt feel that thou hast sinned,
> As never thou didst feel, and wilt desire
> To slink away, and hide thee from His sight;
> And yet wilt have a longing eye to dwell
> Within the beauty of His countenance.
> And these two pains, so counter and so keen—
> The longing for Him, when thou seest Him not;
> The shame of self at thought of seeing Him—
> Will be thy veriest, sharpest purgatory.'

What then did this mean but the word purgatory, so sharp the pain, and yet so exquisite the refreshment, light and peace?

Rest eternal, and unfading light pour in upon the soul, as the will, now perfectly quiescent in its accordance with the will of God, finds perfect peace in accepting pain, till the peace is one with blessedness, and blessedness with joy. Such is the complexity of the suffering offered in sacrifice by the sinner, or the saint, on earth: such in ways still more blessed and unspeakable are the fate and the expectancy of the holy souls who throb and pine and languish, though motionless and happy because perfectly secure in hope, as they sink deep and deeper into the dim distance of eternity.

9

None can be surprised at the immediate success, or the continued appeal, of this poem. Its style is as varied and powerful as its theme is original. It combines mysticism with imagery to link the threshold of the eternal with the agony of death, and to provide us with a moving and consoling apprehension of our entry on the intermediate state.

Few would argue that it is a sustained success, or free from Newman's common failure to achieve an effective end. Its power is akin to that of music, and in itself it is not complete till it is set to music. With Elgar's music, it combines into an oratorio which is unique.

Its strength is like that of the *Divina Commedia*, combining theology with imagination and both with spiritual experience to convey in a unique way a truth of the life to come. Its style, too, is interesting: at one time its blank verse recaptures the cadences of the Jacobean dramatists' blank verse, at another that of *Samson Agonistes*—but its most appealing passages are in the simple verses, thirty-five in all, which begin with the words 'Praise to the Holiest in the height'. The last of these is the hymn second in favour only among Newman's writings to 'Lead Kindly Light'; and it tells in touching words the triumph of redemption. Not only does it with the fine precision of the scholastic accept the distinction between the Divine Essence in the Christ and the Divine Grace which is the power of His Spirit as that meets and mingles with the receptivity of man, but with a just appositeness to its place in the story of a death-bed, it ends with the words:

> 'And in the garden secretly,
> And on the Cross on high,
> Should teach his brethren and inspire
> To suffer and to die.'

Thus it leaves suspended the glories of the Resurrection and Ascension which alone would make its theology complete. Had those been added at the end, they would have given to the close the majesty it lacks.

The themes of Newman's life are, all through, less of triumph than of that strife which is the condition of victory: he kept at the Oratory the portrait as well as the book of the stout severe old Calvinistic clergyman, Thomas Scott, under whose guidance he had first sought to live a holy life. But not only was the poem acclaimed by his critics like the *Apologia*: Hutton leading them; it was immediately praised at Oxford by the new Professor of Poetry, Sir Francis Doyle, in a special lecture.[1]

Such events rapidly drew Newman back from his seclusion at the Oratory to play a fresh part in affairs.

---

[1] Sir F. Doyle: *Lectures on Poetry*, 91–124.

CHAPTER XXII

THE OXFORD INTRIGUE

I

When Newman first left the Church of England, he felt acutely, as we saw, the suspicion with which certain English Catholics regarded him. But the sensational acts of his drama concern the campaign which was carried on against him by other converts.

The reasons they attacked him were more than one. In the first place, his temper was always scholarly and English: secondly, he early came to an understanding with his Yorkshireman bishop, Ullathorne, and also gained the adherence of the Catholic laity: thirdly, his disappointments were disillusioning him, while more recent converts were still indulging their enthusiasm: fourthly, though he was a born leader, he was not himself a man of affairs, gifted to manage men of varying types in all the exacting business of day to day; fifthly, his temper was sensitive; and lastly, one cannot blink the fact, the lustre of his gifts occasioned one of the commonest of human passions—jealousy.

The acrid, though disguised, enmity of the most able of the converts, Archdeacon Manning, was so strong, that it embittered years of Newman's life as a Catholic. Manning, as he rose in the Roman Church from neophyte to Provost of Westminster, from Provost to Protonotary Apostolic, from Protonotary to Archbishop, from Archbishop to Cardinal, was always to be aware that Newman, in spite of his apparent failures, enjoyed a secret superior, inviolate prestige: he was a power that could not be put by: not alone by his historic part in the spiritual revival at Oxford, not only by his mastery of poetry and pathos in the highest art of classic composition, but by a personal intensity as phenomenal as genius he rivalled Manning—he soared above them all,—in alien and singular renown.

2

Yet Manning too is an historic figure: Manning too was complex. Born in 1808, he had come from Harrow to Oxford in 1827
with the reputation of a cricketer and horseman, and the nickname
of 'the General'.[1] His father was a banker living at the rate of
twenty thousand a year: he himself indulged ambitions of a high
political future. And well he might do: for he added to wealth,
brain; to brain, eloquence: to eloquence, fine features and a graceful person.[2] He was one of those triumphant personalities whom
undergraduates call a 'blood'. It was noticed that, like many
handsome and admired young men, he was sure that whatever he
did was right. Although sincere and truthful at heart, he could
cheerfully gull a don: among his traits as an undergraduate, this
tendency was so graceful, so assured, that most people—including
himself—were persuaded it was innocent.[3] He had not yet left
Oxford when his father suddenly lost all his money, and he himself was converted by the pious lady who wrote Line Upon Line.
She made him an evangelical Anglican. He became first a Fellow
of Merton, then a curate in Sussex. There he devoted himself to
the cure of souls. He assumed a leading position in his diocese. He
fell romantically in love, was widowed and heart-broken. At the
age of thirty-five in 1843 he came back to Oxford to denounce
Roman Catholicism in St Mary's, and denounced it in the
strongest terms.

3

But doubts began to assail both him and his friends. 'The waves
rise,' said Aubrey de Vere, 'our vessel leaks, and assumes besides
a good deal the look of a merchant vessel. Near us rides a ship,
vast, majestic and secure. But then there remains an ugly doubt—
may not that stately ship have come from an infected port and
have the plague on board?'

[1] Shane Leslie: Manning, 14–35.   [2] Purcell: Manning, 29–30.
[3] George Moberly: Dulce Domum, 24–35.

Manning's face shrivelled up in an expression where vexation mingled with mischief as he said:

'Or, at least, bugs!'[1]

But it is better after all to reach port having mastered an itch than to sink on the way: and in 1851, after many searchings of heart, he followed Newman into the Papal fold. He made a great sacrifice; but what made Prince Albert say that a mitre would have kept him in the Church of England?

His instinct was that of the administrator. As, while an Anglican, he had accused Newman of being an extremist, so as a Roman Catholic he was to oppose Newman for being a moderate.[2] He threw himself with ardour into the position most specifically Papal; everywhere he made a deep impression among his new friends;[3] and, by an apparent subservience to Wiseman, he gained supreme control at Westminster.

Both the Jesuits and the English Catholics saw their position imperilled, and prepared entrenchments. No sooner, however, had they marched forward than they were routed by superior generalship. Even the able, genial but now obese and diabetic Cardinal had to abandon his confidential and equally plump secretary, Monsignor Searle.[4]

The stalwart English strength of one traditional Catholic still remained, nevertheless, to take a dogged stand. Rough and uncompromising, Monsignor Errington had been named coadjutor at Westminster with rights of succession, and title of Archbishop of Trebizond. Above his massive figure, his eyes, as they looked out through big bluish spectacles over a heavy face where the razor had to be ruthlessly employed from day to day, gave a directness of gaze which, as a sign of strength, was enforced by every line of his face and every muscle of his body. His gaze through those blue spectacles was compared to that of a hawk. His talk likewise was designed for the frank—not to say the brutally frank—expression of his view. He did not ask for new

[1] Aubrey de Vere: *Recollections,* 294.

[2] Purcell: *Manning,* II, 124–99, 317–8.

[3] For Odo Russell's sensational account of this see *Life of Bishop Samuel Wilberforce,* III, 248.   [4] Ward: *Wiseman,* II, 285, 327.

devotions. 'The best form of meditation', he said, 'is to look at a dead body.'[1]

But that rough strength was no more match for the convert Archdeacon than is a boor's cudgel for a rapier in deft hands.

The eyes of Manning were also direct and piercing: but in his whole appearance there was distinction and finesse, as well as deliberation and serenity. His pale features were delicately chiselled, and, though austere, had even a certain sweetness of expression; his figure, slim and elastic, joined with thin cheeks, firm lips, and those piercing eyes to show that here in a prince of men the highest faculties were in fealty to the soul.

Wiseman was not altogether comfortable in his society, but he allowed him power. With no less success when Manning was in Rome did he manage the Pope. He felt for him the most enthusiastic personal devotion, and whom do we trust so much as those who love us?[2] He at once made friends with the one Englishman Pio Nono trusted, the well-cushioned son of a peer, who spoke Italian perfectly and who went in and out of the Vatican as Monsignor Talbot.

Thus it was that Talbot began to have a distrust of Newman. Yet that was no reason for ignoring him and, after the *Apologia* made Newman the centre of attention, Talbot invited him to come to Rome to preach a course of sermons to 'a congregation incomparably more educated' than anyone could expect to find in Birmingham.[3] Talbot received in answer one of those terse letters with which Newman, whether through lack of judgment or of urbanity, had often been apt to set people's teeth on edge.[4] It was an unhappy move. For it naturally sharpened the distrust of Talbot until the Monsignor thought Newman the most dangerous man in England.[5] With such views, he was only too willing to take the side of Manning in those variances between the two remarkable leaders of men who had come from Oxford to Papal Rome to urge opposing policies.[6]

---

[1] Ward: *Wiseman*, II, 215.   [2] *Life of Bishop Samuel Wilberforce, loc. cit.*
[3] Ward: *Newman*, II, 539.   [4] Ward: *op. cit.*, II, 539.
[5] Ward: *op. cit.*, 147.   [6] *op. cit.*, II, 68-9. Cf. Butler: *Ullathorne*, Ch. XIII.

4

Their great clash came over the question of Catholics going to the University. After publishing the *Apologia*, Newman heard from a Catholic friend that he could buy in Oxford, close to the centre of the town, the old workhouse area of five acres of land for £8000. It was an excellent opportunity: enquiries were pressed at once. Oxford was in the diocese of Birmingham. The bishop, Ullathorne, fully approved and indeed for three successive years pressed Newman to go.[1] There was a large piece of land between St Giles and Walton Street, and coming down almost to Beaumont Street within a stone's throw of the Colleges. The price was not excessive; the opportunities were immense.

For what would it not mean at that time when the University was growing in its adaptation to a changing world, when the Catholic Church had regained so much prestige, when the Oxford Movement had so widely changed the character of the Church of England, that Newman should go back there, and once more speak as he had spoken thirty years before?

Furthermore, if Catholic boys were to come up to Oxford and live with the Oratorians, could they not both complete the excellent spirit of his school at Edgbaston, while, by working out all he had said in his *Idea of a University*, they prepared themselves well to seize every opportunity for leadership in England?

It was Oxford which had first brought Newman to see the beauty of Catholicism. It was he who had far more than another reawoken undergraduates to the spiritual life. His early reputation there had assumed the colours of a legend.

And how could his heart resist the call of a place so significant and so dear, of the silver swallow-haunted waters, the grey towers, the college quadrangles, the lawns and gardens, the atmosphere of dignity, of learning and of leisure combined with the college life of privileged and gifted young men?

There was yet another attraction: it was that, not of seizing converts and arousing controversy, but of coming back into relation

[1] Butler: *op. cit.*, 14.

once more with that great institution of which Oxford is in a special sense the shrine, that institution who taught many sober doctrines of everlasting truth, and whose offices threw on the pathway of the just the lamplight of the Divine Word, and who not only in the cadences of her liturgy but also in her reviving sense of saints, of mysteries, of the operations of the Holy Spirit, had held his heart in former years, and had been working in England still—the Established Church, the Church in which he himself as a figure was already becoming historic. Newman could not be unaware of such facts as these.

5

But with these dreams there mingled apprehension. He was already sixty-four and energy was waning: he had had so many disappointments; his community was small; and to represent his Church amid the impacts of new scientific or metaphysical ideas —above all to meet again as an old man, either his old friends or undergraduates so different as undergraduates had become in five and twenty years—from all these encounters he was inclined to shrink.

'I have no hostile feelings towards the Anglican Communion, and nothing but love for Oxford,' he wrote to Pusey. 'Nor would I be a party to any measures different from those which follow from these principles. I have no plans, nor, I may say, expectations. I am too old to be able to speculate on the future: and, if I found an Oratory at Oxford, it may be as much as Providence means me to do. Even so much action as this implies, even to see Oxford, would be to me inexpressibly painful, as the coming to life again of men who have been apparently drowned.'[1]

And yet people seemed to want him: there was a feeling of regard: a promise of welcome: a sense of promise and excitement. 'Unless I had seen it with my own eyes,' a friend wrote, 'I could not have believed how strong is the attachment with which you are regarded by all parties.'[2]

[1] Pusey House: *unpublished*. To Pusey, Nov. 22, 1865.
[2] Ward: *Newman*, II, 62.

Yes, surely, that was reason enough to go; and dear were the hopes he cherished through the encouraging autumn of 1864, while all were hailing the *Apologia*.

Pusey, however, felt nervous lest Protestant controversy should be re-aroused. 'An R.C. establishment of whatever nature (for I know not what is intended) would revive all the ultra-Protestant antagonism unnecessarily.'[1] So he wrote to Copeland. And shortly afterwards Newman was aware that Manning, and his friend, the noisy extremist, Ward, were trying to induce their bishops to discountenance the scheme.[2]

Summoned to meet on December 13, 1864, these bishops made an adverse decision. On the same day Newman wrote to Copeland: 'Only think: among strange facts (it is a secret) of *Manning* and *Ward* co-operating to fulfil *Pusey's* wish of keeping me out of Oxford. And according to appearances they are likely to succeed.'[3]

Pusey became aware of Newman's plaint. 'What I feared', he wrote to Newman on Christmas Eve, 1864, 'was not your taking any line on the offensive, but that it would awaken, on the side of the preachers in the University pulpit, the controversy which has been happily long asleep. However all is in the hands of God.'[4]

Three days later, Newman wrote back to Pusey to say that Pusey's anxiety had no reason. 'I suppose', he said, 'I shall not go to Oxford in the way I proposed or any way.'[5] He pointed out that the Roman authorities could overlook their undergraduates being at Oxford, but could not encourage them. On February 10, Newman wrote again to Pusey: 'For myself of course they rely on my still going to Oxford, but I don't think it will come to pass. The truth is, since the year 1855 influential converts have spread unfavourable reports about me at Rome: and I am told at this time that there would not be this unwillingness there to allow young Catholics to go to Oxford, if I were not mixed up in the plan.

'My bishop, and other bishops are doing what they can to get

[1] Pusey House: *unpublished*. On Nov. 6.   [2] Ullathorne: *Facts and Documents*.
[3] Pusey House: *unpublished*. To Copeland. Cf. Ward: *Newman*, II, 67.
[4] Pusey House: *unpublished*.   [5] Pusey House: *unpublished*.

this right, but of course, I, for my part should take higher ground if I were asked again than I have hitherto taken, nor shall I deem it consistent with my duty or my sense of propriety to go to Oxford without the express and direct sanction of Propaganda, and this I don't think there is a chance of receiving.'[1] And Newman—not without a return to cynicism—sold to the University that first land he had bought.

6

The project, nevertheless, could not so easily die. The Catholics must do more in Oxford. They should be building a big Church. It was for the bishop of the diocese to decide, and he definitely did decide.

Again and quickly, important plots of land came into the market, plots even more central, if less extensive, than the property backing on Beaumont Street. There were others in St Aldates and again on either side of George Street. Those closer to centre of town and university were bought by the Oratorians by the summer of 1866, and Newman, strengthened by the bishop's firm conviction, felt he was indeed the one man to lead a new mission of the ancient Church in Oxford.

On January 21, 1867, he therefore again wrote to Pusey:

'(Fr Harper) refers to my going to Oxford. I suppose it is nearly settled that the Oratory is to go there, but I trust it will be in no hostile spirit to what remains of Oxford's old habits, opinions and practices. What I hear about the dominant teaching just now is simply shocking. *You*, I suppose, would rather a man agreed with me than with the advocates of scepticism and infidelity, and *I* certainly should prefer a man to be an Anglican than an infidel, therefore I do not see what chance there is of our moving in opposite directions. Then again for myself I confess I could not consistently refuse to bring a soul into that communion which I think the only Fold, if he deliberately and intelligently wished it, but I have no intention of making a crusade against under-

[1] Pusey House: *unpublished*. The phrase 'influential converts' refers, of course, to Manning and Talbot.

graduates; and on the other hand it is quite uncertain what influence I *could* exert; and when I think of myself again at Oxford, I think of those actors and singers who, having retired from the public scenes, in their old age come back again to act and make deplorable failures to the disappointment of those who wish them well, and I anticipate that I may be a nine-days' wonder and then break down. But if my coming produced any effect, it is likely that it would tell more or at least not less against scepticism than against the Anglican Church, and therefore on the whole I think an Anglican would be satisfied with the result.'[1]

In the spring of 1867 therefore, exchanging his hesitation for hope, he began to outline the brilliant picture of all that he might do: how he might stem the tide of liberalism, how he might win over old adherents like Mark Pattison, how that moment was peculiarly propitious to assert in the city of promise the traditions which had long since endued her with her unique distinction—how for that reason he would face the publicity and all the poignant memories of the years, how like the dead coming to the dead, he would return to where his heart lingered always—to that Oxford which for forty years he had loved with the ecstasy of the music in her Churches, and the passion of the friendships she had given him.

He had with all the ardour of exhilaration been painting this picture as he walked out one spring afternoon from his Oratory in Edgbaston among the shooting green. For him there was to be a second spring in Oxford. As in high hopes, after sketching his plans to the young priest he was about to despatch, he came back to the door of the Oratory, the servant opening it handed him a long blue envelope. He looked for a moment at the letter in it, then he covered his face with his hands.

'All is over,' he cried out. 'I am not allowed to go.'[2]

7

No one who realised the mind of him who uttered those words can hear them without pity and indignation. Behind them is a

---

[1] Pusey House: *unpublished*.   [2] Ward: *Newman*, II, 139.

THE ORATORY AT BIRMINGHAM

long story of narrow-mindedness, of scandal and of intrigue; each of these is associated with the historic problem of Manning[1]— Manning in relation to something yet more complex than his own remarkable character, the Roman Catholic Church.

In the Establishment Manning had known the worth of moral principles: he had known more than these—the power of a personal relation to a Saviour, truth revealed to the believer, and the haunting power of a liturgy founded on the Bible and on the offices of the Catholic Church.

But in Catholicism the principles of the spiritual life were more acutely defined. There was the original liturgy—richer and fuller. There was also interior prayer of mystical communion where heart spoke to heart. But beside these he met an urgent personal piety; a devotion not only to the Redeemer and to His Holy Name, but to His wounds and His Heart. Jesus was approached as a person, ardent, romantic, tender, with His Mother and with St Joseph, with other special patrons, with a guardian angel. These softened the heart to tenderness; they made worship fervent; they gave Catholicism the warmth of a mother's embrace. Her sanctuaries had an atmosphere as peculiar and fragrant as their incense.

Since the Reformation, the features of the great Church had become more marked, individual and expressive. Many of its adherents concentrated on these alone. They revelled in miracles; they surrendered their mind to more elaborate dogma: and insisting on the intransigence of their Church, fixed their ideas with ever intenser enthusiasm on the prerogatives not only of the Madonna but of the Pope.

Newman was a stranger to none of these things; but he kept them balanced in his sense of the Church in her range of height and breadth. To other converts, these assumed an almost exclusive interest and awoke an enthusiasm which drowned every other consideration. Manning found it simplified everything if he pushed things to extremes, and treated the Pope as in all matters absolute.[2]

[1] Butler: *Ullathorne*, IV, 4, 9.
[2] This is developed in full by Manning in his *Temporal Mission of the Holy Ghost*.

H

8

A crisis in history encouraged them. The Pope, though most generous and genial, had been disappointed with reforms in Italy: he had been forced to put down revolution and assert authority. He, in response to the fervours of a widespread devotion, had defined the dogma of the Immaculate Conception, and, to atone for encroachments on his papal states, he outlined in a pronouncement in 1864 the errors of all revolutionary tendencies. He proposed no compromise in any direction whatsoever. Since, then, paganism was spreading, standards declining and society disintegrating, he opposed them strongly with his insistence on the uniqueness of the Church.[1] This suited certain English converts. It stimulated the uncompromising logic of Ward. It indulged the luxuriant emotions of Faber.

Above all, it fitted with certain instincts for definition and power in the temper of Manning.[2] For these convert extremists, it was but too easy to insist that what the Church allowed to them, she enforced on all; that nothing was so Catholic as their own excesses.

To them therefore the subtler, freer, truer mind of Newman was suspect; they ignored the sober sense of their co-religionists in England; they shivered at the thought of Newman coming back to Oxford to encourage the English Catholics in all the traditions which suited them to exercise an influence on the temper of their countrymen, or to speak in the language adopted by the age;[3] discarding Oxford, those converts affected Naples or copied Cork.

9

So it was that Manning had set to work in 1864. He had long dominated the failing Wiseman: he managed to combine the

---

[1] Aubrey de Vere: *Recollections,* 294.

[2] Ward: *Newman,* II, 60, 69. 'So towering an aim, so grasping an ambition, can never be gratified.'

[3] Purcell: *Manning,* II, 291 and all Chapters XIII and XIV.

bishops: he was not less active in Rome, both with Monsignor Talbot and with Propaganda.[1] Though it was against the policy of these to interfere in diocesan administration, they were induced to believe that all England was affected, and that a real principle was at stake: that, in fact, young Catholics could not go to English Universities without prejudice to their faith.

Talbot, as we saw, was already hostile to Newman. With him placed in his point of vantage, Manning obtained a decision from Propaganda, and managed to persuade the Pope to present as a Papal idea what was originally Manning's own design.[2] For this was Manning's subtlety. He first persuaded his own conscience that whatever suited his own planning was right. He then persuaded others that they had been clever enough to form the projects he suggested. So it was that the Propaganda at Rome sent to Ullathorne the message that if Newman thought of going back to Oxford, he was to be blandly and suavely recalled.[3]

Strachey has told this story with a vividness none can forget; but being mischievous, he subordinates accuracy to amusement: and thus forfeits the delicacy and appeal of the truth. Therefore it is not out of place to give the real facts of the touching episode which came at the end of the affair. When his cherished plans had all failed, Newman decided that in spite of all he must revisit not Oxford, but Littlemore; and one June morning in 1868, in the company of Ambrose St John, he took the train straight there from Birmingham. It was just forty years since he had first gone to the village as Vicar of St Mary's.

When again he saw the place of the central change in his life, a thousand poignant memories came upon him. He leant over the lych-gate and he wept.

At that moment, a young clergyman passing looked with sympathy into the stranger's face. Had he not seen its likeness before? Was it not the original of the miniature[4] he had so often scrutinised in the sitting-room of his principal parishioner? Surely it was—

[1] Purcell: *Manning, loc. cit.*   [2] Butler: *Ullathorne,* II, 9.
[3] Ward: *Newman,* II, 139, 145.
[4] This miniature is now in the possession of Lady Aldenham at Clifton Hampden.

Newman! He hurried to this parishioner, a man of position, insisted that they must make sure; when the clergyman went back, he found the two strangers in the churchyard. 'Are you not', he asked, 'an old friend of Mr Crawley? I feel sure he would be very pleased to see you.' 'Oh no, oh no,' answered the old man. 'I cannot.' And the tears came again.[1] But he did go—to find that Mr Crawley and his daughters remembered him so much more clearly than he them.

On June 25th, 1868, Newman wrote to Copeland:

'We did not go through Oxford. We had five hours there, but not time for everything. It was a most strange vision. I could hardly believe it real. It was the past coming back, as it might be in the intermediate state.'[2]

Lytton Strachey not only alters the details of this scene, but also misinterprets the characters and the significance. He describes the variance between Manning and Newman as 'the meeting of the eagle and the dove; there was a hovering, a swoop, and then the quick beak and the relentless talons did their work.'[3] But these contrasted birds are quite inadequate to furnish a simile for the natures of the two men. For Newman, too, was fierce; though he might meet with frequent set-backs, yet he persevered not the less relentlessly. He might have to wait till Manning was in his grave, but decades do not decide the biggest issues of Church affairs.

If we were to credit Strachey, Newman at Littlemore would be but a beaten man who was never more to count in Universities. But how different is the truth! While Manning's tired waves vainly break as they recede over the naked shingles of his forgotten shore, the tide of Newman flows amain in Oxford—and elsewhere.

'Was there nothing that could be done?' Such is the question that Strachey invents, and he invents the further information that the old man seemed hardly to understand what was being said to him. He suggests that Newman was weeping over the Oxford

[1] Ward: *Newman*, II, 206.
[2] Pusey House: *unpublished*. To Copeland, June 25, 1868.
[3] Strachey: *Eminent Victorians* (1918), 31.

project, and that when he replied 'Oh no, oh no' he was thinking of that, and there could be nothing more to say. Even if
it had been simply the Oxford project, history, as we saw, was
to say much more. Within twelve years, Newman was to be
welcomed back to Trinity. The flying dazzle of a meteor may
catch many eyes: but it may only for its flash outshine the morning star.

The real question asked at Littlemore, however, was not what
could be done for an aged man in tears: it was whether Newman
would revisit an old friend, still in the Church of England. He
began by saying 'Oh no, oh no'. But he did go. And henceforward
he occupied himself much with his old Oxford friends, and heard
again the music of those anthems which for long years had dissolved him into ecstasies, and opened heaven.

It had been said also of Newman that he did not care for his
work among the poor—this was never true. His first cares were
among the poor. He himself instituted his country work, and
built his new chapel out at Littlemore. One who saw him work
among the poor parishioners said they listened to him with an
attention which would have been almost painful had he not been
the lodestar of their lives.[1] Poor and simple people feel always
among them the presence of a heart.

10

In the meantime Manning had been made Archbishop of
Westminster by the special choice of Pius IX. In his frequent in-
terventions at Rome during the difficulties with Archbishop
Errington he had become well known, and not only did the Pope
feel a personal regard for him, but he had the private support of
Monsignor Talbot. None knew better than himself that his
appointment would not be welcomed in England. None knew
better how best to win round opinions to his favour. He was to
reign at Westminster for twenty-seven years, and through that
time to make himself remarked and revered, not only as a figure
of impressive dignity, not only as a social reformer, but as one of

[1] Orielensis: in *Daily Telegraph*, Aug. 13, 1890.

the noblest, the most charitable, the most attractive of churchmen, the devoted friend of the drunkard and the outcast. He now attempted to win back with the rest the confidence of Newman; and again the tense cords tightened.

The trouble went far back. Newman, whose memory was long, did not forget the embarrassing hostility that Manning had shown in that sermon he had contrived to preach against Catholicism at St Mary's on Guy Fawkes Day in 1843.[1] Newman was well aware that it was Manning who worked against him both at Westminster and in Rome in the Oxford matter. When therefore he received in 1867, through his old friend Oakeley, an invitation to be reconciled to Manning, he replied that the best thing Manning could do to convince Newman of his sincerity would be to let the Oxford scheme go through.

Newman's reasons for doubting Manning could not be put down because they were the result of accumulating inferences, and for many of these the evidence was confidential. But together they formed an impression which no one questioned.[2] There was an inveterate distrust.[3] Manning was still anxious to remove a cause of scandal; he knew that the variance between them was so well known that it did much harm, and he wrote a most diplomatic letter pleading for the removal of misunderstandings. Newman's answer stated the unpleasant fact that for four years he had been unable to dismiss from his mind a feeling of mistrust, which was not confined to himself; but his tone was gentler than before, and he concluded without the slightest asperity: 'That God may bless you and guide you in all things, as my own sun goes down, is, my dear Archbishop, the constant prayer of

Yours affectionately

John H. Newman.'[4]

Manning, however, was not mollified by this ending; he replied with a counter-declaration of mistrust. He admitted running counter to Newman in certain things, but denied intrigue. The argument went on from month to month, but Newman was not

---

[1] Purcell: *Manning*, II, 328.   [2] Liddon: *Pusey*, II, 377.
[3] Purcell: *Manning*, II, 245-50.   [4] *op. cit.*, 331.

disposed to take back the statement of facts he had reason to think was established.

'My dear Archbishop,' he wrote finally on November 3, 1869,

'I can only repeat what I said when you last heard from me. I do not know whether I am on my head or my heels when I have active relations with you. In spite of my friendly feelings, this is the judgment of my intellect.

Yours affectionately in Christ,
John H. Newman.'[1]

The historians who have had either close access to documents, or know the state of contemporary opinion, do not think that Newman was mistaken in this judgment. Manning's own biographer gives the documents and no further comment is required. Ambrose Phillipps de Lisle was filled with indignation, and thought it odious to attribute as a decision of Propaganda what was really a personal intrigue.[2] Finally, after long years, the judicious Abbot Butler, in writing on Ullathorne, said that if he, rather than Manning, had become Archbishop, Catholics would at once have been free to go to Oxford.[3]

II

If we still doubt whether Manning played the part which Newman believed, there remain three points which support Newman's judgment. The first is that the need for University education was so obvious that Manning had to offer a substitute—the London University College. This college was never a success, and finally Manning was warned that Catholics were refusing absolutely to send their sons to it. The reasons given were not merely that the place was inefficient for its purpose, but that there also lay serious imputations against the character of the man whom Manning had appointed as its head: and after this doubt had been expressed, it was found that this same man had also allowed thousands of

---

[1] Purcell: *Manning*, II, 346. The full and tell-tale correspondence is given in these pages.

[2] Purcell: *A. P. de Lisle*, II, 9-14. Ambrose Lisle Phillipps had assumed the name of de Lisle in 1862.   [3] C. Butler: *Ullathorne*, II, 31.

pounds to escape from the funds—so that all this money was lost. The whole story was so unpleasant that finally Manning had to write to Rome that he would resign his see rather than have this man sent back to it.[1]

If this were the alternative to sending undergraduates to Oxford: what an alternative!

The second point is that when Manning died and pressure was put on his successor, that successor, in spite of his prejudices, rapidly gave way: for fifty years Catholics have gone to Oxford, and to Cambridge, as later to modern universities, without anyone finding the slightest reason for misgiving.[2]

Newman's plan for them to go and study freely at Universities, while safeguarding their religion and their theology, is now generally accepted, and furnishes a practical reason for studying still more deeply his classic book on University ideals.

The third point will, as this history concludes, show that long afterwards Newman had conclusive evidence in yet more dramatic circumstances of Manning's personal moves against him.[3] In these circumstances one cannot but feel that Manning's efforts to keep Newman from coming back to Oxford were not only short-sighted.

Newman noted, not without irony, as we saw, that in this affair Pusey supported Manning, because of his fear that Newman's return would awaken the hostility of Protestants and retard the Anglo-Catholic Movement within the Church of England. To this it can be answered that since then several religious orders have established themselves in Oxford without the slightest repercussion in the sense that Pusey feared.

The conclusion is that in the whole matter Newman once more proves himself the patron to religion in universities. Before his foresight and his arguments alike, the notion that a young man's

[1] Purcell: *Manning*, II, 497–502.

[2] Snead Cox: *Vaughan*, II, 83–4. The above sentence should be qualified by an admission that when the first Catholics went up to Oxford in 1893, only those from the Oratory School were successful in resisting the temptations of University freedom. The conclusion was that the other Catholic Schools must conform more to Newman's ideas.

[3] See Chapter XXVII.

faith, confirmed by appropriate rules and counsels, cannot take the plunge into a secular university unless he is to drown in doubt; or that the Catholics cannot be prepared to take that leading part for which Universities educate men for the service of Church and State—such a notion is shown to be the vapour of over-heated air which has long since dissolved and vanished.

faith, confirmed by acceptance and rules and custom: so not to the plunge into a secular university unless he is to throw to doubt: or that the Catholic...

CHAPTER XXIII

MANNING AND PUSEY

I

The University question was only one phase of the acute variance between Newman and Manning. It closely concerned their attitude towards the Church of England and towards the Holy See, both in its hold of territories and its relation to spiritual authority: but was it really more a question of principle than of personality? Principle is itself the matter of temperament, and temperament is one with the story of a life.

Newman and Manning had much in common. They both were Englishmen of the cultured class: both were devoted to Oxford and its traditions: both had been earnest Protestants: both had been eminent in the Church of England: both felt compelled to leave it: after doing so both had to face distrust: both were distinguished writers: and they both displayed their genius as priests of the Catholic Church.

Yet from the beginning their gifts marked them among cultured Englishmen as contrasting types. At school Newman played no games, while Manning captained the Harrow eleven. Newman edited *The Spy* while Manning was hailed as 'The General'. At College Newman lived exclusively with one friend, while Manning was a leader of all. While Newman wrote verse in praise of solitude and silence, Manning became President of the Union. While Newman lived as a Puritan, Manning's background was that of sumptuous wealth. While Newman went about in dark clothes and huge wide-rimmed spectacles, Manning outdid the smartest in riding breeches of pink silk.[1]

While Newman's youth lived for piety, Manning, though irreproachable, did not strike his friends as devout.[2] While Newman then shrank away as a recluse, Manning was a polished man of the

[1] Shane Leslie: *Manning,* 26.   [2] *ibid,* 27.

world.[1] When Newman began to gather fame as a preacher, Manning, impressed yet independent, wanted more accommodation with human nature. When Newman became a Tractarian, Manning for long remained Protestant. While Newman delighted in intimate friendships, Manning fell normally and passionately in love with his Rector's daughter. While Newman remained a don, Manning showed great talent for parochial administration. While Newman centred everything on Oxford, Manning knew the country and knew the people. While Newman's eloquence was rich and poetical, that of Manning was precise and definite.[2] The music of Newman's voice was subtle and mournful, that of Manning was ringing and full. Newman was phenomenally sensitive, Manning enjoyed his victories in the combats of life. While Newman was tender and fascinating, Manning was courtly and masterful. While Newman's elasticity suggested peril, Manning's sureness made men feel safe.

While Newman incurred suspicion by leading a Catholic movement in the Church of England, Manning took the much simpler line of denouncing Rome.

When the change was made, the result was what one would expect. Newman saw on either side a truth of lights and shadows, to Manning the Church of England was wholly erroneous because wholly Protestant. Where Newman proved unpractical, Manning displayed the generalship of the born administrator. Where Newman had disappointments, therefore, Manning had successes. While Newman's temper was sensitive and affectionate, Manning was both less confiding and more urbane. While Newman, after disappointment, became less subject to glamour, Manning, after success, became more so. Newman, though seeing the advantage of the papal states both in prestige and in resources, saw that the advantage, while historical and convenient, was to some extent balanced by disadvantages; Manning felt that they embodied a principle essential to religion.[3] While Newman believed that the

[1] Purcell: *Manning*, I, 36. Shane Leslie: *Manning*, 27.
[2] Sir F. Doyle: *Reminiscences*, 105, 112, 146.
[3] See Manning: *The Temporal Sovereignty of the Popes* (1860). *Lost Glories of the Holy See* (1861).

Pope was a dogmatic teacher preserved from error, Manning felt that every inclination of the Pope's mind was an inspiration of the Holy Ghost, and asserted that in every encyclical, bull and pronouncement the Pope was infallible.[1] Thus at last Manning began to feel that in matters of all-important principle, Newman was at fault. Manning was inclined to grudge liberty where Newman insisted that the Catholic Church concedes it. The result was that in things very dear to his heart, very natural to his temperament, and very helpful to his success, Manning saw that Newman was on the other side. He felt that Newman was cold, donnish, disloyal.[2] He even doubted the integrity of Newman's faith in the Catholic Church! 'Collision was inevitable.'[3]

So when we look closer, we see that this clash on principle was but one phase of an antipathy founded on contrasting temper and gifts: and that Manning's animosity was often fostered by that distrust with which the sporting and successful Englishman views persons of more delicate fibre: from that impatience with which the normal type, viewing the less normal, becomes aware that, in spite of obvious differences, this ungaugeable, indescribable, pliant elasticity has within it persistence, speed and viridity. The roots of such a plant as Newman's genius run underground like sorrel and always sprout again.

Manning meant to be generous. 'I always regarded him as so far above me in gifts of culture of every kind that I never had a temptation of rivalry or jealousy. I began with a great admiration, a true affection, a warm friendship.'[4] Then the inevitable divergencies arose, and after that came the crux. For when it was found that Newman could put his case more persuasively, and was being cited against Manning; then it was that Manning, having to add humiliation to his antipathy, began his planning. Thus Newman, harassed yet heroic, won first the sympathy, then the admiration which is the pioneer's reward. Nor does his venture lose to history, as time does her testing work. The world, said Chateaubriand, remembers those who do it great service. The wisdom of Newman's judgment is a freight as precious as the winning outline with

[1] Manning: *Temporal Mission of the Holy Ghost.*   [2] Ward: *Newman*, II, 63–4.
[3] J. E. C. Bodley: *Manning*, 19–20.   [4] Purcell: *Manning*, II, 351.

which his ship in full sail took the breeze and steered for havens
in virgin and opulent lands.

2

Yet none of these considerations takes us to the last phase of this
historic and scandalous rivalry. We shall fail to understand the
complexity of Manning's nature until we remember—and most
have forgotten—that the central principle of Manning's clear-cut
piety was devotion to the Holy Ghost. Manning identified everything for which he chiefly cared with that exquisite divine inspiration which is kindled within the purest spirits as the fire of
love. This it is which makes this practical English administrator
such an intriguing mystery. He was able to define every detail of
his convictions, every practice of his elaborate Catholicism, every
administrative decision in terms of the purest heavenly inspiration.
It was not enough for this zealous and courtly ecclesiastic to
impress people with his fine features, his graceful figure or his
distinct and melodious accents; it was not enough to fascinate
their attention with the delineation of such figures as that marvel
of courage and fun, St Teresa de Jesus, the mistress of affairs—or
St Francis of Assisi who in his exquisite attraction took the birds
of the air and the elements of nature to his heart, nor yet to show
that the Heart of his Redeemer was the well-spring of life and
holiness. Manning mentioned all these; but he related them all to
the same celestial Spirit Who comes into men's hearts as pervasively
as light, as fresh as dew.

3

He would engage in no common controversy: but he decided
in 1864 that he could elucidate his position if he wrote to his old
friend Pusey on *The workings of the Holy Spirit in the Church of
England*. The operation of the Holy Spirit he said extended to
all men, and Anglican baptism conferred the sacramental grace
by which a babe is born anew—and into Christ. 'I loved', he
wrote, 'the Christian England which survived, and all the linger-
ing outlines of dioceses and parishes, cathedrals and churches with

the names of Saints upon them. I loved the parish church of my childhood, and the College chapel of my youth, and the little church under a green hillside where the morning and evening prayers, and the music of the English Bible, for seventeen years, became a part of my soul. Nothing is more beautiful in the natural order, and if there were no eternal world I could have made it my home.'[1] He admired in England noble Christians; he saw in their exalted characters beautiful examples of personal excellence. And still he loved all his old friends—and hoped all would be drawn together in mutual kindness and mutual equity of judgment—but he could not accept Anglicanism as though it were Catholicism.

Pusey felt he must write a reply, and this reply was to be called an *Eirenicon*. This was to argue that in their honour to the Blessed Virgin the Roman Catholics had gone too far: that in its general position the Anglican Via Media was sound, that even in the Roman fold men had fallen short and that controversy had exaggerated the differences between the two communions.

Four years later Pusey addressed to Newman a second *Eirenicon* on the subject of the Blessed Virgin. This went very far indeed in paying her honour, and seemed indeed to stop short only in denying what had never been affirmed—a special guiltlessness in the marriage relations of St Joachim and St Anne.

Yet a third *Eirenicon* was centred on Papal infallibility: in this Pusey went very far in the prerogatives he allowed to the Pope, and indeed it might be said that when it came to a definition, the Vatican Council of 1870 hardly went further than the theology of Dr Pusey, who inveighed not against the Pope as supreme, but against the extreme views held by enthusiasts such as Ward and Manning.

4

With these questions Newman was much occupied for the next five and even ten years. On all of them he exerted a moderating influence: in all of them he argued for that central position which in truth is the very essence of Catholicism. He insists that even

[1] Manning: *The Workings of the Holy Spirit in the Church of England*, 38.

within the Papal fold theologian differs from theologian, school
from school, nation from nation, era from era. He knows that
there are fashions both in opinions and in practices, and that
fashions change.[1] Each age and each mind has its own emphasis,
and emphasis counts for a great deal. It was the Fathers, he said,
who gave him the ladder to climb up into the Church, and he had
no notion of kicking the ladder down.[2] For the rest the Church is
a living body and meets needs and situations as they arise.

He stated, in the ardent yet unexaggerated way in which he
practised and preached it, his devotion to the Blessed Virgin; and
he concluded in Advent with the words: 'May the blessed influence of this time bring us all together in unity! May it destroy
all bitterness on your side and on ours! May it quench all jealous,
sour, proud, fierce antagonism on our side; and dissipate all
captious, carping, fastidious refinements of reasoning on yours.
May that bright and gentle Lady, the Blessed Virgin Mary, overcome you with her sweetness and revenge herself on her foes by
interceding effectually for their conversion.'[3]

5

It was of course inevitable that the defensive statements which
Pusey made should sound in certain ears like aggressive controversy: but he insisted that his aim was conciliation. It was to go
back to Archbishop Wake and to Bossuet, and to look for a
basis of reunion: but the *Weekly Register* naturally enquired how
far Pusey spoke for the whole Church of England.[4] Church admitted that the Eirenicon was not typical of the Establishment but
of the Romeward van.[5]

No one knew better than Newman that it was fanciful to the
last degree for anyone to talk of the reunion of the whole Church of
England, not as it might become in indefinite time, but in fact,
as it was then, with Rome. He saw in the clearest light that its
boast was in its divergences. He remembered with painfully clear

[1] Newman: *Letter to Pusey*, 21.   [2] *ibid*, 26.   [3] *ibid*, 102–4.
[4] A Review of Pusey's *Eirenicon* reprinted from *Weekly Register*, 1865.
[5] Church: *Occasional Papers*, II 406.

distinctness how his own Catholic moves had been received by authorities: he knew above all how deep and wide remained the view which he had himself taken so long to abandon, that Rome itself was—far from being infallible—in error and corrupt.

At the same time he well remembered what he had felt in his long years of doubt and hesitation, and knew that what had helped him most was the generosity of Russell and of Wiseman; and must he yet reject the hope they had entertained that a body of Anglo-Catholics might lead if not their Church, at least a powerful group from it, back into Catholic unity?

His desire therefore was that which tact and his heart alike dictated: to show his old friends every possible courtesy. At the same time, he could not compromise the position he had attained at such cost. He knew and accepted with his whole heart all that he knew to be essential to the dogmatic position of Rome. He could see by the lengths to which Pusey went in his *Eirenicon* regarding both the prerogatives of the Blessed Virgin and the authority of the Holy See, that Pusey personally, and any who would accept Pusey's authority, had gone far down the Littlemore road; and it was extremely annoying to him that they should be led to think that excesses were essentials.

As to the fact of corruptions, he faced it squarely. 'The religion of the multitude is ever vulgar and abnormal; it will ever be tinctured with fanaticism and superstition while men are what they are. A people's religion is ever a corrupt religion. If you are to have a Catholic Church, you must put up with fish of every kind, fish good and bad, vessels of gold, vessels of earth. You may beat religion out of men if you will, and then their excesses will take a different direction, but if you make use of religion to improve them, they will make use of religion to corrupt it. And then you will have effected that compromise of which our countrymen report so unfavourably, from abroad—a high grand faith and worship which compels their admiration, and puerile absurdities among the people which excite their contempt.'[1]

We therefore find him pointing out that Faber's spirituality took extreme forms, and insisting that the true view of papal in-

[1] *Letter to Pusey*, 86.

fallibility was that which was most moderate and reasonable. What comforted him was to think not of definitions but of the Holy Spirit speaking with a living voice through a living Church. 'I do not dogmatise,' he added, 'and I detest any dogmatism where the Church has not clearly spoken. And if I am told "The Church has spoken", then I ask when? . . . I incline one way to-day, another to-morrow.' 'Sad as it is to witness', he wrote afterwards to a Presbyterian friend, 'the ineffectual yearnings after unity on all hands, of which you speak, still it is hopeful also. We may hope that our good God has not put it into the hearts of religious men to wish and pray for unity without intending in His own time to fulfil the prayer. And since the bar against unity is a conscientious feeling and a reverence for what each party holds itself to be the truth, and a desire to maintain the Faith, we may humbly hope that in our day and till He discloses what the time for this is, He will, where hearts are honest, take the will for the deed.'[1]

His friend, Ambrose Phillipps de Lisle, had been intensely interested in two moves for rapprochement with Anglicans. The chief was the Association for Promoting the Unity of Christendom: the other was the formation of a Uniate Church. Catholics had been bidden to withdraw from the Association on the ground that the unity of the Church was founded on the Rock of Peter; they could not give ground for thinking it was anywhere else,[2] and Rome will not compromise for a moment on the theory that the Catholic Church is divided into three branches. On the second project, no word of authority is extant. But Newman wrote: 'It has often happened in sacred and ecclesiastical history that a thing is in itself good, but the time has not come for it. . . . And I reconcile myself to many, many things and put them in God's hands.'

6

Newman in the meantime insisted to Pusey that the coming Council would not say anything excessive. Yet at one moment he lost his confidence and his indignation once more carried his

[1] Ward: *Newman*, II, 395.   [2] Purcell: *A. P. de Lisle*, I, Appendix iii.

pen away. He wrote at last to the bishop to ask why 'an aggressive and insolent faction should be allowed to make the heart of the just mourn. When has a definition of doctrine *de fide* been a luxury of devotion and not a stern painful necessity? Why can't we be left alone . . . ?'[1] Now this was Newman in the vein which more than once had got him into difficulties—and it did so now. The letter was a private one addressed to the bishop, who agreed with it. But the bishop quoted it—confidentially of course—to other bishops; before long the passage about 'an aggressive and insolent faction' appeared in an English newspaper: the *Standard*. When it did, Newman had forgotten it, and denied it; but, on thinking further he was compelled to admit the newspaper was right.

What made the whole subject more difficult for Newman was that he took the word infallibility to mean a permanent and continuous guarantee, in fact, the meaning Manning had given it:

'The Definitions and Decrees of Pontiffs, speaking *ex cathedra* or as the Head of the Church, whether by Bull, or Apostolic Letters, or Encyclical or Brief, to many or to one person, undoubtedly emanate from a Divine Source and are infallible. So again the judgment of the Pontiff in matters which affect the welfare of the whole Church, such as the condemnation of propositions. In all declarations that such propositions are, as the case may be, heretical or savouring of heresy, or erroneous, or scandalous, or offensive to pious ears, and the like, the assistance of the Holy Spirit certainly preserves the Pontiff from error; and such judgments are infallible and demand interior assent from all.'[2]

Newman, taking up the word infallible as Manning had rashly defined it, gave it a precise philosophical application. It is persons and rules that are infallible, not what is brought out into act or committed to people. '*A man is infallible whose words are always true,* a rule is infallible if it is unerring in all its possible applications; an infallible authority is certain in every particular case that may arise, but a man who is certain in some one definite case is not on that account infallible.'[3]

[1] Ward: *Newman*, II, 788–9.
[2] Manning: *Temporal Mission of the Holy Ghost*, 81–4.
[3] *Grammar of Assent*, 218.

As long as Newman gave this meaning to the word infallible, he needs *must* think a definition inopportune and ill-advised, besides the Pope had already defined one dogma in his reign and one, thought Newman, was enough: but the Pope himself was insistent; and though he was already eighty-five he had a wonderful knack of exerting personal influence; Newman has himself described how his unyielding 'faith, his courage, the graceful intermingling in him of the human and the divine, the humour, the wit, the playfulness with which he tempered his severity, his naturalness, and then his true eloquence and the resources he had at command for meeting with appropriate words the circumstances of the moment, overcame those who were least likely to be overcome'.[1]

Meanwhile the infinite sagacity of the Vatican, aided by an Irish Cardinal, prepared a phrase so subtly oracular that it met all occasions. 'People are talking about the definition of Papal Infallibility as if there were and could be but one definition,' Newman had said. 'Twenty definitions might be made, and of those several of them might be perfectly correct, and several others exaggerated and incorrect.'[2] They found one he had every reason to deem correct. It centred on the Pope the solidarity of the Church; it paid full tribute to the personal prestige of Pio Nono, and it guaranteed him indeed, but only in being preserved from error if and when officially speaking for the whole Church, he defined in some preciser detail the faith once for all delivered to the saints; in short, the definition kept the word infallible, but it modified its application in a way which neither Newman, nor many others, anticipated.

In the decades that have passed no pronouncement has been made to which this definition has been obviously applied, and from the very beginning discerning bishops took that guarded line which not only Newman but also Pusey had indicated as judicious.[3]

The pronouncement both excused and made nonsense of his nervousness, because it accepted his contentions.

[1] *Addresses to Cardinal Newman*, 243.   [2] Aubrey de Vere: *Recollections*, 274.
[3] Butler: *Ullathorne*, II, 81–6.

An advanced Anglican might claim therefore that the Council
endorsed the contentions of Pusey. A papalist might suggest that
Pusey vindicated the Council. Such is the finesse of Vatican dip-
lomacy; such is the caution of Holy Church. It was exactly what
Newman had said all along both to Pusey and to Aubrey de Vere.

Nevertheless, everything considered, Newman judged it well
that he had not to discuss such things amid the strife of tongues at
Oxford.[1]

[1] Edward Bellasis: *Coram Cardinali*, 91.

CHAPTER XXIV

GLADSTONE AND THE POPE

I

In the fourth year after the Vatican Council had made its historic definition, the ritualist movement which developed out of Tractarianism had gone so far that Archbishop Tait introduced into parliament a bill for the stricter control of public worship. This was aimed at the Catholic party in the Church of England, and Gladstone in reply wrote an article on Ritualism in the *Contemporary Review*. On the one hand he vindicated the use of ritual, demanding the fullest possible freedom for the Anglican service; but in a second article he had written to enforce strictures on Roman Catholics. In the earlier one, he spoke violently against Rome and the Vatican Council. And he accused the English Catholics of disloyalty to the Country and the Queen. He described the Catholic bishops as 'degraded', the Pope's reign as 'perilous', he spoke of the Council's 'subserviency or pliancy', of 'foreign arrogance' and 'hideous mummeries'.

Not only was his language intemperate, the ideas were inexact. And the Catholics returned several vigorous answers. That of Manning was most interesting: flinging far all mention of the extreme views he had held a few years before, he pointed out how confined, how guarded was the phrase that had been adopted in Rome; but his *volte face* was soon forgotten in the brilliant reply of his rival—in Newman's *Letter to the Duke of Norfolk*.

Gladstone had said the Church ignored ancient history, Newman proved from ancient history that the state had admitted the Church to be above the state's own claims; that the Pope's political influence was severely circumscribed, and that he had no right to absolve subjects from their civil allegiance.

2

Newman then went on to speak of the sovereignty of conscience. 'Disobey it,' said a council of the Church, 'and you incline to hell. Conscience is the aboriginal Vicar of Christ, a prophet in its information, a monarch in its peremptoriness, a priest in its blessings and anathemas, and even though the eternal priesthood through the Church should cease to be in it, the sacerdotal principle would remain and have a sway.'[1] In it the Creator declared His rights over man: it is the stern monition of authority, very different from self-will.

In brilliant pages Newman then identified the authority of conscience with that of the Popes. If the Popes were not obliged to proclaim the moral law, what was their authority? Did the Pope speak against conscience in the true sense of the word, he would commit a suicidal act. The championship of the moral law and of conscience was his *raison d'être*.[2]

The fact is that men so easily allow their own inclinations to stifle the Divine voice within them: they need the judgment of others to reinforce its claim: above all they need the voice of revelation to speak with the mystical authority of faith. 'The general sense of right and wrong, which is the first element in religion, is so delicate, so fitful, so easily puzzled, obscured, perverted, so subtle in its argumentative methods, so impressed by education, so biassed by pride and passion, so unsteady in its flight that in the struggle for existence amid various exercises and triumphs of the human intellect, this sense is at once the highest of all teachers, yet the least luminous; and the Church, the Pope, the Hierarchy, are in the Divine purpose the supply of an urgent demand.'[3] That is why natural religion needs the support of revelation.

3

But if the Divine authority fully functions only when the Church and its head are there to enforce it, yet the Pope is neces-

---

[1] *Letter to the Duke of Norfolk*, 57.   [2] *op. cit.*, 60.
[3] *op. cit.*, 61.

sary only as a Divine authority, only in so far as he supports the
moral law, only in so far as he is its complement, reassertion,
voice, embodiment and interpretation.[1] The dogma of infallibility did not guarantee him in political or personal acts. The
scope of infallibility stops with defining for the Church matters
dealing with revelation. In many matters the Catholic is free;
provided always that he exercises his freedom not unadvisedly
nor wantonly, but soberly, decently and in the fear of God.

'I add one remark,' concluded Newman, 'certainly if I am to
bring religion into after-dinner toasts (which indeed does not
seem quite the thing) I shall drink, to the Pope, if you please—still
to conscience first, and to the Pope afterwards.'[2]

Newman then went back to the Encyclical and syllabus of 1864.
They had been denounced by Gladstone, indeed by many, as
monstrous obscurantism. Newman said in answer that he saw
throughout Europe many demonstrations against religion and
against decency that neither taste nor tradition would have toler-
ated in his youth. A decent public opinion, he said, was then called
'Toryism, and men gloried in the name, now it is called Popery,
and reviled'.[3]

He reviewed the trend of the times. It was to take away from
the nation the unifying sense of the traditional authority of morals
and religion: it was to replace it by progress, liberalism, and the
new civilisation with which the Pope refused to come to terms
because they meant not real advancement or true civilisation, but
a preference of the whims and inclinations of the flesh to the law
of God. That was the problem of the times, and Newman knew
what his deepest instincts were. 'No one', he said, 'can dislike the
democratic principle more than I do. No one mourns, for instance,
more than I over the state of Oxford, given up, alas! to liberalism
and progress to the forfeiture of her great medieval motto,
"*Dominus illuminatio mea*", and with a consequent call on men to
go to parliament for a new one. But what can we do? All I know
is that Toryism, that is, loyalty to persons, "springs eternal in the
human breast"; that religion is a spiritual loyalty, and that Catholicity is the only Divine form of religion. And thus *in centuries to*

[1] *loc. cit.*   [2] *op. cit.*, 66.   [3] *op. cit*, 68.

come there may be found out some way of uniting what is free in the new structure of society with what is authoritative in the old.'[1]

4

As for the syllabus, it was meant as a reminder to bishops of things stated before, and much mischief had been made by people who wanted to see it 'make a row in Europe'. 'For', said Newman, 'the Rock of St Peter on its summit enjoys a fine and serene atmosphere but there is a great deal of Roman malaria at the foot of it.'[2]

Newman went on to the debated definition. He admitted quite openly that he had deprecated anything being said, because he knew how easily mischief is made. But when the definition was made, he recognised the magisterium of the Church; for had not Butler taught him that discoveries were gradual? Therefore a Council might well set to work on such a question, and finally he showed how guarded and moderate the definition was, how different from 'that fierce and intolerant temper which scorns and tramples on the little ones of Christ'.[3] Newman acknowledged the Pope as having Divine authority, but how strongly he reprobated the tyranny of those who set up their own personal judgments as infallible in order to hurl anathemas at others who had every justification for taking a different stand. For in the vast field of things uncertain the Church allows liberty; and her very dogma, dealing as it does with infinite mystery, leaves so much mysterious that it has within it infinite reserves.

[1] *op. cit.*, 72.   [2] *op. cit.*, 94.   [3] *op. cit.*, 125.

CHAPTER XXV

HOW A MIND WORKS

I

What are the qualities which give a man a grip of actual things so as to exert his power among them? What is the reason why a logical case does not persuade people, but leaves them a choice in moral conduct, in politics, in religion? What is the reason why one man believes and another not? Such all-important questions in dealing with men and their convictions began early to exercise the mind of Newman and accompanied him for thirty years. He found when he had written in the *Apologia* the history of his religious opinions, that he had written nothing about the way that he came to hold opinions; considering this, he saw that his psychology was hardly less important than his conclusions.

His story, indeed, would not be complete unless he wrote down the psychology of his faith.

This is the reason why he wrote on it an essay which is certainly not the least important of his writings. Without it, in fact, we should never know the quality of his mind or the essential characteristics of his genius.

In two lectures he gave in Dublin, he disclosed the secret of his power as a writer and as a preacher.

As a writer he found that success came from the fullness with which a mind lived: he advised no technique but that of a desire for precision and clearness of exposition; it is the fullness of living and the elevation of the concepts which change writing into literature; as a preacher he insisted, as we saw, that the success of preaching was the force by which a sermon conveyed from a speaker to his hearers the message of a conviction about *particular* truths. In each case the secret was the apprehension of reality and the power to communicate it. This living power, either of

237

preacher or poet, came from the power of a mind to seize the richness of life; to deal with a thing not as a name but a reality. To be vague is to be feeble; to employ merely general terms is to be unreal and ineffective; one must deal in this world not with notions but with things; one must deal in the world of thought and religion with truths so vividly apprehended that they move among men with dynamic power.

2

So far back as the feast of St Peter and St Paul in 1840, Newman had preached in St Mary's on 'Explicit and Implicit Reason'. His great point was that reasoning is a living spontaneous energy within us, not an art.[1] He knew what Aristotle had said of logic. Yet little of our practical knowledge, few of our conclusions are based on logic. The mind leaps at times to great conclusions, like a giant refreshed; at others it attains to heights of skill which is both instinctive and individual, like that of a mountaineer scaling a peak, or a cliff-climber mounting from the Devon seashore to the moorland above. The mind's subtlety and versatility baffle investigation; it is as swift and luminous as lightning. A hint, a probability, an association, a popular impression, an instinct, an obscure memory may each and all work in with principle or evidence with prejudice, with authority, with temper, inclination and affection, before a mind accepts a proposition or is led on from truth to truth. The most diligent enquiry can give but a vague description of the human mind, or its feelings or its thoughts, and Newman asks 'is it less difficult to delineate, as theology professes to do, the works, dealings, providences, attributes or nature of Almighty God?'[2]

If man cannot explain his own complexity, still less can he compass the mysteries of the Infinite. Every theological definition, even if correct as far as it goes, is inadequate to truths which, being Divine, are complex and unfathomable. God speaks to us at best only by approximations; for all earthly images are far below the illimitable splendours of heaven. How inadequate

[1] *Sermons before the University of Oxford* (1843), 253.   [2] *op. cit.*, 264.

therefore is controversy when religion is the issue! For the critical
judgment can detect the fallacies of argument; it cannot gauge
the scope of mysteries, or follow the latent and implicit processes
by which a spiritual man believes, or a genius creates. Let not the
writer think he is most effective when he argues: the true office of
a writer is 'to excite and direct trains of thought'.[1]

3

Thus Newman had long been prepared to build up his psychology of faith. He wove together his essay, now as a result of
watching the processes of his own mind; now as dealing with
the problems of preaching and persuading; now as dealing with
the theory of knowledge in the way that the followers of Locke
were discussing it academically at Oxford.

Locke used the word assent for the apprehension of a proposition or a fact. The word assent is the one he uses for knowledge.
It is essential to his view of the theory of knowledge. To criticise
Locke and his followers, and to improve on them by building up
a theory of knowledge and then to relate this general theory of
knowledge to faith, and finally to show how faith becomes dynamic in certain traits—above all in a life like his own—such are
the objects of this essay. His object, as James Anthony Froude
rightly said, from the beginning to the end is to combat and over-
throw the position of Locke, that reasonable assent is proportioned
to 'evidence'.[2]

Since its object harks back to Locke and his academic study of
philosophy in Oxford, Newman continues to use the word assent,
and since he is examining his story for what conclusions it could
furnish, he calls his book *An Essay in aid of a Grammar of Assent*.

When he was a boy, he had begun without a fixed belief; his
mind had wandered from God; he had been drawn back to religion by an intense experience which had given him an overwhelming consciousness of the immediacy of God whose Voice
spoke in his own conscience. He had gradually proceeded from
this view, first identified with Calvinism, held in conjunction with

[1] *op. cit.*, 272.   [2] *Short Studies* (1871), ii, 84.

Anglican forms, to the view of a High Churchman, an Anglo-Catholic; then, driven by fresh accumulations of inward experience, reading and reflection, he had reached another stage. When his earlier faith appeared inadequate, he began to wonder why! Yet even as he did so, and after doing so, he saw that the whole subject was for himself, as for others, full of psychological complexities; the arguments which seemed to him overwhelming as arguments were not sufficient to make even himself act. That final decision had to come from some other source.

Not only so, but he found that the considerations which were convincing to himself, availed little to others closest to his mind and to his heart. Must he not then put down all he knew of the subtler interrogations of the mind and the certainties it accepts as final? Must he not put them down—as he saw them sometimes—academically, like a don talking with other dons? So he had done for nearly twenty-five years at Oxford, sometimes as a preacher putting his case on general principles, and sometimes giving rein to those mysterious elevations of his genius which endowed his style with qualities moving and sublime.

That was what he now tried to do, and did do. The result is, as we saw, an essential revelation of his own mind. It is an extraordinarily subtle and far-reaching essay on the psychology of faith; and it is also a piece of writing so much affected by changes of style and modifications of approach, or qualifying considerations, that it cannot be understood except in relation to Newman as a whole man; therefore it is in vain to read this essay unless with sympathy for the mind he is revealing and the problem with which he had to deal.

4

If then we abandon the critical attitude, and try to follow what he is trying to say, what do we find? We find that the basis of his argument is common sense in the light of experience. A friend of his, explaining the book when it appeared, wrote that the basis throughout is distinctly and simply experience. 'The philosophy of the day has appealed to experience: to experience it shall go.'[1]

---

[1] *The Month*, March, 1870, 359.

The philosophy of the day, following the school of Locke, had indeed appealed to experience, but had not given it their ear. They neglected the experience they could not bring under strict logical analysis. The result was that to make a system, they simplified to excess. They sacrificed reality to form, depth to precision. The object of Newman's system was not a system, but the living man with all his complexities: and chief in those complexities came conscience and the belief in God.

Now Newman's object is partly to make psychology more real: partly to lift it into the realm where its scope is enlarged by a special divine gift, the gift of faith. He tries to relate psychology to theology.

But what psychology to what theology? The difficulty about each of these is that one man's psychology differs from another's, and one man's theology differs from another's. All Newman could do was to make *himself* the test, knowing that other believers must have something, perhaps much, in common with him. In all religious enquiry each of us can speak only for himself; and for himself he has a right to speak. A man's own experiences are valid for himself; but he cannot speak for others; he cannot lay down the law; he can only bring his own experiences to the common stock of psychological facts. He knows what has satisfied and satisfies himself; if it satisfies him it is likely to satisfy others.

5

Newman's essay will be justified to some extent by those who gnaw humbly at the meaty bone he throws them. His arrangement of the subject was arbitrary: his method was not logical sequence—in fact, he was aiming at something deeper than a logical argument, at a variety of suggestions and appeals on the subject of certainty and of faith, presented like a musical theme with manifold variations and ever-shifting harmonies. The appeal is to every side of our mental constitution: the justification is not logic but analogy.[1]

We are then confronting a subtle and complex mind, not

[1] *The Month*, March, 1870, 366.

arguing so much as suggesting, and all this is difficult; and yet another difficulty comes from the originality in the view taken, and the novelty in the terms. These terms sometimes compromise with former philosophies, as in the use of the word assent for knowledge or certainty: more often they are entirely new, the excuse being that Newman needs new terms for the new views he is putting forward. All these contribute to make the book a problem not only to the general reader, but to the trained psychologist and the Thomist philosopher. Both have to adapt themselves to new technical terms and to place themselves at the disposal of a mind which is as searching and complex as it is original: and which relates to itself all that it discusses.

6

Putting questions on one side, statements are made either to make an assertion or draw a conclusion. When we take a statement for granted, we *assent* to it. Now Locke had argued that there are different qualities in assent according to our apprehension of the subject it deals with. Newman denied this, and drew a sharp distinction between the statement made with regard to things of which we have no direct experience, and those of which we have. He called the first *notional assent* springing from *notional* apprehension; and he deprecated it. The second he called real assent, which comes from real understanding: for intellectual ideas cannot compete in apprehension with concrete facts.[1] Facts are stubborn things. Experience teaches, seeing is believing. The common-sense touch with reality arouses the feelings and does more than principles and generalities could ever effect.[2] Notions therefore cannot compete in value with facts: words not related to direct experience may enable us to reason: but when they are related to direct experience, memory impregnates them with life to the extent that the life was lived; for this lives again in memory.

But if we want to argue, then of course we argue from merely notional terms. So we reach a paradox: when assent is most in-

[1] *Grammar of Assent,* 9.   [2] *op. cit,* 10.

tense, it is less suited for those logical contentions which Newman calls inference.

7

Though it may be confusing to the philosopher, it is encouraging to the believer, to find Newman, after establishing his view of notional and real assent, immediately applying it to religion. Theology, he says, is notional, being scientific, its terms relating simply to one another. But religion means a real immediate grasp of that which binds the soul to God. And at this point the writer suddenly makes another observation: that Protestant countries prefer religion not to be too concrete: they do not want it made immediate in images, pictures, saints or vivid representations. England with her Bible religion (such as she then had) preferred a religion of words where neither persons nor facts were put too dramatically or immediately before the people in appeal to their feelings and imagination.

It is equally typical of Newman that having made this observation he explains the advantages gained by the English in reading the Bible.

8

He then goes on to define opinion, presumption and speculation: opinion is the acceptance of a statement probably true; presumption is the acceptance of first principles; speculation is the contemplation of reasonable conclusions.[1]

9

We now come to the real field of Newman's interest: those real assents which are sometimes called beliefs, sometimes convictions, sometimes certainties, and which, though rarely perhaps given to moral objects, are dominant when they are. We have within ourselves the conviction of their validity and power. Till we have these we are, whether in conduct, in politics, or in religion, at the mercy of impulses, fancies and wandering lights. 'These beliefs,

[1] *Grammar of Assent*, 54.

be they true or false, in the particular case form the mind out of which they grow and impart to it a seriousness and manliness which inspire in other minds a confidence in its views and is one secret of persuasiveness and influence in the public stage of the world. They create, as the case may be, heroes and saints, good leaders, statesmen, preachers and reformers, the pioneers of discovery in science, visionaries, fanatics, knights-errant, demagogues, and adventurers. They have given to the world men of one idea, of immense energy, of adamantine will, of revolutionary power. They kindle sympathies between man and man, and knit together the innumerable units which constitute a race and a nation. They become the principle of its political existence, they impart to it homogeneity of thought and fellowship of purpose. They have given form to the medieval theocracy, and to the Mahometan superstition: they are now the life both of 'Holy Russia' and of that freedom of speech and action which is the special boast of Englishmen.'[1]

'Man is *not* a reasoning animal,' so Newman had written thirty years before, when the study of Aristotle surrounded him in Oriel, 'he is a seeing, feeling, contemplating, acting animal: he is influenced by what is direct or precise. . . . Life is for action; if we insist on proof for everything we shall never come to action: to act you must assume, and that assumption is faith.'[2] Here then already stated in 1841 was the kernel of his philosophy, the principle which explains both his complex career and his lasting influence. For if it was true in secular affairs, it was true also in religion. 'Religion is a matter of *faith*. It has never lived in a conclusion: it has ever been a message, a history or a vision. . . . Christianity is a history, supernatural and almost scenic: it tells us what its Author is by telling us what He has done.'[3]

10

It is now time for Newman to examine religious belief in the Unity of God, in His Trinity, and then in dogmatic theology. For

[1] *Grammar of Assent*, 85.   [2] *op. cit.*, 91–2.   [3] *op. cit.*, 95.

by now Newman can assert what it means to 'believe' a dogma of faith. A dogma is a statement, standing for a notion or a fact. To accept it as a notion is an act of theology: to accept is as a fact is an act of religion. The religious imagination appropriates it as reality: the mind holds it as a theological truth.

Now it is, he says, a fact that everyone has a conscience—everyone knows what it is to have a good or bad conscience[1]—and from this fact of conscience he argues, following Butler, that it witnesses to the existence of God as judge. He draws a vivid picture of conscience, and the fear and dismay it can arouse. And with it, and with the sense of God as judge, comes acceptance of Him as a being Who is present everywhere and ever accessible, Who reads the heart and can change it. 'A child', says Newman, 'has that within him which actually vibrates, responds, and gives a deep meaning to the lessons of his first teachers about the will and the providence of God.'[2] It is plain that he is referring back to his own childhood.

He then sees how the whole world works by laws under the omnipotence of God. And acting accordingly one discovers that by habits of personal religion one gains the finest hold of theological truths. 'Thus by living a good and religious life, one who believes converses with God as a Living Person with a directness and simplicity, with a confidence and intimacy far exceeding those we know given to those human beings we love and revere.' This any child might have anywhere, but how much is added for one who knows the Bible: and piety to develop needs a religion to satisfy the mind. So it is that 'devotion falls back upon dogma'.[3]

How then does the soul arrive at believing in the Trinity? That comes to a man as a truth which touches his imagination and his heart. It comes to the unlearned, the young, the busy, the afflicted as a fact which is to arrest them, penetrate them and support and animate them in their passage through life.[4] Men may learn statements about this truth of the Trinity and think them out, one with another; all are summed up in the creeds, especially the Athanasian creed; this Newman calls a war song, appealing to the imagination as much as the intellect: dogma is thus completed in the splendours

[1] *op. cit.,* 103.   [2] *op. cit.,* 111.   [3] *op. cit.,* 117.   [4] *op. cit.,* 122.

I

of the liturgy. And when men see the life of the Church and hear as worship her living voice as she sets in the course of the year the cycle of redemption, then they can accept her dogma. They accept it not as a written statement, but as a voice of one to trust implicitly. 'The word of the Church is the word of the revelation.'[1] It is enough for the believer to accept the Church for him to accept the mysterious and vital wisdom of her mind in whatever way she may propose to his faith.

II

So does Newman describe the growth of psychology of faith. Plainly it is a personal confession. It is autobiography. And being true for one man it will be true, as he said, for others, in so far as their minds correspond with his. That is, as we saw, the *raison d'être* of the book.

We have now come to the second part of the book. So far, he had been dealing with knowledge as apprehension; he now deals with it as thought or arriving at conclusions. Returning to Locke, he combats Locke's theory that it is both illogical and immoral to claim to be certain of things we cannot prove. Conviction is one thing; logic is another, and as Newman insists, much inferior. Who does not know that

> A man convinced against his will
> Is of the same opinion still?

We know without proof or argument that there is an outer world, and that Calcutta is the most populous town in India. Truths which are neither instinctive nor can yet be proved are yet absolute for us. But the more we know of a subject the more certain we are, and certainty comes of the fixed conviction that we know what we know. Certainty differs from opinion in its fixity. Certainty in religious faith makes devotion immediate, self-sacrifice generous, and intercourse with the unseen real and habitual.[2]

---

[1] *op. cit.*, 148.   [2] *op. cit.*, 213.

12

Now how does the question of certitude apply to a man's change of religion? Newman's discussion of this is obviously of the highest interest since once he had believed in the Church of England, not in Rome; now he believed in Rome, not Anglicanism. 'When we hear that a man has changed from one religion to another,' he writes, 'the first thing we have to ask is: Have the first and second religions nothing in common? If they still have common doctrines, he has changed only a portion of his creed, not the whole; and the next question is: Has he abandoned those doctrines which are common to his new creed and his old? and then again: Was he certain of the old, or is he certain of the new?'[1]

He takes his own case: that of a Protestant becoming a Catholic; he shows that respect for authority and the Church and dogma were already the ground of his Protestantism; but, on the other hand, one whose basis was morals and the Bible only might well become a Unitarian (as his brother Frank did), because the Bible cannot form a dogma. He takes a third case, that of a believer lapsing, like his other brother: the fact is that such a man never really had an overwhelming certainty of the living truth and power of Christianity, and preferred his own judgment on particular points of belief and conduct.

He then considered the case of Anglo-Catholics, asking why some came closer to Rome, some not. He saw those like himself who were not satisfied that Anglicanism was the perfect wisdom of the Catholic centre, and others like Pusey, who were certain that it was. But when belief in a certain position is as solid and as strong as to amount to a certainty, it will remain; if it is in certain points tentative, it is liable to change.

From a discussion of enduring certainty, Newman goes on to what he calls inference, meaning logical and ordered thinking—in a word, reasoning. Here he comes back to the point that logic does not carry conviction. Genuine conviction requires an instrument more delicate, versatile and elastic, than verbal argument.

[1] op. cit., 238.

And that instrument is nothing less than individual experience which, as Aristotle had said in the *Nicomachæan Ethics*, makes each man an authority in that of which he knows most: the eye of experience beholds the principles of things.[1]

13

Has this any connection with Newman's conversion? It has. He explains how one who first believed the Catholic Church to be corrupt, and instinctively rejected certain of its doctrines begins to question his position, and ask if he is satisfied with the religion he is professing. Where did Protestantism come from? Did not the Catholic Church exist before it?

Then he begins to say 'He is not a Protestant: he is a Catholic of an early undivided Church: he is a Catholic but not a Papist'. Then he has to determine questions about division, schism, visible unity; what is essential: what is desirable: about provisional states: as to the adjustment of the Church's claims with those of personal judgment and responsibility: as to the soul of the Church contrasted with the body: as to degrees of proof and the degree necessary for his conversion: as to what is called his providential position and the responsibility of change; as to the sincerity of his purpose to follow the Divine will whithersoever it may lead him: as to his intellectual capacities of investigating such questions at all.

'None of these questions, as they come before him, admit of simple demonstration; but each carries with it *a number of independent probable arguments, sufficient when united for a reasonable conclusion.*'[2]

14

The conclusion comes not by any verbal enumeration of all the relevant considerations. They are too minute, as well as too delicate and too abundant, for anyone to formulate; but, taken together, they give a man—after much deliberation—a discernment and comprehension which lead at last to a clear, rapid and

[1] *op. cit.,* 334 cf. *Nic. Ethics,* VI, xi.   [2] *op. cit.,* 283–4.

final conclusion which he cannot analyse, but which connects the mind with the deepest realities of an individual life.[1]

So it becomes plain why one believes, and another does not: what to one mind is a proof is not a proof to another: what is certainty to one mind is not certainty to another. So it is that what theology calls the gift of faith is a personal thing corresponding to a psychology and a life, supported indeed by reasoning, but decided finally by a complexity of considerations which are personal, and far more final than any reasoning.[2]

15

Therefore this power to reach conclusions by some other method than logic is the all-important fact for anyone studying either the force of conviction in general, or of religious belief in particular. Some have said that Newman's insistence on it amounts to a discovery; and certainly he gives it a name all his own: 'the illative sense.'

The word illative is of course an adjective connected with the verb to infer: it means the faculty of inferring—the power to reach conclusions. A distinguished writer on the nature of belief identifies it with interpretation.[3] Before coming to his final discussion of the psychology of faith, Newman devotes a chapter to considering it. It acts, he says, 'by that minute, continuous experimental reasoning which shows badly on paper but which drifts into an overwhelming cumulus of proof and, when our start is true, brings us to a true result'.

It does not exclude, but it supplements logic. Founded on a science of first principles, it accumulates the converging probabilities, and concludes by being morally certain. We cannot keep on reasoning verbally, but we must decide on each personal issue as it arises: and so we get a personal gift or habit of deciding effectively on the things that matter most to us. So it is that though there is a final truth, and One to judge us in relation to it,

[1] op. cit., 285.   [2] op. cit., 286.
[3] M. C. D'Arcy: The Nature of Belief, Ch. VI, esp. p. 201.

yet men apprehend truth variously, and one puts the emphasis in one place, one in another. One is more devout, one is more moral.

It was easy to accept the Catholic Church when in Christendom there was no alternative religion; it is not so easy when there are important denominations separate.

Common sense, chance, visual perception, genius, the great discoveries of principle do not come from reason. They have no arguments, no grounds. They see the truth, but they do not know how they see it. It comes to them as an *experience*. Such was the moral conviction, the strong sense, the happy augury which so strongly convinced every Protestant that the Bible is the Word of God, that he thought of no other authority.

This then is Newman's account of this practical standard of judgment, founded not on reasoning but on experience, which leads men to accept propositions, as it accepts the knowledge gained through experience: each is[1]—for him who accepts—*final*.

The question remains, how are we to relate this to a belief in religion? First of all we see it, as Bishop Butler had shown, agreeing with and enforcing the truths we learn from nature. Christianity is the completion of natural religion. Newman's real discussion therefore centres on natural religion.

'By religion,' he says, 'I mean the knowledge of God, of His will, of our duties towards Him.' How do we learn this knowledge? From the course of the world, from the voice of mankind and, far more authoritative than either, from our own consciousness. The great internal teacher of religion is in other words Conscience. 'I am as little able to think by any mind but my own as to breathe with another's lungs. Conscience is nearer to me than any other means of knowledge.'[2] It is fully furnished for its office which is to tell us what God is, how to worship Him, and what is right and wrong.

The dominant aspect of God was to Newman that of Judge. He then went on to say that men, sinning more often than they do well, regard their Judge with fear. They regard Him as one who is angry and threatens evils. They feel they require expiation,

[1] *Grammar of Assent*, 384.   [2] *op. cit.*, 384.

reconciliation: sin, pollution, retribution require intercession and mediation. Everywhere with natural religion comes the need of atonement.

16

But how can we reconcile an idea of justice with that of atonement, with that of sacrifice made for us by another? Only by recognising that sooner or later we must face responsibility; and meantime we become aware of what Unamuno called the tragic sense of life in men and peoples. God's control of the world seems so indirect, his action so obscure. 'It is as if others had got possession of His work.'[1] And what does this mean but to say what Newman had said so powerfully in the *Apologia,* that some huge and appalling calamity had disordered creation? 'How are we to explain it, the existence of God being taken for granted, except by saying that another will, besides His, has had a part in the disposition of His work, that there is an intractable quarrel, a chronic alienation between God and man?'[2] God has hidden the light of His countenance because under evil influence we have dishonoured Him. This is the grim truth we learn from conscience, and there it solves the world's mystery, and accounts for the problem of man's woe.

Yet in spite of the anguish, and then the tumult of the world, and the certainty of death, religion has always brought with it a sense, not merely of fear, but of hope, of mercy and blessing. The world is not all misery and lamentation: our hearts are often filled with food and gladness. Nay, there are signs in history of a gradual advancement according to principles of wisdom and justice, and in them 'the spontaneous piety of the human mind discerns a Divine supervision'.[3] Judgment is applied in human life, and men know 'that punishment is sure, though slow, that murder will out, that treason never prospers, that pride will have a fall, that honesty is the best policy, and that curses fall on the heads of those who utter them'.[4]

[1] *op. cit.,* 391.   [2] *op. cit.,* 393–4. Cf. *Callista,* Ch. XIX.
[3] *op. cit.,* 397.   [4] *op. cit.,* 400.

17

Everywhere then is this sense of order and justice: not less universal is the phenomenon of prayer. And with prayer comes the sense of an answer, and of holy leaders, and this leads back to the idea that others help and redeem us from our faults. We cannot deny life as we know it, and it simply is a fact of human life that 'we all suffer for each other, and gain by each other's sufferings, for man never stands alone here, though he will stand by himself one day hereafter, but here he is a social being and goes forward to his long home as one of a large company'.[1] And so strong is this sense of man's solidarity as man, that we admire heroes as specimens of what our natures may be, and feel an exhilaration in the spectacle of a courage and a holiness to which we hardly try to attain. And if men offer sacrifices, the thing offered must be unblemished.

So much is the universal instinct of natural religion.

18

From this Newman proceeds to the powerful passages in which, as a conclusion, he sets out under the name of revealed religion the case for Christianity. He does not go by way of logic: for he has proved already that logic is of small account in matters of intense conviction. Only those will be persuaded who are already disposed to believe and act accordingly: only those will succeed in persuading who, having intense conviction, have also that understanding sympathy which gives them the power to put their case in language their hearers can understand.

But the book 'is composed with elaborate art which is more striking the more frequently we peruse it. Every line, every word tells, from the opening sentence to the last.'[2]

[1] op. cit., 400.   [2] J. A. Froude: Short Studies, ii, 84.

CHAPTER XXVI

THE NATURE OF BELIEF

I

The state of mind of those who are disposed to hear the case for Christianity, says Newman now, is 'a belief and perception of the Divine Presence, a recognition of His attributes and an admiration of His Person viewed under them, a conviction of the worth of the soul, and of the reality and momentousness of the unseen world, an understanding that in proportion as we partake in our own persons of the attributes which we admire in Him, we are dear to Him, a consciousness on the contrary that we are far from partaking them, a consequent insight into our guilt and misery, an eager hope of reconciliation to Him, a desire to know and love Him, a sensitive looking-out in all that happens, whether in the course of nature or of human life, for holiness, if such there be, of His bestowing on us what we so greatly need'.[1]

Men will be aware of God above all in His attributes of Holiness, Truth and Love. Foulness, falsity and cruelty therefore will above all strike them as hateful and cause bitter remorse. Sin will awaken the sense of retribution made personal in God's vengeance though that is too mysterious for us to trace till all is known.

2

There is, of course, the argument from miracles; there was Paley's argument from probability. But Newman was insisting all through on the need of something more than argument. 'I say plainly, I do not want to be converted by a smart syllogism: if I am asked to convert others by it I say plainly I do not care to

[1] *Grammar of Assent*, 412–3.

overcome their reason without touching their hearts.'[1] No one can be persuaded unless he feels first the *need* of religion.

3

So far Newman had tested his philosophy of life to take man as he found him by the principles of Aristotle: he had therefore consulted moralists other than Christian. He had looked out on the various religions of the world. But now the time had come to fix his gaze on the central historic fact which he had considered so carefully at Littlemore twenty-five years before: the fact of Christianity.

What had he found the Church to be? He found it among the religions of the world an active, elastic, dynamic, unique and constant energy of truth and life, of holiness and love. Its announcements were both practical and momentous, suited alike to barbarians and to the most refined civilisation. Its history had meant both victory and reverse in its combat with philosophies, with civil powers, with masses, but it had a grand history of achievements, being as vigorous in its age as in its youth; through history it exhibited prerogatives so special, a pre-eminence so distinguished that he was overcome with admiration, and convinced into acceptance.

Newman now proceeds to relate Christianity to history. He does so by dealing with nine different points: The Jews; the correction of their mistakes; the mixed character of the Church; the explanations Gibbon gave for the triumph of the Church and his refutation of these explanations. Newman wrote of the uniqueness of the Christ, the hold of His religion over the lower classes, the impression made on Pliny, the spread of the early Church, the power shown in and by martyrdom. All these led him up to his own immediate observation of the Church as a contemporary and urgent power—proving Christ to be the best answer to the needs of human nature—an unchanging Divine reality corresponding to the unchanging reality of man.

[1] *op. cit.*, 419–20.

4

Each of these points Newman develops with magisterial eloquence and sustained power to a majestic culmination. Here then
is the most massive accumulation of evidence for his peculiar
genius.

Greece, he says, is the classical home of intellectual power,
Rome that of political wisdom, Palestine that of religion. The
pre-occupation of the Jews is with nothing less than God: they
knew Him as One and as Almighty. Their august doctrine begins
with them: their laws and government are moulded by it: their
politics, literature and philosophy are formed by it: the poetry
which expresses it has never been displaced.

Their history is sublime and tragic. At the moment destined for
the consummation of their blessings, they were overthrown and
their tribes dispersed into exile. So it is that their name is clothed
both with sacred prestige and with peculiar reproach. Yet from
early in their history, this disaster had been prophesied—for their
sin promised their calamity, and when the time came they—as a
people—rejected their ineffable opportunity: the Prophet and
King whom they had been expecting to rule the world was condemned because His kingdom was not of this world, but Divine.
Such was the old dispensation: 'it was created for a great end, and
in that end it had its ending.'[1]

5

For the Christ they were so eagerly expecting came not to set
up their tribe in worldly dominion, but to set up a Church 'which
aimed at the benefit of all nations by the spiritual conquest of all'.
How triumphantly He in this Church fulfilled the Jewish expectancy: seeing that it 'from the first filled the world, that it has had
wonderful successes; that its successes have on the whole been of
extreme benefit to the human race; that it has imparted an intelligent notion about the Supreme God among millions who

[1] op. cit., 437.

would have lived and died in irreligion, that it has raised the tone of morality wherever it has come, has abolished great social anomalies and miseries, has raised the female sex to its proper dignity, has protected the poorer classes, has destroyed slavery, encouraged literature and philosophy and had a principal part in that civilisation of human kind which, with some evils, has on the whole been productive of far greater good.[1] The Christ, while fulfilling Jewish prophecy, transcends it, and inaugurates for the first time a universal religion which exerts not a temporal power but a power, far more august, to which our natures bow—that of the Spirit working through tribulation.

The new Church is not meant to be exempt from the weakness of man's corruption. As soon as it is founded, it is warned that there will be corruption within it, even in central places.

How had Gibbon explained the Catholic Church? He had noted in it a combination of five characteristics: *esprit de corps,* clerical administration, a claim to miraculous powers, perfection of virtues, and organisation. But in the first place, how is one to account for so striking a combination? and secondly, how could any of these by themselves persuade? Most people are inclined to deride the ideal of hell, few are fascinated by austere virtues. You cannot conquer simply by organisation—that comes afterwards.

6

The real answer is neither these things nor their combination. It is the portrayal of the Christ. 'It is the image of Him who fulfils the one great need of human nature, the Healer of its wounds, the Physician of the soul, this image it is which both creates faith and rewards it.'[2]

It is the love He inspires which is the miracle: and this is all the more astounding when one sees its power among the lower classes, the poor and ignorant. They heard of Christ Crucified. Without seeing Him, they loved him. They heard that He lived in them and they in Him, and so it was that working-men were

[1] *op. cit.,* 439.   [2] *op. cit.,* 458.

overpowered, and, in their turn, became persuaded. In the words
of Libanius, they left their tongs and anvils to preach about the
things of heaven. They faced martyrdom. 'And in skins of beasts,'
said Tacitus, 'they were torn to pieces by dogs; they were nailed
up to crosses, they were made inflammable so that when day
failed they might serve as lights'[1]—and in all this they exercised a
persuasion that won the hearts of those that mocked them first to
compassion, then to admiration; thus they proved irresistible.

Pliny in a long passage attested their power. One sees the true
explanation in a long citation from the Epistle to Diognetus,
which hymns the power of the Christ to give the souls of men
strength, glory, honour, light and life.

For page on page Newman quoted the triumphant sufferings of
the martyrs. He told of Symphorian of Autun, a youth of noble
birth who when told to worship an idol replied, 'Give me leave
and I will hammer it to pieces'; of a girl of eighteen of Cæsarea,
who, while her sides were torn open with iron rakes preserved a
light and joyous countenance; of a hundred and fifty Christians
at Utica who, when told to burn incense to an idol or they should
be thrown into a pit of burning lime, jumped into it of their own
accord. In short, wherever a Christian was martyred, a new proof
of faith was given, which was received with songs of thanksgiving
and triumph.

7

Thus Newman came to the grand conclusion of his argument:
natural religion is incomplete. It needs a revelation. That revelation is Christianity. Natural religion, recognising sin, sees the need
of a remedy. That remedy is the mediation of the Christ.

Man knows his own needs. The Church's magnificent answer to
them is the secret of her success. In her energy, in her hold over
different classes, in her power to sustain martyrs, and in spite of
new and fearful adversaries, Christ's religion remains mysteriously
potent. 'It has with it that gift of staunching the one deep wound
of human nature which avails more for its success than a full

[1] *op. cit.*, 403.

encyclopædia of scientific knowledge and a whole library of controversy, and therefore it must last while human nature lasts. It is a living truth which never can grow old.

'Some persons speak of it as if it were a thing of history, with only direct bearing upon modern times: I cannot allow that it is a mere historical religion. Certainly it has its foundations in past and glorious memories but its power is in the present. It is no dreary matter of antiquarianism; we do not contemplate it in conclusions drawn from dumb documents and dead events, but by faith exercised in ever living objects and by the appropriation and use of ever recurring gifts.'[1]

In the rites and ordinances of the Church, man comes in touch with the Unseen and Eternal Powers: he joins in that sacrifice for the sins of the world, which, made once for all, is yet daily perpetuated in the signs which mysteriously renew the reconciling work of Christ from its beginning to its end. In Holy Communion, He, the Christ, soul and body and divinity, enters into and indwells every believer who receives Him. He abides personally in the Churches. And thus He, by receiving His own into union with Himself, makes them partakers of the Divine nature.

Such is the gift with which the Church fulfils us; the fullness of Him that filleth all in all transcends every instinct and desire with gifts of grace. What more can any ask than is given by such a Church? *Its very divination of our needs is in itself a proof that it is really the supply of them.*[2]

'The Deliverer of the nations', Newman continues, 'has not done His work by halves.[3] He is not Himself complete in a single relation to ourselves. But His Spirit is in the Communion of Saints.' We live in a great company. Saints and angels, therefore, are our protectors. The dead join with the living and the living with the dead. The Christ is one also with a visible hierarchy on earth and a continuous succession of mysteries. His word, His name, His image are daily brought before us. 'While human nature continues in life and action what it has ever been,' so He too lives in our imaginations by His visible symbols as if He were on earth, with a practical efficacy which even believers cannot deny to be the cor-

---

[1] *op. cit.*, 480.   [2] *op. cit.*, 481.   [3] *loc. cit.*

rective of that nature, its strength day by day, and that this power of perpetuating His image, being altogether singular and special, and the prerogative of Him and Him alone, is a grand evidence how well He fulfils to this day that sovereign mission which, from the first beginning of the world's history, has been in prophecy assigned to Him.'[1]

Newman completed his argument by relating a consideration which was mentioned of Napoleon in the Conversations at St Helena, and which Newman had used for his students in Dublin. The great conqueror had emulated Cæsar and Alexander. But, he asked, when all is said, who really cares about them? Their names flit about like ghosts. Their home is in the schoolroom. So it is with all the world's greatest heroes.

'But on the contrary (he is reported to have continued) there is only One Name in the whole world that lives: it is the name of One Who passed His years in obscurity, and Who died a malefactor's death. Eighteen hundred years have gone since that time, and still it has its hold upon the human mind. It has possessed the world, and it retains possession. Amid the most varied nations, under the most diversified circumstances, in the most cultivated, in the rudest races and intellects, in all classes of society, the Owner of that great Name reigns. High and low, rich and poor acknowledge Him. Millions of souls are conversing with Him, are venturing on His word, are looking for His presence. Palaces, sumptuous, innumerable, are raised to His honour; His image as in the hour of His deepest humiliation, is triumphantly displayed in the proud city, in the open country, in the corners of streets, on the tops of mountains. It sanctifies the ancestral hall, the closet, and the bed-chamber; it is the subject for the exercise of the highest genius in the imitative arts. It is worn next the heart in life; it is held before the failing eyes in death. Here then is One who is not a mere name, who is a reality. He is dead and gone but still He lives—lives as the living energetic thought of successive generations, as the awful motive power of a thousand great events. He has done without effort what others with lifelong struggle have not done. Can He be less than Divine? Who is He but the Creator

[1] *op. cit.*, 482.

Himself, who is sovereign over His own works, towards whom
our eyes and hearts turn instinctively because He is our Father and
our God?'[1]

8

Such was Newman's final appeal for the Christ and His Church:
the evidences they set before the believer were addressed not
merely to reason but to the imagination and the heart: the evidences they produced were 'too various for enumeration, too
personal and deep for words, too powerful and concurrent for
reversal'. Taken together, they present both the object and the
proof of its existence, crowding experience with overwhelming
cogencies of their reality, and so forcing a faith absolute and final.[2]
'Christianity is received', he said, 'as the counterpart of ourselves,
and as real as we are real.'[3]

Such is the faith, appealing to Newman's deepest convictions,
because his convictions were one with the instincts of his nature—
such is the psychology of faith, which he makes cogent in great
writing to endure with time.

---

[1] *Grammar of Assent*, 484.   [2] *loc. cit.*   [3] *loc. cit.*

CHAPTER XXVII

THE FINAL VICTORY

I

Newman had felt the burden of the years; and though he relished the appreciation which returned to him, it was not without a certain sense of age and mourning that told him he had passed his summer evenings, and that if colours gilded his views, they were October colours: their beauty had the tenderness of death: and he was pensive as the birds whose coverts the dying season has made bare. The music of his voice became more plangent. He was fighting still against democracy and liberalism; liberalism understood as the temper which ignoring the authority of revelation betrays the very basis of real religion, democracy as the insurgence of the multitude against the standards of excellence, set them by a Church, a court and a governing tradition.

But Newman was not occupied with these things incessantly: he was a human being with the lightest touch on all affairs and absolutely free from all portentousness. Nothing so much disgusted him as adulation: 'He protested with whimsical fierceness', said Church, 'against being made a hero or a sage; he was what he said and nothing more.'[1] And if any tried to put him on to a throne, he threw them off with quite uncompromising gestures. In this world nothing is complete and much is ridiculous, and his was a humour in which the grotesque and pathetic sides of life were recognised at every moment. He was always ready for a jest and a smile at any false steps made by others or by himself.

His manner was as it had always been, direct, warm and easy; as Gerard Hopkins said, genial and almost, so to speak, unserious.[2] Looking back on all he shared with his Anglican friends, he spoke

[1] Church: *Occasional Papers*, II, 481.   [2] Hopkins: *Letters*, Vol. I, 5.

with interest, appreciation, generosity. Among other things he
said he always answered those who said the learned had no excuse
in invincible ignorance, that, on the contrary, they had that
excuse the most of all people.[1] In a parlour was a bird's-eye picture of Oxford, and under it in Latin the words *Son of Man
thinkest thou these dry bones will live? Lord God, thou knowest.*

'Anyone', wrote one of his oldest friends, Dean Church, 'who
has watched at all carefully his career, whether in old days or in
later, must have been struck with this feature of his character, his
naturalness, the freshness and freedom with which he addressed a
friend or expressed an opinion, the absence of all mannerism or
formality. . . . Quite aware of what he was to his friends and to
the things with which he was connected and ready with a certain
quickness of temper which marked him in old days to resent anything unbecoming done to his cause, or those connected with it,
he would not allow any homage to be paid to himself . . . with his
profound sense of the incomplete and the ridiculous in this world,
and with a humour in which the grotesque and the pathetic sides
of life were together recognised at every moment, he never hesitated to admit his own mistakes.'[2]

2

Yet none denied the power of his personality or the atmosphere it created. In himself he looked more fragile than ever, and
though he continued to walk eagerly had a figure much bent.
His features were all extremely marked—eyes, nose, lips, profile—
but their texture seemed as dainty as porcelain. 'He looked', said
Furse, 'as delicate as an old lady washed in milk.' So frail, so
exquisite did he seem, so quick and soft and tender were the
cadences of his low speech, that a stranger felt afraid to speak too
loud lest the noise should hurt him. He himself spoke, not loud,
but in silvery whispers, keen and quick. 'His soul was in his voice
like a bird in its song.'[3] In everything, there was the same appealing charm, insinuating, wistful, and his presence was like the
embodiment of his voice. Its cadences were so subtle, so touching

[1] Hopkins: *Letters, loc. cit.*   [2] Church: *op. cit.*, II, 480–1.
[3] Ward: *Newman*, II, 370.

OXFORD IN NEWMAN'S TIME

that they moved his hearers like the notes of his violin, as though for all its sweetness and its courage, the speaker's heart was broken; though he was so courteous, so easy; though he spoke so often the things of a light wit, yet they left an echo of melancholy; men went away from him enthralled, yet sad. He seemed a master of high tragedy, so marvellous the intermingling of pathos with grandeur, and of sweetness with power. And yet— how was it?—there could be felt with all this the experience of combat, and of fierce combat.

The quiet dignity of his presence concealed much strength, almost fierceness, of will; and the sensitiveness and refinement of his nature which it was impossible for him to conceal made an 'atmosphere' in his presence by which no one could remain unaffected. He usually said little and was true to his own definition of a gentleman as 'one who does not willingly give pain'. But at times, and sometimes unexpectedly, he would speak his mind plainly and sharply, and when he did it was remembered.[1]

3

The most vivid picture of Newman at this time comes from one who listened to the sermon he preached on the Easter Day of 1874:

'Bold yet gentle, energetic but reflective, calm yet seeming to droop somewhat with a languor born of anxious yet not always satisfying thought, revealing full cognisance of everything around but significant also of an isolation quiescent though not always perfectly serene; a face still powerful but weighted, and an expression of fatigue of years and something more. It is quite possible that imagination—and especially a Protestant's imagination—sees more in Dr Newman's face than he would own to be written there, and one would be a confident physiognomist to insist against his own positive declaration on a theory which he would pronounce at variance with his self-knowledge. Perhaps the outlines and mouldings of his thin and rugged, though gentle, countenance are deceptive. Still the fact remains that Dr New-

[1] *Expositor*, 4th Series, 1890.

man's life has been nothing if not a continual expenditure of intellectual strength. Though he proudly and gratefully boasts of the calm and comfort he has enjoyed ever since he knelt at the feet of the Church, he is distinguished from his fellow Catholics and fellow converts by opinions and methods of thought such as coincide better than any mere expression of spiritual content with the expression which so irresistibly tells a more tempestuous story in the contour and shading of his face.

'He proceeded to deliver his Easter sermon. It was eloquent, it was sensitive, it was in its main thought boldly ingenious; but its principal beauty was its exquisite simplicity. And this was aided in its effect by the preacher's manner. It was that of a good old father, much beloved, who had retained amidst physical weakness the strongest mental powers, talking naturally to his dearest children, without a phrase of gushing affection—for between such a father and such children they are needless—of the things he most desired them to remember. There was no appearance of oratorical preparation, nor of the speaker's invariably rounded readiness. Occasionally, though the right word came, there was a hesitation and a feeling about for it. And never, except in the natural yet placid zeal of a strong desire to make what he was saying understood and permanently apprehended, was there anything like the emphasis and stress of the pulpiteer.

'The scheme of the discourse was easy and almost conversational. It was the greatest day of the year and there were many ways of looking at it. We might think of the miracle of the Resurrection. We might remember how Christ's life went not from strength to strength, but from weakness to weakness, from indignity to indignity, from suffering to suffering, until in the great mystery celebrated on that day, He made strong that which had fallen in Adam.

'But what Dr Newman wished to impress upon us that day was that there were two worlds: one a world of order and constant law, in which we live, the other a world of miracle. It was in order that we might not worship the ordinary world that the higher world of the supernatural was exhibited to us in the miracles, and in the greatest miracle of all. It was to be expected,

and was quite right that at the time of Christ's death and resurrection, so now, the politics and history of the world should pursue
their own line by their own rules; but as the miraculous events, so
now, faith in them, bore witness to a world beyond politics and
history, without the recognition of which man's life would be imperfect and unspiritual.'[1] For the eternal world was open to believers in the mystery of the Church. And those who received
Holy Communion were made partakers of the risen Christ.

Such with grave and earnest application in enforcement of the
duty of promoting the Divine glory each in our own way was
Dr Newman's Easter sermon. And great was its charm.

'Analysing it, we should probably find its secret as hinted above
in its simplicity; and this lay in the execution, rather than in the
idea of his discourse. The notion of two worlds—one of regular
and constant law, and the other of irregular and exceptional viola-
tion of law—is not a simple one, or if simple, is simple only in its
audacity as a philosophical theory: but no one would attribute to
it such a fault as audacity or could deem it complex or subtle as
set forth by Dr Newman. There was no resisting the gentle yet
firm persuasion of a speaker who had the double art of solving
without magic the difficulties of theology, and expressing in
various ways, all equally lucid, all apparently obvious, the formulas of his solution. Miracle, which had perhaps come to be a
trial, seemed to be once more a help to faith, and half an hour's
grave speech by a venerable teacher showed even to those of its
hearers who could not acknowledge the authority of his Church,
or the daily miracle of its altars, how intimately the supernatural
was bound up in the spiritual in the experience of each human
being.'[2]

4

The years which had curved Newman, and whitened his silky
yet abundant hair, had not staled the infinite variety of his talk,
rusted the edges of his feelings, nor tarnished the polished steel of
his prose. He could not but be aware of the prestige which had
revisited him, nor was he unthankful for it. But, though his wit

[1] *Oriel College MSS.*   [2] *ibid.*

was unwearied—if he spoke at all—no one could fail to be aware that he felt weighted by a double burden, the burden of being mistrusted by others, and of apprehension at the shape of things to come. He knew only too precisely that he was the subject of suspicion and attack, especially from certain co-religionists in London.

Not less was he sure that the growth of irreligion in England, and in Europe would, with the declension of moral principles, bring disaster. The gloom of forty years before encircled him still. Men, he said, thus took atheism for faith before they worked out a religion. 'I have all this time thought that a time of wide-spread infidelity was coming, and through all those years the waters have been rising as a deluge. I look for the time after my life when only the tops of the mountains will be seen like islands in the waste of waters.'[1] The conviction was not new: he had held it, we know, from his early Oxford days: but as he grew older, the feeling of nearing catastrophe weighed on him more painfully as he toiled over moor and fen.

5

Old friends were dying. Bellasis and Hope-Scott both went, and, in his own community, Father Joseph Gordon, and the school matron, Mrs Wootten: in the spring of 1875, bereavement was to take the closest of all, his devoted Ambrose St John. They had been jubilant as he seemed to recover, when there was in the night a sudden relapse, and all was over. 'From the first,' wrote Newman to his friend Rogers, now Lord Blachford, 'he loved me with an intensity of love which was unaccountable. At Rome twenty-eight years ago he was always so working for me and re-lieving me that, being young and Saxon-looking, the Romans called him my guardian angel. As far as this world was con-cerned, I was his first and last.'[2]

A few days after he died, Newman was to preach at the Ora-tory. Everyone expected a sermon on the friend he prized. But Newman did not mention Ambrose St John. He spoke of the wonderful power to console which was to be found in the Blessed

[1] Aubrey de Vere: *Recollections*, 286.   [2] Ward: *Newman*, II, 410.

Sacrament, adding in a low voice of intense conviction simply the words, 'I know'.

6

In the year 1868 Newman began to make arrangements for a complete reissue of his works. These included not only his sermons, but even the controversial pieces he had written as an Anglican. Where his mind was changed, he published a statement to mark what he now considered the necessary adjustment: but he did not pretend that time, or his change of faith, had provided him with a complete answer to everything for which he had contended as an Anglican.

A letter written to an Anglican clergyman in 1873 is an evidence to his tact and insight.

'Revd Sir,

'I hope I am not taking a liberty in writing to you. I am sanguine you will not feel it as such.

'Your son has written to tell me what pain he has caused you and his own deep distress in consequence.

'I do not know him except by his letters but I perceive clearly enough his great affection and reverence for his Father; also I believe he is one of those in whose case the Church of Rome is the only possible protection against infidelity. They would be unbelievers if they were not Catholics. They need a spiritual authority with claims upon their faith, and they find themselves unable to discern those claims in any religious body except the Church of Rome.

'There is scarcely a doubt that your son, had he remained in the Church of England would have only in profession been a member of it and in his heart would have believed nothing. The spread of infidelity just now is appalling: were I now in the Anglican Church I should deplore as a calamity a friend's leaving it, but I am sure I would rather he left than that he denied heaven and hell, and the redemption of mankind by our Lord's death. I should feel he was much nearer to me as a member of the Roman Church than as an unbeliever.'[1]

[1] Keble College: *unpublished*. To the Revd William Nevins.

7

At this time he received a letter which touched and gratified him to the quick. It had occurred to one of the Fellows of Trinity that the most distinguished son of the College should be welcomed back to her, and Oxford honour once more the aged exile who had so deeply loved her. Trinity elected him as her first honorary Fellow.

When Newman walked again in those dear haunts where he had lived so happily sixty years before—where, as he said, 'I began the battle of life with my good angel at my side', one touching relationship was renewed; he found still living his tutor, Tommy Short, who had helped and encouraged him in the obscurity of his boyhood.

When he rose to speak in the College hall, all were aware that the prince of preachers was again among them; he spoke still in that simple, natural, genial manner which was the echo of his soul. The voice still had the old haunting music, the articulation was still perfectly clear; his choice of words was not less exquisite. Though a man of nearly eighty, he was still that magical personage who had pierced to the soul a generation of Oxford men, and changed the temper of the Church of England.

'There was something tenderly pathetic to us younger people,' wrote Lord Bryce, 'in seeing the old man come again after so many eventful years to the hall where he had been wont to sit as a youth, the voice so often heard in St Mary's retaining, faint though it had grown, the sweet modulations Oxford knew so well, and the aged face, worn deep with the lines of thought, struggle and sorrow.'[1]

8

Such was the return of 1878. And in that same year, the good old Pio Nono died in Rome. He was succeeded by a diplomat of unexcelled finesse, who determined to use his lightning mind to win back the thinkers of the age to agreement with the Church.

[1] Ward: *Newman*, II, 430.

His eyes were not only as brilliant as those of his predecessor but infinitely sharper. He searched the horizons: he scrutinised the urgent and immediate: the instinct of his Italian mind was to seize each possible occasion and use it finely for the needs of the Church. Wherever possible, he would ally with able minds: for to him scrutiny was a passion, and truth welcome, even when it showed no mercy to pious, or conventional, ears. His idea was to show that the Catholic Church could join with the arrowy intellects of the time, because swifter than them all. A statesman, he built his plans on wide foundations. 'You will know my policy', he said, 'when you see the name of my first Cardinal.'

This inspiration was not peculiar to himself. It accorded perfectly with the feeling of the leading layman in England. When the Duke of Norfolk went to Rome to offer his homage to the new Pope, he pointed out how high and how well-won was Newman's renown—though he admitted that his outstanding work for the Church was to some extent discounted by the party who pretended that the bigger the bigot the better the Catholic. The truth was that Newman's supreme appeal lay in his fairness —he blended, as no other did, childlike tenderness with intellectual insight. To honour such a man, said the Duke, would cause England a lively satisfaction.

In the summer of 1878 the Duke and Lord Ripon had put their case to Cardinal Manning:[1] but when they arrived in Rome some months later, they found that the enthusiastic letter written by Manning at their request had not reached the Pope. Strachey's account is this time perfectly correct; but we must not therefore conclude that Manning had not forwarded the letter. No, not that! He had entrusted it to Cardinal Howard to deliver personally, and Cardinal Howard took months and months to reach Rome.[2]

When therefore the Duke made his suggestion to the Pope, the Pope wondered. Why, it was natural to ask, had no suggestion on so important a matter come from the Cardinal-Archbishop

[1] Purcell: *Manning,* II, 554.
[2] See Strachey: *Eminent Victorians,* 104–5. Purcell: *Manning,* II, 557. Butler: *Ullathorne,* II, 109. Ward: *Newman,* II, 436–7.

of Westminster? The Duke, when stopping at the British Embassy in Paris on his way home, wrote to Cardinal Manning to press the question.[1]

When at last the letter Manning had been asked to write did reach the Holy See, the Pope acted quickly. He determined to override that opposition to Newman in England of which the Duke had told him.[2] Very soon after receiving the required letter from Manning, the Pope wrote back to him, and by January 30, the information had reached Newman's bishop, Ullathorne. Ullathorne wrote immediately to Newman saying that for Newman to receive this honour would add weight to the books he had written: it would prove against his detractors that he had the confidence of the Holy See. 'Although at your venerable age', the bishop concluded, 'you might be inclined to shrink from a position so new, and apparently opposed to your simple habits, yet I fail to see how these habits need be much interfered with further than you are inclined to allow. The Pope would scarcely, I think, require you to live in Rome unless it were your desire. The chief object of His Holiness is evidently to confer on you this dignity and honour in token of his confidence and respect. And you know that Cardinals out of Rome are not required to keep up much state that would be cumbrous or expensive.'[3]

It is very plain that the bishop knew what he was talking about. This plan to make Newman a Cardinal, said the bishop, 'has more in it than meets the ear, as you will readily understand'.[4]

The news was to Newman a supreme encouragement and consolation. So he was not to die without a sign that his work enjoyed the solemn approval of the Church! His only difficulty was that he was too old and infirm to live in Rome, as the rule was for those Cardinals who were not Archbishops.

[1] Purcell: *Manning*, II, 557.
[2] *Memoir of Sophia Palmer, Comtesse de Franqueville*, 190.
[3] Butler: *Ullathorne*, II, 110–1.   [4] *op. cit.*

9

He went as soon as he could to see the bishop at Oscott and draft a reply: a reply which should make it clear that though he was not strong enough to live in Rome, he would most gratefully accept the honour. 'But how can I intimate or in any way suggest such things?' Newman asked his bishop. 'It would be altogether unbecoming.' 'Write your letter', the bishop answered, 'and leave it to me to make the necessary explanations.'[1] So Newman wrote humbly that the Pope's offer was altogether above him, and 'I pray and entreat His Holiness in compassion of my diffidence of mind, in consideration of my feeble health, my nearly eighty years, the retired course of my life from my youth, my ignorance of foreign languages and my lack of experience in business to let me die where I have so long lived.'[2] Now this was not a refusal: it was a request for a concession not to live in Rome—and put in the only way it could be put from Newman to the Pope.

That there could be no *possible* doubt as to the meaning, however, Ullathorne wrote very clearly, yet very courteously, to Manning, saying that though Newman had far too humble and delicate a mind to dream of anything that would look like hinting at any kind of terms, nothing stood in the way of his grateful acceptance except the idea of having to leave his Oratory. 'But', added Ullathorne, 'it was plain that the Pope intended him to remain in England.'[3]

To make assurance doubly sure, Ullathorne wrote again the next day in still warmer terms: 'Dr Newman is very much aged and softened with age and the losses he has had, especially by the loss of his two brethren, St John and Caswall; he can never refer to these losses without weeping, and becoming speechless for the time. He is very much affected by the Pope's kindness—would, I know, like to receive the real honour offered him, but feels the whole difficulty at his age of changing his life, or having to leave

[1] Butler: *Ullathorne*, II, 112–3, 115.   [2] Butler: *Ullathorne*, II, 112.
[3] Purcell: *Manning*, II, 558–9.

the Oratory, which I am sure he could not do. If the Holy Father thinks well to confer on him the dignity, leaving him where he is, I know how immensely he would be gratified, and you will know how generally the conferring on him the Cardinalate would be applauded.'[1]

In case even *that* should not be enough to make the case clear, Newman wrote one more letter direct to Manning: 'I could not be so ungracious whether to the Holy Father, or to the friends at home who have interested themselves in the matter, as to decline what was so kindly proposed.'[2]

Hardly had this letter been sent, however, than Bishop Ullathorne began to feel uncomfortable. Cardinal Manning gave no sign that he understood what either Newman or the bishop had written. On the contrary, rumours—not altogether unexpected, but not the less nasty—came to the bishop's ears: it was being pretended in London that Newman had refused the honour.[3]

Now from whom did those rumours come? And what did they mean unless to give the impression that Newman had been discourteous to the Holy See? And if there were an impression of discourtesy, might not that affect the feelings of the Vatican so that Newman's answer could be misread?

Ullathorne was himself a Yorkshireman, as shrewd as he was robust. He was well aware that Manning had never liked the proposal of making Newman a Cardinal. Manning had said heated things about it to the bishop himself. 'You don't know Newman as I do. He simply twists you round his little finger; he bamboozles you with his carefully selected words, and plays so subtly with his logic that your simplicity is taken in. You are no match for him. You are no match for him!'

Those words were not wise words to use to that Bishop of Birmingham; Ullathorne had made a strong reply, in which among other things he said that Newman was an avowed hater of all duplicity and intrigue, that there was no honester man on earth, and Manning had to hear once more what he knew too well—that Newman's banner, no matter how grim and exhaust-

---

[1] Purcell: *Manning,* II, 560.   [2] *ibid.*
[3] Ward: *Newman,* II, 443.

ing the episodes of the campaign, no matter what stratagems were employed against him, would wave at last victorious.

Ullathorne knew, however, that Harrow had not called Manning 'The General' for nothing: he had guessed that an ambush was being planned. He therefore went so far as to write direct to Rome, and put the whole story very plainly indeed.[1] Nine days later, when the mischievous rumours had been published in *The Times* as a fact, Newman wrote with equal directness to the Duke of Norfolk:

'This statement', wrote Newman to the Duke, 'cannot come from me, nor could it come, for it was made public before my answer got to Rome.

'It could only come then, from someone who not only read my letter, but, instead of leaving to the Pope to interpret it, took upon himself to put an interpretation upon it, and published that interpretation to the world.

'A private letter, addressed to Roman authorities, is interpreted on its way and published in the English papers.'[2]

The Duke of Norfolk noticed something more; that the rumours were now being supported in *The Tablet* by a former enemy of Newman, Herbert Vaughan, now Bishop of Salford.[3] How much this suited the narrow party who had always said that Newman was not a good Catholic and that he was not trusted by his own people! The Pope, they had said, snubs him, and now they went on—he snubs the Pope.[4]

All this might well create such an unpleasant feeling in Rome that the former delay might become very long indeed—long enough for a frail old man to die.

10

'The feeling of the Ultramontanes towards the most illustrious of English Catholics,' notes the *Pall Mall Gazette* at this juncture, 'could not have been better shown than in an article on Catholicism and Culture which appeared in the first number of the new

[1] Butler: *Ullathorne*, II, 114.   [2] Ward: *Newman*, II, 444–5.
[3] Purcell: *Manning*, II, 563.   [4] Butler: *Ullathorne*, II, 562–3.

series of the *Dublin Review*. The writer of that article undertook
to reckon up the English Catholics who had made for themselves
a name in letters. The list was not a long one, and the Reviewer
frankly owned that it was not. It must have been a great temptation to him to have included in it the man who as regards the
substance of his writings stands on the same level with Pascal and
Bossuet, while, as regards their form, he has shown a mastery of
the varied resources of the English tongue which gives him an
equal pre-eminence in the literature of his own country. But the
Dublin Review rose superior to the temptation and had the
magnificent courage to omit Dr Newman's name.'[1]

II

The intrigues now being carried on against Newman aroused
a widespread contempt and indignation. Now that the facts are
known, we can guess what, on reading Dr Newman's letter, the
Duke of Norfolk thought of Cardinal Manning. He wrote to
him at once and strongly. On February 22, he begged the Cardinal to explain to the Pope that the affair had not only been
misrepresented, but that the misrepresentations had been made
public in a way for which no one could account; and which, if
not contradicted, might well have given in Rome itself a false
idea of Newman's answer. The Duke concluded by saying that,
as he was himself the first to mention the matter to the new Pope,
he wished to thank the Pope for acting according to his suggestion.

The following day, the Duke, now evidently incensed, wrote
to the Cardinal again to say that neither he nor his friends, nor
Newman nor his friends had spread the false report. Then who,
asked the Duke, had given the false report to the Cardinal?[2]

Who indeed?

When a personal antipathy is strong, when this antipathy em-
braces principles, when these principles touch religious zeal or
high politics, then it happens that a masterful mind envelops
facts in such an atmosphere that they can no more be seen than

[1] The documents quoted in Purcell: *Manning*, II, 564-5.
[2] *ibid.*, 562-3.

POPE LEO XIII

the desert is seen when an Arab finds the sun obscured by the whirling dust of the khamsin. A man's will in such a case determines how much he can see or hear; and will is the name of the deep motive power at the springs of character. It would be unfair in such cases to pass judgment as on a normal man. Deceit is not deliberate; the man is himself betrayed by what is not necessarily false, but is certainly faulty within; and an admiring friend of Manning had noted from the beginning not only that pride was his ruling passion, but also that imagination worked upon his weakness and deceived him in many points that touched him the nearest.[1]

So it was that surrounded as he had been by men who hated Newman as much for the strenuousness of his sincerity, as for the admiration it evoked, by men who in their bigotry refused to count Newman among the English Catholics, Manning's instinct led him into that error of judgment which hastened—and will for ever enforce—the verdict of history on his rivalry with the supreme churchman of his time. The dazzling meteor must soon flare out, the morning star shines on.

The facts of the episode are now clear. But they do not mean that a memorable prelate was simply a mean and jealous intriguer. Could we see into the hidden counsels of the hearts, we need not judge that a figure so English and so Papal had basely lost his sense of honour.

There is in the psychology of man a sort of instinctive defence which a man who is strong, but not strong enough, sets up against another who, being a genius, soars beyond him—abler, loftier, more searching; and this instinct is apt to give a man inadequate instructions. While admitting receipt of all the letters, Manning said quite plainly, and no doubt sincerely, that he read in every one of them a refusal.[2]

[1] Shane Leslie: *Manning*, 40.
[2] Shane Leslie: *Manning*, 183. Purcell: *Manning*, II, 508–9. The laymen, Snead-Cox, Wilfrid Ward, and Sir Shane Leslie all refrain from quoting the details of Manning's moves. They left it open to the non-Catholic Lytton Strachey to give these moves a mischievous interpretation. It is the judicial Benedictine, Abbot Cuthbert Butler, who records the value of Purcell's historical work.

Manning, to tell the truth, was no less an Englishman than Newman. But we cannot live for ever on logic any more than on the superiority of youthful prestige and strength. It is by sympathy, not superiority that we win the hearts and souls of men. Manning in his old age devoted himself to the cause less of the Papacy than of the poor, and as the champion of the outcast worked valiantly in fields beyond the range of Newman's genius, fields where he gained a fame to which history pays its just tribute.

12

Manning, if he duped himself occasionally, had not gone mad. By the time that he had received in Rome the two letters of the Duke of Norfolk, he saw the daylight clearly. He must act at once and strongly. He must report to the Holy See. He must explain to Newman, to Ullathorne, and to Norfolk, his lamentable, his colossal mistake. And he was equal to it all. He congratulated Newman with the public impressiveness the occasion demanded.

Thus Newman's enemies were routed. 'The cloud', he said, 'is lifted from me for ever.'[1] The high precision of his views on religion, and on universities; his liturgical spirit, his searching, scholarly knowledge of the Bible, his welcome to classical culture and contemporary science, his sane views on Papal infallibility, his indignation at the insolence and aggression of extremists, his English temper, patriotic, yet judicious, the flights and nobleness of his genius were after careful consideration established for ever by the marked approval of the Holy See: and his works in the twinkling of an eye became the classics of Catholicism.

13

Old and frail, he found it an effort to make the journey to Rome: three days after he arrived, on April 24, 1879, he was received affectionately by the Pope, and on May 12 he received the formal notice of his election, the *biglietto*, which immediately

[1] Ward: *Newman*, II, 446.

precedes the ceremony of being made a Cardinal. In his formal answer he spoke of the tendency to regard one religion as good as another, and to encourage each one to think as he felt inclined. Newman saw the mind of the times—to leave everyone a choice, not to judge religion as a fact but to tolerate it as a possible convenience for certain individuals. Justice, morality, benevolence were all in accord with this spirit: it particularly suited the English and their variety of denominations. But it was none the less dangerous to true religion, though that he believed would triumph, nevertheless, in some way he could not foresee.

Each Cardinal is attached to a separate church in Rome. To this outstanding Englishman was given the title of that dedicated to England's Patron Saint: San Giorgio in Velabro.

The ceremonies in Rome soon exhausted him: he was often tired and ill: in six weeks he had been able to say his Mass only three times, and had to return to England by the shortest route, so that he had to give up seeing Miss Giberne at Autun.[1]

14

And now came a great reception given for him by the Duke of Norfolk, and many addresses of congratulation. To each he replied with his peculiar felicity; the series of answers, therefore, takes one far into the spirit of his Catholicism. A new and brighter sun was shining into his life, to give him a glow of serenity more than he had ever known. Sweet after luckless campaigning was victorious peace: welcome after such strenuous labours such consoling rest. England and his Church both offered him their homage, and his sensitive heart grew calm in thankfulness, as his dignity found its proper scope in the princely rank now accorded. In this sunshine of respect and veneration his rich nature, like chrysanthemums in the summer of All Saints, flowered out in a late blooming with a keen perfume all its own. The dignity and impressiveness inherent in his person were now framed and outlined by his rank as Cardinal. But it did not in the least change the simple sincere natural ease which had always made the soul

[1] Ward: *Newman,* II, 458–62.

K

of Newman one with that of the boys and men he loved to have around him.

As Cardinal he was once more entertained at Trinity College; once again he was heard in a pulpit at Oxford—a pulpit, it must be confessed, that was not in the centre of the town. The Catholics were to suffer for many a year for Manning's mistake: and when Pusey died, and Liddon resigned, Newman felt what a tragedy it was that no great figure had been there to maintain the supremacy of God's honour and glory over the mere devices and designs of men's ordinary hearts.

CHAPTER XXVIII

DEEP CALLS TO DEEP

I

The remaining years were not eventful. 'Cardinal New-man receives very few visitors at the Oratory now,' said a notice in *Birmingham Daily Mail* on August 4, 1886. 'A brain that is as restless and active as ever leaves a man, whose years fall short only by one of those of the century, little time for anything but the work for which there is only the twilight remaining. They are only a privileged few—his Grace of Norfolk, and one or two others, close and firm friends of the Oratory and of its "Father"—to whom the Cardinal opens the door of his seclusion . . . his visitors seeing still the same resolute strong face, the same keen piercing eye which marked the man who carried on the greatest controversy of our time. The marks of time are to be seen, but they are physical only. His voice is weaker but it is as sweet sounding as ever, and in his talk there is all the old firmness of expression together with that gentle sweetness of tone which those who know him always speak of as one of his chief personal charms. He wore spectacles as a young man; he reads easily without them now except when the light is bad. But the receding years have stranded each its ripple on his face and his unimpaired energy is of the

> Great spirits yearning in desire
> To follow knowledge like a sinking star
> Beyond the utmost bound of human thought.

Though it minimises it cannot prevent one noticing the feebleness of a body that carries the weight of over fourscore years. There is in his manner the slowness of perception of external objects, the abstracted air which is invariable with old men. Sometimes he will forget for a moment a visitor's presence, and in the course of conversation will momentarily relapse into the self-communion that has in the long years of deep thought become habitual, and then will awake with a start to the consciousness of external objects.'[1]

He never lost his acute sense of the catastrophe impending over a world that felt competent enough in itself to ignore religion, that corrected neither its impulses by the graces nor its plan by the revelation of which the Church was the instrument and the guardian.

2

While he adhered to his own communion as unique, he was most courteous in all his dealings with those outside it, seeking always the union of hearts, sceptical of the facile pronouncements of self-confidence.

A story is told too of an archdeacon who wished to pay him a visit, and before doing so wrote to ask what marks of respect it was customary to show in greeting a Prince of the Church. The arch-deacon was told he would be welcome; with the additional message that on the guest's arrival, the Cardinal would himself give the information desired. When the minister entered, Cardinal Newman stretched out both his arms to receive his guest. 'These', he said, 'are the formalities that are required when you come to see me.'

Yet another guest who had been with him at Rednal on a wet day was abashed to find as he prepared to leave that Cardinal Newman was at his feet brushing his shoes. He protested strongly. 'Ah,' said the Cardinal. 'We couldn't let you go worse than you came.'[2]

3

'A strain of justice runs through his invectives,' wrote *The Times* on May 11, 1879, 'and even in the heat of controversy large

[1] *Birmingham Daily Gazette,* Aug. 3, 1886. The Cardinal retains many of the tastes as well as the exquisite simplicity of youth. He is very fond of sweets.
[2] Private information.

human ways and far extending sympathies are visible. Hence the charm of Dr Newman's words to people who have no sympathy with the direction of his arguments. Hence, too, the fact that he interests opponents almost as much as friends. He has gone far away from Protestantism, becoming its most dangerous and subtle opponent, and yet he has never ceased to be an interesting subject of study to many true Protestants. His free swift spirit occasionally overleaps the barriers of his creed . . . he loves at bottom English ways and is proud of the memories common to all of us, whatever our faith may be. He does not go abroad for models of sanctity. He likes the English type of Catholic better than any other. He loves that dear mother tongue of which he is a master. The Protestantism of England cannot obliterate in his eyes the virtues and basis of solid worth.'[1]

As for the Protestants' feeling for Newman, another wrote: 'He is separated from them by what seems an abyss. He is clothed in the highest dignity in a Church which is not theirs. But the place which he fills in the mind of his countrymen is the same as ever. His words are always welcomed with respect and sympathy. He is received with demonstrations of honour whenever he leaves his retreat.'[2]

Those who knew him best knew what range and variety of understanding his unassuming lightness of touch habitually compassed, what depths of sympathy it sounded. In the pervading fragrance that his personality exhaled, they recognised the power no less of prince than priest. Where too many were content with demanding a shibboleth, he was admired because he understood, while the note of pathos in his accents reminded his hearers that sensitiveness but increases delicacy as the consecrated heart in detachment makes love more tender because more Divine.

Reverence and devotion attended his failing steps. Seldom have the lightnings of genius or command flashed from a sweeter personality or a more delicate wit.

[1] Bloxam MSS. in Magdalen College Library.
[2] *Life of Lady Georgiana Fullerton*, 205.

4

But if controversy were pressed too far, he was still able to
answer. And when the Principal of Mansfield College, Dr Fair-
bairn, wrote in the *Contemporary* to say that Newman in order to
exalt the claims of the infallible Church was profoundly sceptical
of human reason, Newman answered vigorously in defence of
his old Aristotelian view that logic was but one way, and not
always the most practical, of arriving at conclusions, adding from
an early sermon the wise apothegm that controversy was for the
most part vain because for those who agreed fundamentally, to
argue was needless; and that for those who disagreed fundamentally, to argue was vain.

In earlier years he had encouraged lay scholarship. He felt that
the scholars and thinkers of the Church had two great tasks to
perform: one was to scrutinise the origins of Church History, the
other was to face modern research on the Bible itself.

In February, 1884, Newman published in the *XIX Century* an
article on the Inspiration of Scripture. It was already a current
view that Catholics held views and accepted interpretations of
Scripture which modern science and research had utterly discredited.

Better than to deny or defend such an allegation was to explain
the Catholic view of the Bible and its inspiration. That a Catholic
cannot disagree with the Church is of course true; to what then
must he agree? There is much room for diversity of opinion, but
yet Newman thought caution necessary in promulgating striking
novelties which, even though true, might unsettle ill-educated
minds. 'The household of God had claims on our tenderness in
such matters which criticism and history have not.'[1]

The Church holds the Canonical books to be inspired. But in
what respect? In teaching with regard to faith or moral conduct
in those things which hold us right in the relations of our souls
and characters to God. 'It seems unworthy of Divine greatness',

[1] *XIX Century*, Feb., 1884, 187.

says Newman, 'that the Almighty should, in His Revelation of Himself to us, undertake mere secular duties and assume the office of a narrator as such, or an historian or a geographer, except so far as the secular matters bear directly upon the revealed truth.[1] Neither the Council of Trent, nor the Vatican Council, in dealing with the inspiration of the Bible, says a word directly as to its inspiration in matters of fact.'[2] But since its pages breathe of providence and grace, of our Lord and of His work and teaching from beginning to end, it views all it says in relation to Him, and in such a relation should be viewed as true, even in matters of fact.

A complicated question remains. The Bible is a collection of heterogeneous writings: it is the outcome of many minds, times and places: it is complex, unsystematic, in parts obscure. Its contents are copious and various: it appears to contain some incompatible ideas. What are we to decide about these unless we have with the Bible the safeguard of some authority? If the Bible is inspired it certainly needs an interpreter: and, said Newman, the Church is its infallible interpreter. On that both Trent and the Vatican Council insisted: but till the authority has spoken, liberty of interpretation is allowed, provided of course that on a doctrinal text there is not such continuous and universal support from the Fathers, and such a corroboration in defined dogma, as would make it clear what was the mind of the Church.[3]

The great point for a scholar to remember is that he is handling the Word of God which, by reason of the difficulty of always drawing the line between what is human and what is divine, cannot be put on the level of other books as it is now the fashion to do, but has the nature of a sacrament which is outward and inward, and a channel of supernatural grace.[4] For on teaching about faith or morals, the authority of the Church must never be forgotten.

Newman then asks, are the books inspired or their writers? The answer is this: 'The books are inspired because the writers were inspired to write them.'[5] But it does not follow that the writers knew they were inspired, or were conscious of the range of mean-

[1] op. cit., 189.   [2] op. cit., 189.   [3] op. cit., 191.
[4] op. cit., 192.   [5] op. cit., 192.

ing the Church would find in their words. 'The Psalms are inspired; but when David, in the outpouring of his deep contrition, disburdened himself before God in the words of the *Miserere* could he, possibly, while uttering them, have been directly conscious that every word he uttered was not simply his but another's? Did he not think he was personally asking forgiveness and spiritual help?'[1] Some writers of Scripture apologise for their style of writing: others say they are abridging other work, or collecting information. A canonical book may be composed of pre-existing documents: but if so there must be a certain authority given to the compiler in relation to faith and morals. Nor does the Church guarantee authorship, or that a book as in the Canon is all the work of the person to whom it is imputed. The Church admits that there may be interpolations and additions.[2] She does not insist either on the titles of the canonical books, or their ascription to definite authors. 'For instance,' says Newman, 'the Epistle to the Hebrews is said in our Bible to be the writing of St Paul and so virtually it is, and to deny that is so in any sense might be temerarious; but its authorship is not a matter of faith as its inspiration is, but an acceptance of received opinion, and because to no other writer can it be so well assigned.'[3] Newman goes back to Melchior Cano, the theologian of Salamanca, who already before the Council of Trent said 'It does not much matter to the Catholic faith that a book was written by this or that writer, so long as the Spirit of God is believed to be the author of it'.[4] Nor does inspiration extend to minute and personal matters, or to chronology: for St Matthew is vague in the order of time. And there may be errors in transcription. Miracles, however, are doctrinal facts.

Such is Newman's exposition of what the Church insists on Catholics holding on the Bible. It was not his wish that his answer should be in every respect the right one, but that the idea of inspiration should be explained according to the judgment of the Holy See.

Although this view was published in 1884, there is little that time has done in sixty years of biblical scholarship to modify

[1] *op. cit.*, 193.   [2] *op. cit.*, 196.   [3] *op. cit.*, 192.   [4] *op. cit.*, 193.

it: it could be taken as an excellent exposition of the present attitude of the Roman specialists towards the Bible. But like most of Newman's work it was expressed with a precision that was too much for certain of his contemporary co-religionists. In spite of his being venerated as a scholar, in spite of his being a Cardinal, it was in fact immediately and vehemently assailed by an Irish priest professor named Healy in the *Irish Ecclesiastical Record*. The contention was that of a fundamentalist who claimed that no clause whatever in the Bible is open to charge of error of any kind, and that every Catholic must believe every word of the Bible to be *literally* true! Healy insisted, in fact, on just that view which had brought on his Church severe attacks from scholars and repeated accusations of obscurantism.

Newman's answer to this is a fine example of his delicate irony. He had shown in the *Apologia* that the most effective answer to abuse is simply to quote it. He thus began now: 'a not over-courteous, nor over-exact writer in his criticism of my essay on Inspiration gives as his judgment upon it that its "startling character must be evident to the merest tyro in the school of Catholic theology".'

He had done most of his work in that opening sentence. 'But it is a pity', Newman goes on gently, 'he did not take more than a short month for reading, pondering, writing and printing. Had he not been in a hurry to publish, he would have made a better article. I took about a twelvemonth for mine. Thus I account for some of the professor's unnecessary remarks.' This was the Newman of Oriel, still the same as fifty years before, as he who had answered strident undergraduates with the words 'Very likely'. He goes on to quote St Thomas Aquinas for authority to take much more freedom in interpretation than he, Newman, actually had done. 'Holy Scripture', said St Thomas, 'contains every meaning which can be made to agree with it, as long as one does not outrage its literal exactness.'[1]

Newman insists that the Church not only has a reason for what she says but also for what she refrains from saying; and therefore

---

[1] *Inspiration of the Canonical Scriptures: a reply*, 19. *Omnis veritas quæ, salva litteræ circumstantia, potest Divinæ Scripturæ aptare est eius sensus.*

one should respect her silences. She certainly does not guarantee things apart from faith or morals.

Healy had said that error cannot co-exist with inspiration any more than sin with grace. But, says Newman, the parallel confutes him. Even those in grace are not guaranteed in every particular from sin. 'Good Christians are each "the temple of God", "partakers of the Divine Nature", nay "gods", and they are said "to bear God in their own bodies", and priests, I consider, have not less holiness than others; yet every priest in his daily Mass asks pardon "for his innumerable sins and offences and negligences". . . . Yet the Professor tells us though sin is possible in spite of grace, that error is impossible because of inspiration. I have not dared to speak against any great decision of the great doctors, St Augustine and St Thomas, but I feel it sad indeed that from a Professor in a School of Theology, so widely known and so time-honoured, they should sustain the indignity of so unsatisfactory an advocacy, and that too against one whose ecclesiastical station might have advantageously suggested criticism in a milder tone.' Such was the final word of the Cardinal, and it was not less effective by its mildness.

The great man had asked in the Preface to this reply: What was the conclusion of the matter? 'The Scriptures are inspired, inspired throughout, but not inspired by immediately divine act, but through the instrumentality of inspired men in all matters of faith and morals, and being inspired because written by inspired men, they have a human side which manifests itself in language, style, tone of thought, character, intellectual peculiarities, and such infirmities, not sinful, as belong to our nature.'

5

It was peculiarly fitting that Newman's last publication should be a vindication of the study of the Bible and the Church. For this both points the incessant drama of his life and the secret of his style. Both are those of one who from early youth to ripest age loved his Bible. From it he learned the poetry of nature, the

wholeness of man, the use of passion and imagination, of literature and drama, to combine into an infinitely nobler revelation
of Christ's religion than can be made by any code of theology,
while it leads on by its constant nourishment of a living Church
to the ringing statements in those creeds, which the Church also
calls symbols; these formulate what is revealed to the intellect of
the infinite mysteries of God.

The Bible, like Newman's favourite hymn of triumph, the
Athanasian creed, leads him in this last article to insist once more
on a truth peculiar to his Catholic life, the august and infinite
scope opened to man's soul by heavenly grace. To His chosen,
God almighty extends a participation in His own divineness: for
what is grace but the presence of the Holy Spirit within them to
fill them with all the fullness of God? It leads them ever in their
life to know what passes knowledge, the stillness and the peace
where adoration grows silent in the sense of blessing, as the heart
of the believer exchanges its inmost treasures with those of the
Heart to which it turns.

Newman left no discourses on that mystery—but the words he
chose as Cardinal for his motto were just those—*heart to heart*.

6

When had he not known that mystical communion? His
earliest verses at Oxford were a hymn to silence: he lived there
never less alone than when alone. He learned there in friendship
the sweet secret of communion. He read while still at Oriel, and
again at Littlemore, all that St François de Sales tells of this
mystical ardour which the Divine Love kindles in His adorers.

That study of St François de Sales never ceased; so fervent was
Newman's devotion to this master, that pictures of him took the
largest place on the walls beside the altar in his room. He never
moved to or from the refectory but he saw in the vestibule two
portraits painted by Miss Giberne, one of St François de Sales,
one of his friend Ste Jeanne Françoise Fremiot de Chantal.

Heart to heart. Those words which are the centre of his faith hint also the secret of his appeal. There was at all times in his personality a well both of intimacy and distinction. From a coign of vantage he looked into the soul. He spoke to its depths in the simple words:

> 'The night is dark and I am far from home
> Lead Thou me on.'

When too his excellence of style evoked men's admiration, they were drawn into an ecstasy of sympathy as moving as the old German hymn to the still and holy night when the Redeemer is born.

7

After he had been made a Cardinal, and all England had become aware of him, he had felt the stress of former years. He was growing very old: little by little his intellectual powers faded into a life of purer spirit. All his writing must be given up; then the offices of the Church; then the recital of her simplest forms, till his devotions became the contemplation, heart to heart, of the mysteries of redemption.

All were aware, as he approached the age of ninety, that the dawn of eternal life was near, and at the end, after just two days of illness, borne away on a tide too full for sound or foam, he passed into the boundless deep of light and peace.

8

It was August 11, 1890. His death renewed the eloquent tributes of his Church and of the country. The newspapers filled their columns with his story, concentrating on his portrait of a gentleman and still more on the leading of his kindly light. The bookshops found their copies of his works soon exhausted. The whole country paused for a moment and bowed its head to one it could not but venerate.

The great church which the Oratorians had built in London was filled to the doors to hear what on this occasion would be the words of Cardinal Manning. He might not have stilled for ever his long resentment at the temper—or at the triumphs—of the man of genius, but to the great admiration of all his hearers one Prince of the Church, with that noble distinctness of utterance which none could rival, paid his homage to the other.

Manning could remember the days when undergraduates began to gather at St Mary's in Oxford to hear the new Vicar: and then passing thence himself he recalled the work of the subsequent sixty years. 'He had become a Catholic as our forefathers were. And yet for no one in our memory has such a heartfelt and loving veneration been poured out. Of this the proof is enough. Someone has said: "Whether Rome canonises him or not, he will be canonised in the thoughts of pious people of every creed in England."

'No living man has so changed the thought of England. His withdrawal closes a chapter which stands alone in the religious life of the century. It has for the most part been wrought in silence: for the retiring habits of the man, and the passing weight of age made his later utterances few. Nevertheless his words of gold were "as the hammer that breaks the rocks in pieces", and as the light that works without sound. It has been boldly and truly avowed that "he is the founder of the Church of England as we see it. What the Church of England would have been without the Tractarian movement we can faintly guess, and of the Tractarian movement, Newman was the living soul and the inspiring genius."

'Moreover his hymns are in the hearts of Englishmen and they have a transforming power. He has taught us that beauty and truth are inseparable: that beauty resides essentially in the thought.

'His writings are in your hands. But beyond the power of all books has been the example of his humble and unworldly life: always the same, in union with God and in manifold charity to all who sought him. He was the centre of innumerable souls, drawn to him as leader, guide and comforter through long years, and especially in not more than forty years of his Catholic life. In them he was a spring of light and strength. . . .[1]'

Such in its force and its justice was Manning's tribute to New-

[1] Purcell: *Manning*, II, 749-52.

man. With the judgment that marked the administrator and the man for the people, he had taken his points from the papers.[1] And what he said was echoed not only in Anglican pulpits, but in many of other denominations. Amid encircling gloom, Newman had pointed England to the kindly light, which led him over the fen, the torrent and the crag to halls of radiance where mercy sits enthroned.

[1] The newspapers in the Oriel College MSS. show how closely Manning followed them in both points and phrases.

CHAPTER XXIX

THE TEMPER AND GENIUS OF NEWMAN

I

It is only when we see in the *Grammar of Assent* the place that Newman gives to the wholeness of man: to his reason, passion and imagination—that we see why he takes a towering place among his contemporaries in Church history, and enjoys among men of letters secure renown.

For Newman was at home with classic genius.

He had in fact found his first master in Cicero. It was in writing on Cicero that he first showed how excellently he could himself write. And Cicero remained at once the model of his eloquence, and its precise teacher. 'Our model orator', said Cicero, 'will often turn one and the same subject about in many ways, dwell and linger on the same thought, frequently extenuate circumstances, frequently deride them; sometimes depart from the subject and direct his view another way, propound what he means to speak; define what he has effected; recollect himself; repeat what he has said; conclude his address with an argument; distribute into parts, leave and neglect something occasionally; guard his case beforehand; cast back upon his adversary the very charges brought against him, describe the languages and characters of men; introduce inanimate subjects speaking; avert attention from the main point; turn a matter into jest and amusement; anticipate an objection; introduce similes; employ examples; speak with boldness and freedom, even with indignation: sometimes with invective: implore and entreat; heal an offence; occasionally decline a little from the subject; implore blessings; denounce execrations; in a word, put himself on terms of familiarity with the people he addresses.'[1]

'*Ut fiat iis, apud quos dicet, familiaris*'—To be of one household

[1] *Cicero*, 230.

with those to whom he speaks. That was the art which made
Cicero the greatest of orators: it was that which Newman had
learnt from Cicero to make his own. As Newman himself wrote:
'By the invention of a style which adapts itself with singular
felicity to every class of subjects, whether lofty or familiar, philosophical or forensic, Cicero answers even more exactly to his own
definition of a perfect orator than by his plausibility, pathos or
brilliancy.'[1]

Cicero had aimed at seeing what was various, whole and sublime in his subject. He aimed at appeals to feeling, and adorned
his style with the splendour of imagery. If he could not surpass
the elegance of the Greeks, he could be more vigorous; if less
subtle, he could be brighter; if less exalted in precision, he could
outstrip them in richness of effect.[2] So Quintilian had written.
Newman quoted it and learnt. He compared Cicero to one who
by his arranging his garden with taste and variety compensated
for the lack of space.

2

No influence pressed on him so constantly as that of the Bible
and the Prayer Book. His inward ear lives by those rhythms, as
his ideas mingle his sensitive perceptions with eternal themes:
'Times come and go, and man will not believe that that is to
be which is not yet, or that what now is only continues for a
season and is not eternity. The end is the trial, the world passes;
it is but a pageant and a scene; the lofty palace crumbles, the busy
city is mute, the ships of Tarshish have sped away.'[3]

At one time he enters into the quick of experience:
'Do you know what it is to be in anxiety, lest something should
happen which may happen or may not, or to be in suspense about
some important event, which makes your heart beat when you
are reminded of it and of which you must think the first thing in
the morning? Do you know what it is to have a friend in a distant
country, to expect news of him, and to wonder from day to day
what he is now doing, and whether he is well?'[4] It would be

[1] *Cicero*, 238.   [2] Quintilian: *Orat.*, 40.
[3] *Plain Sermons*, VIII, 247.   [4] *Sermons to Mixed Congregations*, 296–7.

difficult, would it not, to get simpler English than this, or more effective for the purpose of appealing to the heart?

With a like deft directness he portrays those shepherds of Bethlehem who suddenly heard the voice of the heavenly host:

'A set of poor men, engaged in a life of hardship, exposed at that very time to the cold and darkness of the night, watching their flocks, with a view of scaring away beasts of prey or robbers; then, when they are thinking of nothing but earthly things, counting over the tale of their sheep, keeping their dogs by their side, and listening to the noises over the plain, considering the weather and watching for the day, suddenly they are met by far other visitants than they conceived.'[1]

But from this homely directness, he could turn to effects elaborately beautiful. The most picturesque is outlined by irony, for Newman is thinking of what an ordinary English business-man would fail to see around Athens:

'He would not think of writing word to his employers how that clear air of which I have spoken, brought out yet blurred and subdued the colours on the marble; how they had a softness and a harmony, for all their richness, which in a picture looks exaggerated, yet is after all within the truth. He would not tell how that same delicate atmosphere freshened up the pale olive till the olive forgot its monotony, and its cheek glowed like the arbutus or beech on the Umbrian hills. He would say nothing of the thyme and the thousand fragrant herbs which carpeted Hymettos; he would hear nothing of the hum of its bees; nor take much account of the flavour of its honey, since Gozo and Minorca were sufficient for the English demand. He would look over the Ægean from the heights he had ascended; he would follow with his eye the chain of islands which, starting from the Sunian headland, seemed to offer the fabled diversities of Attica when they would visit their Ionian cousins, a sort of viaduct thereto across the sea; but that journey would not occur to him, not any admiration of the dark violet billows with their white edges down below, nor of those graceful fern-like jets of silver upon the rocks, which slowly rise aloft like water spirits from the deep, then

[1] *Plain Sermons,* IV, 323.

shiver and break, and spread, and shroud themselves, and disappear in a soft mist of foam.'[1]

He was indeed an intellectual. His brain, said Gladstone, was 'hard enough to cut the diamond, and bright as the diamond which it cuts'.[2] He was trained in logic: the philosopher of his youth in Oxford was that Aristotle whom Dante had called 'the first of all who know'. He was therefore trained from the first in the sinewy work of the logician, and wrote early with academic exactness. For this reason he grew naturally as a theologian into the mind of the supreme Christian Aristotelian St Thomas Aquinas; and was already a Schoolman before he left the Church of England. Not only was the philosophy of Aquinas the philosophy he had studied at Oriel in the *Nicomochœan Ethics*: but he found also in St Thomas the compendium and dictionary, as it were, of all those theological doctrines of the Fathers to whom he had returned when he began to write about the Arians. They became more and more his main preoccupation until they led him to the conclusions he set down in his *Doctrine of Development*. 'The Fathers', he said, 'made me a Catholic.'[3]

3

His elastic mind was trained all the time by the classical studies of Oxford, trained from St Clement of Alexandria, and his *Stromata,* to continue the work which Philo had begun—to reconcile the metaphysics of Aristotle and Philo with the Old Testament, as later with the New. Newman completely abandoned his early Calvinism and grew into a religion which took to itself the splendours of the Classics. He thus—and again he showed his affinity with Aquinas—perfected his humanism with the Christian revelation, and set his faith in the broad basis of human nature on those noble flights of passion and speculation, where it had already not only the sense of law but of things divine.

Nor did he stop with the Classics and the Bible; not only

[1] *Historical Sketches*, III, 21.   [2] Gladstone: *Vaticanism*, 15.
[3] *Letter to Pusey*, 26.

Jerusalem, Greece and Rome, but Egypt and Asia furnished materials for the palaces of his thought: when in 1841 Newman wrote his article on *Milman's view of Christianity*, he set out in one of his least-known but most magnificent passages the huge range both of his humanism and his Christian faith:

'A great portion of what is generally received as Christian truth is in its rudiments or in its separate parts to be found in other philosophies and religions. For instance, the doctrine of a Trinity is to be found both in the east and in the west: so is the ceremony of washing: so is the rite of sacrifice. The doctrine of the Divine Word is Platonic: the doctrine of the Incarnation is Indian: of a divine kingdom is Judaic: of angels and demons is Magian: the connection of sin with the body is Gnostic; celibacy is known to Bonze and Talapoin; a sacerdotal order is Egyptian; the idea of a new birth is Chinese and Eleusinian: belief in sacramental virtue is Pythagorean; and honours to the dead are a polytheism. Such is the general nature of the facts before us.'

From it Milman had argued that heathen ideas had adulterated the purity of the Church. Newman answered rather that the Church vindicated those scattered adumbrations of her truth:—

'We prefer to say, and we think that Scripture bears us out in saying, that from the beginning the Moral Governor of the World has scattered the seeds of truth far and wide over its extent, and these have variously taken root and grown up in the wilderness, wild plants indeed, but living; and hence that, as the inferior animals have tokens of an immaterial principle, yet these have not souls, so the philosophies and religions of men have their life in certain true ideas, though they are not directly divine. What man is amid the brute creation, such is the Church among the Schools of the world; and as Adam gave names to the animals about him, so has the Church from the first looked round upon the earth, noting and visiting the doctrines she found there. She began in Chaldea, then sojourned among the Canaanites, and went down into Egypt, and thence passed into Arabia till she rested in her own land. Next she encountered the merchants of Tyre, and the wisdom of the east country, and the luxury of Sheba. Then she was carried away to Babylon, and wandered to the Schools of Greece. And wherever she went, in trouble or in triumph, still she was a living spirit, the mind and voice of the Most High, sitting in the midst of the doctors both hearing them and asking them questions, claiming to herself what they said rightly, correcting their errors, supplying their defects, completing their beginnings, expanding their surmises, and thus gradually by means of them enlarging the range and refining the sense of her own teaching. So far then from the creed being of doubtful credit because it resembles foreign theologies, we even hold that the special way in which Providence has imparted Divine knowledge to us has been by enabling her to draw and collect it together out of the world. . . .

'We are not distressed to be told that the doctrine of the angelic host came from Babylon, while we know that they did sing at the Nativity; nor that the vision of a Mediator is in Philo if in very deed He died for us on Calvary. Nor are we afraid to allow that, even after His coming, the Church has been a treasure house giving forth things old and new, casting the gold of fresh tributaries into her refiner's fire, or stamping upon her own, as time required it, a deeper impress of her Master's image.'[1]

4

Newman knew the instinct of the Catholic Church far better than to imagine revelation to be one entire, solitary act. He judged it rather as Butler had taught him to do, from the analogy of nature. The Christian doctrine, like the human frame, is fearfully and wonderfully made, at sundry times, and in divers manners; it is various, complex and progressive. 'The Church, like Aaron's rod, devours the serpents of the magicians.'[2] On the one side with shallowness of views and bigotry, is doubt, on that of depth, insight and largeness of mind, conviction becomes triumphant: 'They are driven to maintain on their part that the Church's doctrine was never pure: we say that it cannot be corrupt.'

It is in the combination of this majestic assurance with views of widest range that we see the secret of Newman's intellectual

[1] *Essays Critical and Historical*, II, 232.   [2] *ibid.*, 233.

supremacy. He takes from Aristotle and Aquinas their essential doctrine of the nobility which God has given to man, and of the generosity with which having marvellously created human nature in His image, He yet more marvellously redeems it to share—through grace—that infinitely higher life which is that of His uncreated Spirit.

In Newman's combination of gifts, religion therefore found a means to impress the world.

5

Style he described as the expression of a perfectly defined thought. Precision then was his first aim: but precision for him meant something more than clearness because the outlines of his concepts were complex, and his purest simplicities subtle in variety of texture and of tint.

What Cicero had provided in Latin, Addison, Gibbon and Dryden provided in English. The sound and vastness of Gibbon haunted his dreams; he learnt from Dryden that energy divine, that combination of vigour with noble taste which marks his essays as the beginning of our clear and classic prose.[1] Addison had been his earliest model. Newman claimed, however, that style as style had never been an end with him: he had never written for writing's sake, but only to express his thoughts clearly and exactly.[2]

6

His first triumph, however, is to be both elegant and natural.

'Newman', says Hopkins, 'does not follow the common tradition of writing. His tradition is that of cultured, the most highly educated conversation; it is the flower of the best Oxford life. Perhaps this gives it a charm of unaffected and personal sincerity nothing else could still—he shirks the technique of written prose —and shuns the tradition of written English.'[3]

While on the one hand Hawkins at Oriel had insisted on exactness, Newman always avoided and derided anything that seemed

[1] Edward Bellasis: *Coram Cardinali*, 78.   [2] A.M. II, 426.
[3] Hopkins to Coventry Patmore: *Further Letters*, 222.

pedantic. His talk was never donnish, and from youth to old age, he had a fancy for the stories heard from the boys and the young men about him. There is only one pedantic word which catches him in its mesh—the horrid word 'desiderate'—when generally 'want' would have done as well. Another favourite, 'realise', takes one further into his secret. But he could be bold in the use of such a colloquial word as 'chuck', and the ease of talk runs through all his letters; the talk of schoolboys, often, for even as a Cardinal when he had enough he would say 'I guess I'm choc'; when an old man he does not scruple to write to Pusey of 'ratting'; just as Manning, with the natural boyishness which makes honour sit so well upon a gentleman of England, talked to Bodley of his crimson cassock as 'these togs'.

The fact remains that though Newman said he never sought for style, there is a great difference between his letters and his sermons, lectures, or books; except when he is describing his Mediterranean journey he reserves his appreciation of beauty for his formal work. The reason is no doubt that to portray beauty cost him painful effort—he had to write and rewrite to obtain his effect—and he was unable to consecrate so much toil to effects that few were expected to see. His copious letters for the most part lack that stamp of elegance and beauty which makes his sermons not only famous but which places them beyond the rivalry even of Donne or of Jeremy Taylor.

What is the secret of these sermons? 'Their English is simple, clear and refreshing as pure water,' said Dean Hutton, 'answering to every thought of the speaker's mind.'[1] 'The charm of Newman's style', says Augustine Birrell, 'necessarily baffles description; as well might one seek to analyse the fragrance of a flower, or to expound in words the jumping of one's heart when a beloved friend unexpectedly enters the room . . . it is pellucid, it is animated, it is varied: at times cold, it afterwards glows with fervent heat; it employs as its obedient and well-trained servant a vast vocabulary, and it does so always with the ease of the educated gentleman.'[2] Sometimes each word is precisely weighed, and

[1] *Cambridge History of English Literature*, X, 268.
[2] Birrell: *Selected Essays*, 184–5.

pronounced with dignity, like that of a judge giving his judgment
—yet at other times Newman is not judge, but the pleader, eager
yet accomplished, who uses every device commended by Cicero,
of rhetoric, imagery, irony or variety, in order to bring others to
share in the full reality of his own conception.

A man of both exquisite sensitiveness, and of impassioned zeal,
he lives by the heart; living so, he is a master of pathos. But the
pathos is as refined as it is tender. For in it are inviolate reserves,
while the caution of the scholar maintains the utmost scruple in
appraisal; and if his spirit is singularly impressionable, or his fancy
singularly brilliant, both are disciplined by long and strenuous
training in those classic schools where words are sculptured with
the same restraint as the sepulchral reliefs of ancient Hellas.

7

Nothing Newman wrote surpasses the sensitive and elaborate
eloquence of his passage on nature's gifts to Athens: no others of
his letters are comparable in style to those he wrote describing
Sicily. As his palate was delicate, so was his eye appreciative, and
it was instructed by his interest till it gave his concepts a richness
of vitality that set him at his best in the foremost rank of writers:
what he has finely said of a representative poet is true of himself:
'His aim is to give forth that which he has within him; and from
his very earnestness it comes to pass that whatever be the splendour
of his diction or the harmony of his periods, he has with him the
charm of an incommunicable simplicity. . . . His page is the lucid
mirror of his mind and life.'[1]

For such an effect two things are necessary. One is certainly
technique in expression. It is so to know the work of men writing
finely and clearly that we catch their tradition. But that in itself
must be accompanied by an access of vitality which enlarges a
man's own soul till he both appreciates lavish detail and welds it
together in one sense of wholeness and grandeur itself made great
by its vision of order, and its sense of what is boundless and
august. A genius speaks not only to himself; but, because his con-

[1] *Idea of a University* (1873), 292.

ceptions are inspired, and his heart generous, he has treasures to share with his fellow men. Taking up the heritage of the past, he speaks also for time to come. In his sacred trust he discerns the order of eternity; his voice has within it the harmony which vibrates from the spheres into his soul. He 'fertilises his simplest ideas, and germinates into a multitude of details, and prolongs the march of his sentences and sweeps round to the full diapason of his harmony as if . . . rejoicing in his own vigour and richness of resource.'[1]

Nowhere is Newman more classical than in his account of great literature; for he sees that since style is the life which a concept takes within a man and which he communicates to others by expressing it, his concepts will be great in so far as he invests great subjects with the sympathy which only greatness can accord: 'That pomp of language, that full and tuneful diction, that felicitousness in the choice and exquisiteness in the collocation of words which to prosaic writers seems artificial, is but the mere habit of, and way of, a lofty intellect.'[2]

Style must be social because it inherits and maintains tradition: but at the same time its distinction comes from the fact that each man sees what he sees with a directness that is his own. Inevitably therefore he moulds his words to his own peculiarities. 'His thought and feelings are personal, and so his language is personal.'

When Newman is writing his sermons, therefore, or when at various times he frees himself from academic constraint to portray the vividness of his experience or the sweep of his imagination, he takes us into the temple of literature; that temple which he found gorgeous alike in the eloquence of Cicero, in the poetic drama of Job, or in the elaborate disquisition of the Epistle to the Hebrews. He was not only the master of pathos, but a painter of visible beauty, joining the concrete detail of Mantegna to Richard Wilson's impressions of the coloured sky. But his description is not an end in itself—it is, like the most eloquent passages in St Augustine's *Confessions*, a means to take men's minds to heaven: 'Leave then the prison of your reasonings, leave the town, the work of man, the haunt of sin; go forth, my brethren, far from

---

[1] *op. cit.*, 280.   [2] *op. cit.*, 280.

the tents of Kedar and the shrine of Babylon: with the patriarch go forth to meditate in the field and from the splendours of the world imagine the unimaginable glory of the Architect. Mount some bold eminence and look back, when the sun is high and full upon the earth, when mountains, cliffs and sea rise up before you like a brilliant pageant with outlines noble and graceful, and tints and shadows soft, clear and harmonious, giving depth and unity to the whole; and then go through the forest or fruitful field, or along meadow and stream, and drink the fragrant air which is poured around you in spring or summer or go among the gardens and delight your senses with the grace and splendour and the various sweetness of the flowers you find there; then think of the almost mysterious influence upon the mind of some particular scents, or the emotion which some gentle, peaceful strain excites in us, or how soul and body are carried away captive by the concord of musical sounds, and when you have ranged through sights and sounds and odours, and your heart kindles, and your voice is full of praise and worship, reflect—not that they tell you nothing of their Maker—but they are the poorest and dimmest glimmerings of His glory; and the very refuse of His exuberant riches, and but the dusky smoke which precedes the flame, compared with Him who made them. Such is the Creator in His eternal uncreated beauty that were it given to us to behold it we should die of very rapture at the sight.'[1]

8

Though Newman is often eloquent and always clear, he is a writer who will be variously judged: he had moods which were donnish and fierce, and many have felt ill at ease with one whose sensitiveness was edgy, and whose edges were sharp to cut. Much of his work is technical, and to tell the truth, his theology, though competent, is not fully alive till he is preaching to young men. 'We have', said Oliver Elton, 'to watch and wait for Newman as an artist. For an artist he can be: but what long and sterile tracts, what belts of unwatered, thin vegetation separate his solitary

[1] *Sermons to Mixed Congregations* (1849), 314.

peaks and happy valleys. In his histories, his disputes, his apologies and his fiction how much even on a liberal showing is ephemeral.'[1]

Nor is this all: he at every turn raises issues which no one can judge on literary grounds alone. He cannot be considered except in relation to his religious moves; and everyone knows where they end.

'It is of course not everyone who will be captivated by Newman or who will like what he has to say. There will be among many', said Church, 'the strongest and most decisive disagreement, there may be impatience at dogmatic teachings, indignation at what seems overstatement and injustice, rejection of argument and conclusions; but there will always be the sense of an unfading nobleness in the way in which the writer thinks and speaks.'[2]

None can fail to be impressed, either, with his sincerity. And in one place that sincerity has in it something so pure and so universal that his voice speaks for souls in all their moods. Such is the voice that England knows best as Newman's. None can resist his dogma when he says:

'Simply to His grace and wholly
Light and life and strength belong,
And I love supremely, solely,
Him the holy, Him the strong.'

or

'So long thy power hath blest me, sure it still
Will lead me on.'

or

'Praise to the holiest in the height,
And in the depth be praise,
In all his works most wonderful
Most sure in all his ways.'

It is this pure essence of religion that we find in the Newman whom religious England as a whole recognised at once and will always trust and love—because those words of his are themselves pure trust and love; they diffuse his brightness everywhere. And

---

[1] Elton: *Survey of English Literature*, 1830–1880, I, 198.
[2] Church: *Occasional Papers*, II, 450.

if any go on from this to the best of his preaching they will see that no one can surpass him when he surpasses himself.

Of his sermons 'It is not too much to say that they have done more than anything else to revolutionise the whole idea of preaching in the English Church'. Said Church again, in them one seemed to hear after many masterly pleas and arguments, 'a voice, very grave, very sweet, very sure and very clear, under whose words the discussion springs up at once to a higher level and in which we recognise at once a mind face to face with realities, and able to seize them and hold them fast'.[1]

9

As a writer, then, Newman can do supreme things—but he is quite content for lengths of time to do mediocre things. It is not merely as a writer that we can appraise him. But his closest rival as a preacher is one whom he himself received into the Catholic Church—Gerard Manley Hopkins. Hopkins had his sensitiveness. He had his fullness of conception, his eagerness, his fine taste, his Oxford training, and he is fresher than Newman for not having his years in College. Where Newman is a don, Hopkins is an enthusiast. His poetry has a roll, an excitement, a carol and surprise that far exceed Newman's gift of poetry. But each had reality in their own concepts and made words great in the grandeur of soul and sense meeting and engendering. For each

'A juice rides rich through bluebells, in vine leaves
And beauty's veriest, dearest vein is tears'.[2]

Newman never attained to such an ecstasy of sensation as made his young friend write:

'blue-bleak embers,
Fall, gall themselves and gash gold vermilion.'[3]

For his genius was not peculiarly poetic.

[1] Church: *Occasional Papers*, II, 446.   [2] Hopkins: *Poems*, 71.
[3] Hopkins: *Poems*, 29.

10

Yet the free, unconstrained movement of Newman's style tells anyone who knows what writing is of a very keen and exact knowledge of the subtle and refined secrets of language. With all that uncared-for play and simplicity, with that precision and sureness there was a fullness, a curious delicate music, quite instinctive and unsought for. Pater particularly noticed the melody of his prose, ranking him with Cicero and with Michelet as masters of a rhythm which gives its musical value to every syllable.[1] This music is often as sprightly, poignant and intense as that of Mozart, but echoes at times the symphonies of Newman's own favourite musician: like Beethoven, his voice speaks from the great deep, it reverberates like thunder rolling across the sky and on its gales we hear the onrush of the storm. His English is 'graceful with the grace of nerve, flexibility and power'.[2] Hopkins himself called him 'our greatest living master of style—and widest mind'.[3]

The Academia said of him that he had a power of illustration which arrayed truth in the fairest garb, a style which was the mirror of exact and lucid thought. 'The justice and candour and gravity and rightness of mind is what is so beautiful in all he wrote.'[4] It might be added to this that there was in his eloquent passages an exuberant wealth of detail with a vividness of delicate imagery which leaves an impression of high and at times unearthly excellence.

> "Tis, but I cannot name it, 'tis the sense
> Of majesty and beauty and repose.
> A blended holiness of earth and sky.'[5]

11

It is sometimes asked: If there is in Newman a consummate mastery of style, what is there else? It is true that none of his works

[1] Pater: *Style in Works* (1901), V, 6, 12.
[2] Church: *Occasional Papers*, II, 450.   [3] Hopkins: *Further Letters*, 43.
[4] Hopkins to Edward Bond: *Further Letters*, 43.
[5] Wordsworth: *Excursion*, Part II, quoted in Pater: *Appreciations* (1889).

is wholly acceptable as literature: it is also true that few of his effects are supported to the end: for at the end the cadence is apt to break. It is true finally that there is often an insistence which is sometimes egoistic and often irritating. But it is not the less true that in his great passages Newman established religion in a new dignity. He puts it where no man of culture can ignore it; he shows it to be essential to an undisputed masterpiece.

What is the secret? On the one hand he gives religion the quality of his own sensitiveness, intense and delicate: he gives it wings to take its flight over wide space and time, or ride the storm of tragedy. In whatever connection he depicts it, he lends it the appeal of his sincerity, and invests it with a chaste exactness: while his perfect taste raises it again and again to elegance and beauty. Not least he adds to it the sense of his personality and his affection. He shows it as urgent, eminent, and fine. Never content to be theological, he establishes the reign of religion over not only reason, but passion, imagination and intuition.

If these are Newman's tributes to religion, his debts are heavier. His style, his taste, his exact and wide-ranging mind would not have set him where he is, had he not added to them his zeal for a holy life, and his enthusiasm for the Catholic idea. We cannot think of Newman apart from his sermons, or of them apart from the Bible. It is his faith which inspires him to his noblest flights, chastens him to his high sincerity, and gives him his most moving effects. It is religion which we hear in the *Apologia's* picture of a godless world, in the majestic rhythms which close *The Grammar of Assent*, and in the sadness of *The Parting of Friends*. His was a zeal so intense for the Church that it mastered and enforced every faculty of his genius; the Catholic faith not only set before him themes of rich and varied beauty but it drew for him from the bourns of time and space treasures unsearchable and sublime.

12

It is when we reflect how in so eminent a stylist religion is inspiring, that we can fix the rank of Newman among the churchmen of his age. As a personality none of them but falls when he is in the tournament. Among his co-religionists, Hopkins as poet, Manning as administrator excelled him. Wiseman and Ullathorne merit tributes, but they do not dispute his place in the history of English religion, nor does Church, nor Pusey, nor Tait, nor Moberley, nor Samuel Wilberforce, nor Kingsley, nor Maurice, nor Liddon. They were excellent preachers and writers and deserve to be read more. But none of them either did so much in history as he, or so long commanded respect. They, in a word, can no more vie with Newman in his peculiar distinction or in the momentum of his churchmanship than in his renown among men of letters.

His role was to win respect for the Catholic tradition. He gave it first of all a new hold over the Church of England so that her services were remoulded, her temper changed; and still, after a hundred years, he shines on for her, son of her morning. But secondly, he did what could not have been done had not taste and pathos joined with strength the appeal to his Protestant and classical beginnings. He taught his countrymen that, in spite of everything, the Church of Rome is still there, not only universal, one, apostolic, and unwearied, but also in spite of all the misconceptions, all the failures, all the misdemeanours of men, a healer of the maladies of Christendom and the central gate of heaven.

13

First then, as a member of the Church of England, and secondly as one who taught her to look with new eyes on Christendom in its great international Church, Newman takes his place in history. And he does so because he was lofty, sensitive and an Englishman. He triumphed early, yet knew no cloudless splendour nor unchequered fortune. Had he been more of the technical theologian —or even of the saint—he would have exercised his powers less widely. His temper or defects of ability emphasise the underlying nobleness, and while he invites admiration, the very fact that one so noble appears to fail awakens the sympathy of just men. He conquers, in short, because he disarms.

Even stronger over us than his distresses is the courage of his

honesty. He saw life whole; and at every turn he balanced truth
with truth. He insists that we must pursue holiness; he, at all times,
adores the sovereignty of the Most High; he demands authority
for a particular revelation—but, after allowing this to bind him
to the Holy See, he insists all the more on the high prerogatives
of the mind. And here again we see how much he is moulded by
Oxford. 'The Lord is my Light' is the motto on her book, but,
as a University, she, maintaining the dignity of all science and all
learning, made youth the heirs also of diverse truth.

Newman too insists that profane learning is moving, lofty and
exact: 'Lines that were the birth of some chance morning or evening at an Ionian festival or on the Sabine hills have lasted generation after generation for thousands of years, with a power over
the mind and a charm' which the current literature of the day is
unable to rival: Virgil seems a prophet or musician: 'His single
words and phrases, his pathetic half lines giving utterance as the
voice of nature herself, to that pain and weariness yet hope of
better things which is the hope of her children in every time.'[1]

Newman loved not only classics but culture and colour. As
Cicero was his exemplar, so following Aristotle, he insists that
poetry transcends our wonted themes: 'While it re-creates the imagination by the superhuman loveliness of its views, it provides
solace for the mind broken by the disappointments of actual life,
and becomes, moreover, the utterance of the inward emotions of
a right moral feeling, seeking a purity and a truth which this
world cannot give. It follows that the poetical mind is one full
of the eternal forms of beauty and perfection.'[2]

14

It was to universities that he looked to harmonise the transcen-
dent powers of the creative imagination with the mind of the
Church: 'I wish the intellect to range with the utmost freedom,'
he said to his undergraduates in Dublin, 'and religion to enjoy an
equal freedom; but what I am stipulating for is this, that they
should be found in one and the same place and exemplified in the

[1] *Grammar of Assent* (1870), 74-5.   [2] *Critical Essays* (1871), 10.

same persons to be at once oracles of philosophy and shrines of devotion.'[1]

From this tempered judgment and elastic strength came also his fineness as a writer. His formula of 'order and warmth' has been commended to those who conserve political tradition.[2] It gives the secret of his own nature when he speaks of poetry being marked by dignity, emotion and refinement.[3] His eminence therefore as a Churchman, which links his story with his ideal of a University, is one with his endearing elegance as a person, and the lustre with which he invests recurring exquisite cadences of words. These, once heard and learnt, return and echo through the flying years—calling us to hold the Church in veneration, to yearn for the eternal beauty, to cherish, as in good Universities the whole- ness of truth as it is given to different types of mind to see it, to love one another with a pure heart fervently, and even in the dark, to work, virtuous and vigilant, by the kindly light of Divine worship and Divine mercy which burns till, in the dusk orient, perfection's dawn silvers on the wide world's encircling gloom.

[1] *Occasional Sermons* (1857), 15.
[2] See Keith Feiling. *Nineteenth Century Biography*. This contains a most valuable study of Newman as a Conservative.
[3] *Critical Essays* (1871), 10.

SUBJECT INDEX

In this Index:

Anglicanism refers to the Church of England in general

Anglo-Catholicism to the Church of England as affected by Newman

Popery to the Roman Catholic Church in the eye of a Protestant

Catholicism to the Roman Catholic Church in the eye of a believer

INDEX OF NAMES

INDEX OF NAMES

311